Kill — Do Not Release

World War II: The Global, Human, and Ethical Dimension
G. Kurt Piehler, *series editor*

Kill—Do Not Release

Censored Marine Corps Stories from World War II

Douglass K. Daniel

Fordham University Press | New York 2025

Copyright © 2025 Fordham University Press

All rights reserved. No part of this publication may be reproduced, stored in a retrieval system, or transmitted in any form or by any means—electronic, mechanical, photocopy, recording, or any other—except for brief quotations in printed reviews, without the prior permission of the publisher.

Fordham University Press has no responsibility for the persistence or accuracy of URLs for external or third-party Internet websites referred to in this publication and does not guarantee that any content on such websites is, or will remain, accurate or appropriate.

Fordham University Press also publishes its books in a variety of electronic formats. Some content that appears in print may not be available in electronic books.

Visit us online at www.fordhampress.com.

For EU safety / GPSR concerns: Mare Nostrum Group B.V., Mauritskade 21D, 1091 GC Amsterdam, The Netherlands, gpsr@mare-nostrum.co.uk

Library of Congress Cataloging-in-Publication Data available online at https://catalog.loc.gov.

Printed in the United States of America
27 26 25   5 4 3 2 1
First edition

For the members of my family who served in the armed forces:

Otis L. Darner
US Marine Corps, World War I
US Army, World War II

Arthur B. Daniel Jr.
US Navy, World War II

James Alfred Taylor III
US Army, World War II

D. V. Douglass
US Army, World War II

Alice Jane Douglass
US Army, World War II

James D. Douglass
US Army, Vietnam War era

Contents

	Introduction	1
1	**A Dangerous Publicity Campaign**	7
2	**In the Jungles of Guadalcanal**	23
3	**Somewhere in the South Pacific**	45
4	**Four Bloody Days on Tarawa**	71
5	**From New Britain to the Marshalls**	97
6	**Sweeping the Marianas: Saipan, Guam, and Tinian**	122
7	**Payback at Peleliu**	149
8	**Invisible Heroes: Black Marines and Sailors in the Pacific**	161
9	**Thirty-Six Days on Iwo Jima**	182
10	**Okinawa and Imperial Japan's Last Stand**	202
11	**Life in the Marine Corps**	219
	Epilogue	239
	Acknowledgments	249
	Notes	251
	Bibliography	275
	Index	279

Photos follow page 148

Kill — Do Not Release

Introduction

Jim G. Lucas had been reporting from the Pacific theater of World War II for more than a year when American forces landed at the Japanese island of Saipan in June 1944. Unlike the civilian journalists who traveled with the troops, Lucas was a US Marine. He had left his job as a reporter for the *Tulsa Tribune* (Oklahoma) to enlist and then endured eight weeks of training at boot camp. He carried a weapon and was prepared to capture or kill the enemy—a rifleman first, the Marines would say of everyone in their ranks. Yet Lucas was among a handful of Marines with specialized equipment: They carried portable typewriters and plenty of typing paper in their packs for Saipan, ready both to fight and write. The noncommissioned officers had the unique title of Marine combat correspondent.

The Marine Corps was the first of the American military services to recruit journalists, train them, and assign them to tell the stories of their men at war. Motion picture and still photographers, artists, and radio broadcasters were recruited as well to give the Marines a presence across the spectrum of American media. Their stories were written or broadcast for stateside audiences eager for any kind of war news. Foremost, however, their stories were meant as a recruiting tool for the Marine Corps and as a first draft of Corps history. Not until Marine writers were regularly placing their stories in local, state, and national media did the Army and Navy seek to compete for public attention by deploying journalists of their own.

Saipan would prove to be the bloodiest battle yet in the Pacific campaign. Lucas was a veteran of such amphibious assaults and had witnessed the heavy casualties that followed. Nonetheless, he was shocked and moved by the scene at a battalion aid station on the island just five days into a conflict that would rage for three weeks. On that afternoon, truck after truck raced dozens of wounded Marines to tents for medical treatment. Some were just as quickly taken away—they were beyond help. Others did not bear the physical wounds wrought by bullets or shrapnel. They had a glazed look, walked with what could barely be called a shuffle, or fell to the ground at the sound of field artillery, even their own. In the eyes of one Marine, Lucas saw the stark terror of living through days of enemy mortar fire. All the wounded looked so young to Lucas, who was four days away from his twenty-ninth birthday.

"They were your boys," Lucas wrote in a dispatch describing that awful June afternoon to readers back home. "You never saw them like this. When you last saw them, they were cocky and sure, all stretched out in their dress uniforms, and proud as peacocks that they were Marines." He closed his report by writing: "I wished that the men who make wars could have gone to that aid station and seen the things we saw there. But I knew immediately it wouldn't have done any good. The men who make wars have seen these things, and they call them the final goal of human endeavor."

Lucas's three-page account went through the usual channels for all stories from Marine writers. Shortly before Saipan he had been promoted from technical sergeant to second lieutenant, but his rise from combat correspondent, called a CC, to public relations officer, a PRO, did not give his reports any special privileges. US Navy censors would evaluate his work as usual, scrutinizing his stories per their training to exclude certain facts in all dispatches: details of military activity that could inadvertently aid the enemy, battlefield gore, and a wide gamut of issues of taste. They were on general alert for any material that could cast a negative light on the war effort or the Marine Corps, which was part of the Navy.

The destination for stories by CCs and PROs was the Division of Public Relations at Marine Corps headquarters, just outside Washington, DC. A team of former journalists and other men with communications experience edited the stories and decided where to send them. They too would have been wary of stories that could make the Marine Corps look bad in the eyes of the public. Stories might be rejected for distribution for various shortcomings, including mediocre writing or a topic unlikely to catch the interest of civilian editors. Time was a factor as well; it could take weeks for stories to reach DPR headquarters, where they could be put aside if deemed "old news." The national wire services and major newspapers and magazines were prime outlets, but any publications with connections to Marines mentioned in the stories, even the writer's hometown paper, were fair game. Ultimately, the civilian press decided what merited space in their publications.

Yet there would be no venue for Lucas's account of the wounded Marines at the battalion aid station on Saipan, not even his own paper in Tulsa. In fact, the Lucas story probably would not be read outside of official channels. Written in capital letters in dark pencil at the top of the first page: "KILLED—NAVY." Nearby were the words, in red pencil, "No—Cmdr. McCarthy." No reason was stated, though censors and other officials probably thought Lucas's description was too grim for an American public deep into the third year of a war with no end in sight. His concluding message may have been seen as problematic. Sowing doubt among readers about the cause for which so many lives were being lost would not bolster public support.

Today, Lucas's battalion aid station story is among thousands of Marine dispatches, published and unpublished, preserved by the National Archives and Records Administration (NARA). One can only guess without examining each story, but the majority probably had been approved for distribution during the war. After all, they were conceived, written, and edited for that purpose. Not only were the approved versions routinely published, but the more celebrated of the dispatches provided the foundation for books by Marine writers during the war and a collection published two years after the war. At least a few former Marine writers kept copies of what they had written and turned to them for their memoirs. The official versions of some stories landed in the Marine Corps Archives at Base Quantico, Virginia, and may be part of collections elsewhere. Thus, most of the published work of the CCs and PROs was readily available in some form outside of the National Archives for decades, but not their original material with editing marks and censors' instructions.

This collection focuses on those Marine dispatches deemed unfit for the eyes of the American public at the time they were written. Stories passed by a Navy censor usually carried an official stamp; by the time of the assault on the island of Iwo Jima, in 1945, the stamp read CINCPOA (Commander in Chief Pacific Ocean Area) and included these words: "Examined for military security; no objection to publication; subject to deletions and amendments indicated." Seldom was the name of a censor or a division editor noted on stories, making it difficult to determine who exactly made content decisions. Written on the first pages of stories rejected in whole were unambiguous instructions: "kill" or "do not release" or, simply, "no." Often stories passed for distribution contained sections crossed out in red, presumably by a censor. Included in this collection are some stories that were marked "filed" in dark pencil, a sign that they were not rejected by an official Navy censor but were evaluated within the public relations division's editorial system and apparently withheld from distribution for some reason after passing the censor.

It cannot be stated with certainty that the censored stories and other unpublished dispatches in this collection have never been cited in postwar books or other publications; however, evidence strongly suggests that this is the case. The writers' individual files were not declassified until years after the war—many were stamped as declassified in 1958—and then eventually housed at the National Archives. Today they are held in the NARA facility in College Park, Maryland. They may have been unknown to or overlooked by most researchers. In fact, when the former Marine public relations officer Herbert Merillat wrote the book *Guadalcanal Remembered* in 1982, he noted that much of the material he had drawn on for an earlier book, *The Island*, in 1944, had disappeared, and he assumed there had been "a periodic housecleaning" at Marine Corps headquarters. He may have been referring in part to the dispatches written by him and others at Guadalcanal in 1942. Institutional histories of the CCs, including a book supported by the Marine Corps Combat Correspondents Association, make no mention of the original World War II–era dispatches now maintained at NARA.

Two of the last surviving Marine writers, Cyril J. O'Brien and Millard Kaufman, told me in 2005 that they did not know if the CCs' original stories still existed. (O'Brien had copies of some of his work; Kaufman did not.) When I sought such original stories for a separate project, archivists at NARA and the Marine Corps Archives had no knowledge of any such material. Urged on by Kaufman—the former public relations officer could not believe the Marine Corps would have thrown away their stories—I inquired again at NARA with a fuller description of the material being sought. The request prompted an archivist to return to the records of the Division of Public Relations within the massive Marine Corps records collection, then to examine material categorized as "individual news release submission files of former public information personnel, 1943–1947." The accurate if uninspired heading led to scores of archival boxes of the CCs' original stories. The NARA finding aid was subsequently updated to better describe its contents.

Two objectives have guided the selection of censored or otherwise unreleased stories from the vast amount of material at NARA. First, they should shed light on what Marines experienced during major island battles of the Pacific campaign. Just like the stories that were distributed, these unreleased dispatches carry the perspectives of the Marine writers, based on either their interviews with fellow Marines or their own experiences, often both. Second, those selected should prompt an exploration of why they were withheld and what those decisions reveal about how the Marine Corps sought to engage the public. Indeed, mayhem and death were regular features of the stories that reached the public, raising questions about what led censors and others to determine that these stories had crossed some line. Answers can be surmised by reading the regular directives the combat correspondents received from the Division of Public Relations along with Navy regulations for disseminating information to the public. Reflections by CCs and PROs in interviews and memoirs long after the war are also informative.

Some of these withheld stories cast a shadow on actions by Marines at war in their suggestions of racism, insensitivity, callousness, and brutality. They also show courage, sacrifice, and even humor under the most intense pressure imaginable. In other words, these unpublished stories speak to the dichotomy of war. They also show competing interests at work within an open society: keeping the public informed while allowing for censorship in the interest of a greater good. If these stories had appeared in newspapers and magazines at the time, readers likely would have been divided in their reactions—and division could not be risked when the fate of the nation, if not the world, was in the balance. In any discussion it should be noted that civilian reporters in the theater of war were subject to the same military censorship. Editors and publishers in the United States made similar decisions not to publish accounts of some events and disturbing facts as part of the effort to maintain the public support required to win the war.

While presenting censored and otherwise withheld stories, this collection also provides a history of Marine combat correspondents in World War II. (Overall military strategies and objectives, gleaned from previously published studies, are included only for background and context.) At the time, the effort to combine journalism with public relations was unique among the American military services. Many of the Marine writers had been journalists and probably chafed at the very notion of public relations—in the eyes of most journalists, the public relations professional was an adversary in the quest to find the truth and report it. Now *they* were the ones providing information with a decidedly skewed perspective. Regardless of instructions for what to cover and how to cover it, the CCs and PROs often fell back into their journalistic ethos and a natural bent to tell a good story. Their history is replete with its own heroes, including men wounded or killed while carrying out their duties as Marines.

Read today without the pressures all Americans faced during World War II, some of these censored and unpublished stories may bring out sentiments similar to those Jim Lucas felt at the battalion aid station on Saipan eight decades ago. "If you think war is a glamorous thing," he wrote, "I wish you could have gone with me this afternoon to the row of camouflaged tents back of a wrecked railroad crossing which we call a battalion aid station." Many consider deep engagement in armed conflict to be the wrong time to discuss the nature of war—and by others the most critical time of all.

A note about the presentation:

In the interest of brevity, general references to Marine combat correspondents (CCs) should be read as including public relations officers (PROs), who operated under the same goals and restrictions even though they did not carry the same title. Together they are called "Marine writers." The distinction between noncommissioned and commissioned officers has been noted when relevant.

The typed pages of the dispatches held at the National Archives are often filled with editing marks with various purposes. At times words appear to be struck through to make a sentence more concise; entire sentences and even paragraphs may be penciled out because of space limitations or, in the opinion of the editor wielding the pencil, to move the story along, drop a frivolous point, or eliminate unnecessary detail. Censors had a different purpose, of course, and could strike words, sentences, or paragraphs they believed to violate regulations. The CCs likely changed their copy before turning it in, adding a word here and there or striking a word or two. All such markings on a typed page can make for difficult reading.

I have exercised my own editorial discretion to make these stories as readable as possible while maintaining the integrity of what came out of the CCs' typewriters—their raw copy as it was handed to the editors and the censors—and indicating what was removed by others. Only significant omissions by censors and editors are noted, not slight changes.

1 A Dangerous Publicity Campaign

The contingent of US Marines on a lonely speck of land in the Pacific called Wake Island were just finishing their breakfast when a radioman received a frantic transmission. The source was an American Army air base more than 2,300 miles away. Hickam Field and the neighboring naval base at Pearl Harbor were under attack from Japanese planes swarming over Hawaii. The Wake Island Marines knew exactly what to do, having undergone a general quarters drill just two days earlier. In forty-five minutes, every defensive position on Wake and the two neighboring islands that made up their V-shaped atoll were manned and ready to repel an assault from the air and sea. The only question was when the attack would begin—just before noon, it turned out—and how long it would last.

President Franklin D. Roosevelt would declare December 7, 1941, a date of "infamy" because of Japan's surprise attack. On the Wake Island calendar, that infamous day was officially December 8, owing to its location west of the International Date Line. The Navy had begun building an air station there early in the year to take advantage of American control of an atoll between Hawaii and Japan with strategic importance to both nations. Far more civilians were working on the project, about 1,200 contractors, than there were military personnel protecting it. Only about 450 Marines with a dozen fighter planes and seventy-five or so Army and Navy personnel stood against an invading Japanese force of dozens of bombers and several ships, two of them aircraft carriers. As many as 2,000 Japanese marines were prepared to land on Wake's shores to wrest it from the Americans.

The defenders held out for seventeen days. With no reinforcements coming to the rescue and the risk of massive civilian deaths growing, the Marines on December 23 literally waved a white flag, in this case tied to a mop handle. Casualties among American military personnel and civilians numbered more than 170; almost all the military losses were Marines. The Japanese paid for their victory with nearly 400 dead, untold wounded, and the destruction of several planes and ships.

The siege of Wake Island would be compared to the battle of the Alamo, another fierce but futile fight against an overwhelming enemy that became a storied moment in American history. At the time of the events in the Pacific, however, the American public as well as military officials knew little about the courage and heroism displayed by Marines and others holding off the Japanese. No civilian or military journalists were on hand, which left the dissemination of information to American and Japanese officials. While Navy communiqués announcing continued resistance at Wake Island made headlines, they lacked the detail and color of on-the-scene news reporting. When the Japanese overpowered the Wake defenders, the *Chicago Tribune* described the resulting Navy communiqué as "a laconic statement, barren of details of a combat that when all facts are known promises to become a classic episode in American arms." The newly expanded world war was in its first weeks, but already there were cries for heroes.

Intense public interest in Wake Island was an argument for the Marine Corps to take charge of reporting the activities of its own men. Pushing that point of view was the Division of Public Relations at Marine Corps headquarters in the new Navy Annex, a collection of buildings in Arlington, Virginia, across the Potomac River from Washington, DC. The DPR was only five months old when war erupted with Japan and its Axis cohorts, Germany and Italy, but the introduction of public relations to the Marine Corps predated even the First World War.

In the early twentieth century, the publicity operations of the Marine Corps centered on recruitment, the lifeblood of any military service. In 1907, the Corps opened its first publicity bureau, a single Chicago office, likely a result of increased enlistment quotas stemming from the Spanish-American War (1898) and the insurrection in the Philippines (1899–1902). The service began operating a national Recruiting Publicity Bureau in 1911, first in New York and later in Philadelphia, to handle press relations, publicity campaigns, advertising copy writing, and, starting in 1916, film production.

Two events influenced the Marine Corps to expand its organizational approach to managing its public image. First, Marine exploits at France's Belleau Wood and other engagements during World War I prompted headlines around the country and enhanced its reputation as a fighting force. Second, the practice of public relations gained credence in corporate America about the same time. Public relations practitioners established professional norms while initiating campaigns to defend or improve the public perception of controversial entities, for example, the oil and tobacco industries. In government, the Wilson administration turned to public relations to develop support for its programs. The close of the first quarter-century of Marine

Corps public relations saw a dedicated public relations section opened at service headquarters in 1933.

After Germany invaded Poland in 1939, the United States increased preparations for what many believed was the nation's inevitable role in a worldwide conflict. The commandant of the Marine Corps, Major General Thomas Holcomb, recognized that the Marines would compete more than ever with the Army and Navy for recruits. To lead the new Division of Public Relations he made what initially seemed an odd choice in Colonel Robert L. Denig, who had served with Holcomb in France during World War I. Denig was fifty-six and on the verge of retiring as commander of the Marine barracks in Bremerton, Washington. More puzzling, the man whom Holcomb was putting in charge of the public relations operation at that critical time had no experience in communications of any kind.

The deficiency was not lost on Denig when he traveled across the country to meet with Holcomb. Years later he recalled the moment with dry amusement. "I went in there and he said, 'Well, Denig,' he said, 'what do you know about public relations?' I said, 'I don't know anything about it. I never heard of it before. What is it?' Well, he said, 'You'd better learn because that's what you're gonna be.' That's my introduction to public relations." Refusing the assignment may not have occurred to the old-school Marine. Officially, Denig retired June 30, 1941, but he was reactivated the next day, with a promotion to brigadier general and assigned to his new command, a division then relegated to a tiny office with one sergeant and two civilian clerks.

The Division of Public Relations oversaw all news, information, and other material produced for public dissemination, but recruitment remained its top priority. Denig knew he needed a right-hand man with at least some of the experience he himself lacked. He recruited George Van der Hoef, a thirty-year-old University of Chicago graduate who had been working for several years as a publicity official with the Federal Housing Administration. Denig had Van der Hoef commissioned as a major and assigned to be his executive officer and the DPR's assistant director. "He put me wise to a lot of things that go on that I didn't know anything about," Denig said. In spite of his ignorance—or perhaps because of it—Denig was open to new ways to promote the Marine Corps.

One idea they worked on that fall involved placing journalists with Marine divisions to report on their activities for hometown newspapers and other print media. First and foremost, they would want stories about the average Marine—called "Joe Blow" at boot camp—whether he was a combat hero or one of the innumerable cooks, mechanics, drivers, and other personnel who kept the war machine humming. After the siege of Wake Island, the lack of information about the Marines' plight and heroism became a catalyst for the proposal. It turned out to be a hard sell. Amid the immediate demands of publicity and recruitment following Pearl Harbor, Commandant Holcomb appeared skeptical of the notion of reporters in Marine uniforms. He eventually authorized Denig to try to recruit ten men for what amounted to a preliminary test of the idea's feasibility.

In early spring 1942, Denig dispatched his division's lone sergeant to newsrooms around Washington to announce that the Marine Corps was signing up reporters as correspondents who would accompany troops into combat and write about them. The pitch proved to be more attractive than Denig could have imagined. Mirroring the patriotism-fueled fervor for enlistment around the country, plenty of young men in Washington's newsrooms wanted to get in on the war. The first class of CCs numbered more than a dozen from the ranks of the *Times-Herald*, the *Post*, the *Star*, the *News*, and the International News Service. Impressed by Denig's success, Holcomb allowed his public relations general to expand the informal recruiting effort to other cities. In addition, some journalists who had already joined the Marines learned of the combat correspondents' formation and sought transfers. Some Marine veterans working as journalists returned to the service with the goal of becoming a writing Marine.

Denig and Van der Hoef were eager to assign their division's reporters to accompany combat-bound Marines as the United States planned its Pacific offensive. In April, Van der Hoef persuaded his friend Herbert L. Merillat, a twenty-six-year-old Rhodes Scholar and Yale Law School alumnus working for the Treasury Department, to accept a commission as a public relations officer. "I liked the idea of joining a small, elite service instead of getting swallowed up in the bureaucracies of the Army and the Navy," Merillat recalled. "Above all, the Marine job would give me an opportunity to write." Merillat waved off a commission in the Navy Reserve and instead became a member of what would one day be called "Denig's Demons."

Like Van der Hoef, Merillat had neither journalism credentials nor Marine Corps experience—not even boot camp training. Before a week had passed, Merillat, now a second lieutenant, was on his way to North Carolina to join the First Marine Division. With him was thirty-one-year-old James W. Hurlbut, who had served in the Marine Corps for five years before working for the *Chicago Tribune*, the *Chicago News*, and the Washington radio station WJSV. Now a sergeant in Denig's public relations division, Hurlbut the CC was teaching the newly commissioned PRO, Merillat, about journalism and the Marines. Such was the hurried nature of wartime activities.

The Marine Corps took the proposal public in early June when Holcomb announced that newspaper reporters with at least five years' experience were being accepted for enlistment as combat correspondents. After training to fight, Holcomb said, they would be given the rank of sergeant and sent overseas with combat units. The demand for journalism experience tended to skew the average CC's age several years beyond the typical recruit, who was between eighteen and twenty-one. Most in the initial class of combat correspondents were in their mid-twenties; the oldest was thirty-two.

An Associated Press report noted that Holcomb stated that none of the service's high standards and physical requirements would be sacrificed. In practice, however, the physical requirements and the level of experience were flexible. Denig was open to seeking waivers for those whose eyesight or other physical traits fell short of standards. Among those who needed a waiver even to get to boot camp was Samuel E. Stavisky, then an assistant city editor with the *Washington Post*. The Army had rejected him when he tried to enlist the day after Pearl Harbor, and the Navy followed suit the next day, both citing poor eyesight. When Stavisky called Denig after hearing about the formation of the combat correspondents, the general wasted no time and told him, "You're in." So was Richard J. Murphy Jr., blind in one eye but, more important to Denig, a reporter for the *Washington Evening Star*. The newspaperman and broadcast journalist Alvin M. Josephy Jr., rejected by the Navy because of his eyesight, was advised to pack extra pairs of glasses when he joined Denig's division. Waivers aside, potential CCs still had to prove their stamina and their accuracy with a rifle alongside other recruits undergoing training at South Carolina's Parris Island or at the Marine Corps Base in San Diego.

Two enticements proved to be critical to recruiting journalists and supporting their mission to cover the average Marine: seeing action and achieving rank. By promising them a combat assignment, Denig assured those willing to put their professional careers on hold that they would join fighting men and not be assigned to a desk job. Also, an almost immediate sergeant's rank after boot camp was a valuable perquisite; a Marine might serve for a decade or more before gaining those stripes. Both factors were important in terms of reporting; it would be easier for a noncommissioned officer facing the same risks to relate to and gain the cooperation of the very people the CCs were created to cover. In other words, he would be one of them. "If you were in there as a major or captain you wouldn't have the same camaraderie with the enlisted," a combat correspondent, Cyril J. O'Brien, observed many years later. Some journalists were commissioned public relations officers who would report and write as well as oversee their sergeants, and some sergeants would be promoted to PRO after outstanding performance. Only the noncommissioned officers, the sergeants and, later, those of lesser rank, would receive the title "Marine Corps Combat Correspondent" in their dispatches.

Recruits enduring the physical and mental pressures of boot camp in South Carolina or California needed reassurances from the Division of Public Relations in Washington that they were not forgotten. Beginning in June 1942 and continuing throughout the war, DPR headquarters distributed once or twice a month a mimeographed bulletin that served as a newsletter. At first it took a breezy air, sharing news of weddings and births as well as tidbits of information about writing assignments and promotional projects. In time the bulletin became the DPR's primary method of communicating policy, criticism, requests for specific material, and other information to personnel stationed around the world. Its voice turning more official and stern as the months passed, the bulletin could be congratulatory and encouraging or scolding and sarcastic, often in the same edition. The bulletin and a log also kept track of stories, serving the dual purpose of assuring individual CCs that their copy had been received and published while subtly shaming less productive writers.

By mid-July 1942, the first eleven recruits had returned to Washington as Marine privates to undergo orientation at the Division of Public Relations, performing writing and editing tasks while awaiting their promotions to sergeant and an overseas assignment. They lived either in the barracks at the Navy Yard or civilian quarters in the city. Reporting to DPR headquarters by eight each morning but Sunday, they might receive a lecture from Denig about their future work as well as lectures from other high-ranking Marine officers about censorship and security regulations. When writing news releases or other material they worked with the kind of typewriter they would take with them overseas; the CCs found that the small Hermes portable fit nicely in the lower half of their packs. By four-thirty in the afternoon they were off-duty. The respite was short-lived for most; the average CC spent just a few weeks at headquarters before being transferred to a battle-bound Marine division. Their ranks continuing to grow, more than thirty CCs were undergoing orientation later that summer.

Selling the American public on the combat correspondent concept was not assured. More critical and perhaps at greater question was the degree of acceptance in civilian newsrooms to what could be taken as an encroachment on their turf. To win over the public in general and journalists in particular, Denig and Van der Hoef traveled around the country to speak to civic and business groups and appear at professional gatherings of journalists to seek cooperation in promoting the Marine Corps. After Van der Hoef returned from a convention of the National Editorial Association, the bulletin reported in July 1942 that he had found many editors "woefully ignorant" about the Marine Corps but enthusiastic about the possibilities the combat correspondent program presented. "Especially do they want to get information about the boys from their home towns serving abroad." Throughout the war the bulletin would maintain a drumbeat on the point that "Joe Blow" stories served an essential purpose even if their audiences were limited. Reports on major battles would include the names of rank-and-file Marines, not just generals and other commanders. It was a publicity gimmick of sorts but also a journalistic way of engaging all readers with the reality of the war effort—names and hometowns carrying the various regional and ethnic flavors of America would likely register with readers everywhere.

In their interaction with editors and publishers and in news stories about the program, Denig and Van der Hoef assured the press that Marine combat correspondents would assist civilian reporters and not compete with them. Some in the press remained wary of "government competition," but CCs were reminded in the bulletin that their job was not aimed at "scoring beats over accredited civilian reporters." Such concerns appeared to diminish over time as the CCs wrote the locally oriented stories that most civilian correspondents with major publications passed over. The Marine writers provided information to civilian press and could be quoted in civilian reporters' stories, often by name. In practice, some civilian correspondents used such material without attribution in stories that reached American news media long before the CCs' own stories, which could limit interest in the CCs' work when it was not focused on local men in uniform. Losing space or prominent play—even bylines—was accepted to adhere to DPR policy of not competing with the civilian press. Still, the Marine writers were understandably rankled—"even unhappier if the man to whom a story was given wasn't believed to be a good reporter," Benis M. Frank observed in his history of the initiative.

The Division of Public Relations would spend much of the next three years fine-tuning its operations as it sought to ensure that its combat correspondents functioned as a sort of hybrid in the world of news media. In almost every sense they were reporters covering a story—the biggest story of their lives—but they were also practicing public relations by promoting the best qualities of their client—in this case the Marine Corps—and soft-pedaling if not ignoring their client's flaws. Evidence of the tension that existed to some degree between a CC's journalistic training and his orders to promote the Marine Corps can be found in the stories that Navy censors and DPR headquarters rejected. Civilian journalists would have felt similar professional anxiety when facing an event that was news by the profession's traditional definitions yet might go unreported for the good of the war effort.

Journalists who became Marine combat correspondents were not left to their judgment alone when deciding what to report and how to report it. Through predeployment orientation at headquarters and through the bulletin, the Division of Public Relations provided guidance on subjects, style, content, and presentation. To process the stories and other material that came from those in the field, the division developed a structure similar to that of a newspaper city room in which reporters wrote stories and editors reviewed and changed them before determining their placement in pages. Establishing the "city room" at DPR headquarters fell to Captain David E. Nopper, who had worked for the *Washington Post*, *Baltimore Sun*, and the Maryland statehouse bureau of the Associated Press before joining up in 1942. The structure Nopper devised was not only familiar to the combat correspondents who came from the news media; it also provided the operation a more journalistic character.

The copy chain began when a CC completed a story and turned it over to his PRO, who conducted an initial edit. A Marine or Navy security officer, working in the theater of battle or in Pearl Harbor, Washington, or another behind-the-lines location, then checked the story for any information that could benefit the enemy or violate other standards. Commanding the Navy's own public relations operation—and acting as its chief censor—was a veteran *Los Angeles Times* newsman, Waldo Drake. He was the first public relations officer for the Pacific Fleet, his tenure beginning six months before the Pearl Harbor attack. Tempering Drake's journalistic drive to get out the story were years as an officer in the naval reserve, including duty with its intelligence service. "He believed he needed to control what correspondents were permitted to write or they'd reveal secrets that damaged operational security," observed Hamilton Bean in his study of Drake's pivotal role in Navy public relations, *Nimitz's Newsman: Waldo Drake and the Navy's Censored War in the Pacific*. Civilian correspondents chafed under what they saw as Drake's heavy hand. The journalists-turned-Marines likely felt similarly bedeviled as Drake and his team of censors determined what could and could not be distributed by the Marine DPR.

Forwarded to division headquarters, the story was edited in the so-called city room for style and other content matters. It was then revised or even rewritten before being typed, mimeographed, and branded an official Marine

Corps press release. DPR personnel determined which news outlets would receive the story, ranging from regional and national wire services to major newspapers, small dailies, and weeklies. Personnel at districts around the country ensured that local media received copies of stories, among them a subject's high school newspaper and a former employer's newsletter or bulletin board. In the summer of 1944, DPR headquarters began producing what it called a clipsheet, a nine-column page designed to showcase the week's best stories. It was mailed each Monday to 4,900 daily and weekly publications.

As part of the effort to promote the Marine Corps in any venue, the DPR developed stories for news and consumer magazines, special interest publications, professional journals, and industry and other nondaily publications. The division established a New York office to deal specifically with magazines, though its focus would be those with a wide national circulation. The DPR bulletin warned CCs that bylines in the *Saturday Evening Post* and *Colliers* were nearly impossible, but they were told that such publications would gladly accept exclusive material with the understanding the magazines could do with it as they pleased. The US government paid the CCs as they did other Marines, of course, and division headquarters reminded them that they were not allowed to solicit or accept paid assignments as freelance writers.

Weeks could pass as a story traveled through the copy chain and reached the civilian press. The initial stories from Guadalcanal in the second half of 1942 took two to four weeks to reach newspaper readers. Air mail was the mode of delivery for stories from the field to DPR headquarters, just one factor contributing to the time lag. Radio or telegraph or telephone lines were not employed routinely, possibly because of expense and the priority of more important transmissions. Security clearances as well as editing by the DPR's city room staff of two to three people were other factors. The division did seek to shorten the delay for extraordinary events. For example, when Marines landed at the western Pacific island of Saipan in June 1944, the DPR's city room worked around the clock to process stories and approved 315 for distribution in two days. Large numbers of stories, photographs, motion picture films, and radio recordings from Saipan continued to arrive at DPR headquarters for weeks thereafter.

For much of what the combat correspondents covered, the number of days that passed before their stories reached readers did not matter. CCs were assigned to write about the average Marine before, during, and after a battle or the Marine serving in a noncombat zone. Outside of battle, the story could be anything from a profile to a humorous piece that allowed its subject a moment of public recognition for doing his part in the war effort. The DPR stylebook, a writer's guide that set standards for policy as well as the mechanics of writing, reiterated the reason and need for such stories.

> While the daily activities of the men in your unit, and their environment, are ordinary stuff to you, they are matters of great personal concern to people in the States whose sons, husbands and neighbors are, as we say, somewhere in the South Pacific. Don't let routine and daily contact with your news sources dull your appreciation of their news values back home.
>
> When you are not in combat write the individual stories of men who are standing by awaiting their turn; when you go into combat write the stories of the men behind the stories—and you will be giving the American people one paramount part of the war coverage we ask you to be determined they shall have.

Division headquarters demanded that each Marine referred to by name in a story be identified by his hometown as well as his military serial number, the latter a way of helping headquarters check that the name and other information were correct. Of particular concern were photographs, a never-ending source of headaches as editors tried to ensure captions were correct, photos and stories were available simultaneously, and film was not damaged in transit.

The bulletin at times carried some of the most basic rules of news and feature writing: focus on a key point, write tightly, and avoid repetition; show instead of tell; check for style, spelling, and accuracy. Stories came in at 800 words on average when press associations informed the DPR that 300 to 400 words or fewer were enough for stories that were not major news. "We don't want, we can't use, flowery writing. We want direct writing. Say what you have to say with punch, with the fewest words possible," the bulletin advised. Another admonition: "Don't pad. The illusion seems to persist with some that a story is judged on the basis of quantity rather than quality." Nonetheless, complaints from division headquarters continued and grew sharper.

Weak storylines were a regular topic in the bulletin. The DPR frequently listed those not worth the CCs' attention or those whose interest among civilian editors had waned. They included pets, general accounts of trips, appeals for mail from home, general morale pieces, books the troops were reading, and worship services. The personal approach had limitations: The bulletin advised CCs not to refer to a Marine's girlfriend as the woman he intends to marry because sometimes it turned out not to be the woman's plan and she was embarrassed when such statements appeared in the local newspaper. DPR headquarters complained that some CCs were still having trouble finding something to write about and pointed to a story arriving in May 1943 relating to the attack on Pearl Harbor. The bulletin commented sarcastically, "At that rate we'll soon be trying to tell the folks about the Revolutionary War."

Newswriting veterans, college graduates among them, may have chafed at what could be taken as the bulletin's patronizing attitude. Cyril J. O'Brien, who had been a reporter for the *Camden Courier-Post* (New Jersey) when he joined the Marines as a CC at twenty-three in 1942, recalled the CCs as a professional cadre. "The only training we had to have was training as Marines," he said. "We were just as much Marines as any rifleman who fired an M-1. We didn't have to have newspaper training because we were all reporters already. The Marine Corps sure as hell couldn't teach us anything about journalism."

However, the public relations officers who published the division bulletin clearly did not share O'Brien's opinion. They routinely praised their scattered staff but also scolded them, at times by name, for failing to write succinctly, follow style, and provide correctly spelled names and other accurate information. "We don't appreciate having to do elementary copy-editing on your material. Make your stories easy to get out once they arrive here, if you care about your reputation at headquarters." It may be that the news experience of many CCs was limited and that in their ranks were many average writers, a reflection of the range in quality within the civilian media. For their part, combat correspondents complained that following the stylebook required a great deal of concentration for men often under small arms and mortar fire. In response, DPR headquarters lifted most style rules in October 1944, advising CCs to "write as you please."

Journalism experience and working within a journalistic structure did not change the fact that Marine combat correspondents were assigned to the Division of Public Relations and were expected to adhere to the mission of promoting the service. Officially, their stories were referred to as "press releases," not news stories. More significant in terms of content were admonitions such as one that appeared in a bulletin in August 1943: "Remember, you are always writing as a representative of the Marine Corps; you are a spokesman; your dispatches are semi-official; what you write either brings credit to, or reflects upon, the Corps." Their public relations function no secret, the news media veterans who joined the Marine Corps to report and write were called on to put aside the independence and impartiality that were expected in news writing at the time.

Two primary areas of censorship in wartime reporting—security and taste—applied to civilian correspondents as well as the CCs, but in different respects. For civilians, censorship for security was imposed by the government and could be specifically defined; taste was a form of self-imposed censorship and more subjective. The US government had rapidly increased its censorship of defense information after Pearl Harbor and established the Office of Censorship to monitor domestic and international news. Media agreed to adhere to a voluntary censorship code and were notified when the office found violations, although it seldom took any action. The journalism historian Michael S. Sweeney has noted that Army and Navy censorship of the civilian press in combat zones was mandatory but that domestic press censorship was voluntary, calling it "one of the shared sacrifices of war for American journalists."

The Marine writers were advised at division headquarters about matters of taste before deployment, and the DPR security guide included a brief section on "certain matters of policy" not directly related to security. Besides avoiding "boastfulness," the security guide advised exercising "good taste" and keeping in mind civilian readers. In a separate category was a caution about reporting "bloodshed," advising that death or suffering should not be described in "gory detail" because it would be painful to friends and relatives and "would do little to heighten morale." This guidance may have been abundantly clear if not obvious; unlike the frequent admonitions about security and writing, directives about bloodshed did not appear in the regular bulletin.

"Good taste" fell into the murky realm of what was considered fit for public consumption. "The censorship was mostly for taste," former combat correspondent Cyril J. O'Brien recalled decades later. "I didn't know enough about strategy and all that to say anything that would be in any way classified. I didn't know enough to say anything classified. . . . There was no need to write about blood and guts all over anybody or something like that. You didn't talk about a lot of blood streaming out and things like that. You could say someone was hit, but you didn't talk about a lot of gory things."

Newspapers and general-interest magazines did not, as a rule, publish foul language and other material they considered offensive to their readers. Those who had worked in news media would have already developed a sense of what was not allowed, and the division's city room likely followed common journalistic practice. Still, DPR headquarters chided the CCs for lapses. "Stories in obvious bad taste, having no value whatsoever for Marine Corps public relations, have been showing up too frequently of late," the bulletin advised in August 1943. Cited were a story about the "love life" of dogs and another about a town's red-light district. Some prohibitions, such as photographs of graves of canines and other animals marked by crosses, appeared to arise on an ad hoc basis. Casual profanity such as "damn" and "hell" was frowned on if occasionally used, and scatological humor was turned away. What was considered too coarse for civilian publications reflected the social mores of the times.

One subject that was not addressed in the bulletin was the use of derogatory racial terms for the enemy. With the attack on Pearl Harbor, referring to "the Japs" became commonplace in American media, including radio and motion pictures. Also regularly employed in CC stories was the term "Nips," but it was usually removed and replaced with "Japs." Occasionally there appeared references to "Tojos," a nod to the Japanese prime minister and military leader Hideki Tojo, as well as the adjective "yellow" to describe a Japanese combatant's racial identity, including the rhyming term "little yeller fellers." While "Japs" was ubiquitous in public relations copy, the other terms and references to "yellow" skin were usually deleted from stories by censors or DPR editors. Similarly, such racist terms rarely appeared in the bulletin. One exception: A bulletin entry referred to a Spanish-language magazine as a "slick in spic." The complicated relationship between the Marine Corps and African Americans and its impact on the public relations endeavor—a form of racial segregation—is the subject of a later chapter.

Unlike lapses in taste that could offend readers, security matters carried life-and-death consequences. Avoiding the unintended disclosure of information that could aid the enemy was an ongoing concern at DPR headquarters and with security officers who censored the CCs' stories. The Marine writers attended lectures about security before their deployment and had access to the division security guide outlining prohibited subjects as a reminder. The DPR stylebook contained a security section on prohibited subjects and information. A division bulletin in June 1943 carried a list from Pacific Fleet detailing subjects prohibited for civilian correspondents to report. Nonetheless, the DPR bulletin frequently indicated that stories were mentioning subjects that should not be reported for security reasons. Prohibited subjects included radar, armor and special weapons, aviation-related activities aboard carriers, code names for areas and places, and any words in a coded message lest they help the enemy break the code. To be treated with care were such subjects as successful escapes from enemy incarceration, troop movements, special vehicles or weapons, and other information that could aid the enemy if too many details were provided. Taken together, the regular warnings about security issues from DPR headquarters, frequent copy deletions, and outright rejection of entire stories refuted the views of combat correspondents like O'Brien who mistakenly believed their lack of knowledge of classified information meant their stories presented no security issues. Many CCs did not fully comprehend their exposure to sensitive information or, at the least, appreciate the potential for creating problems.

Public relations officers in the field or working in division headquarters not only edited copy for style, effective writing, and taste; they were also tasked with censoring material they believed would damage the image of the Marine Corps. Security officers may have done so as well if they considered the service's image a security concern. As early as 1942, Navy officials advised its personnel that a civilian correspondent's report would be passed by censors if it "does not injure the morale of our forces, the people at home, or our Allies; does not embarrass the United States, its Allies or neutral countries." Such a broad mandate for censorship, included with more specific examples, could be applied to practically any material from civilian or military writers that a censor viewed as problematic.

The editing marks on the original dispatches of combat correspondents and public relations officers did not indicate the identity of the editor. However, they suggested a widely shared skepticism for stories in which Marines were anything other than hard-charging, self-effacing, tough, and heroic—qualities that would attract young men to their ranks. Instances in which Marines might have looked reckless, frivolous, or silly could draw rejection. DPR headquarters, under Navy censorship guidelines, sought to quell stories that played up traditional rivalries between the Marine Corps and the Navy or Army. Disobeying orders, even if in the conduct of a heroic effort, was not to be publicized. Some stories that were seen as problematic for the Marine image as a humane if tough war fighter were edited or rejected. Stories about Marine encounters with Japanese soldiers were routinely distributed, but not if their behavior could be regarded as immoral even in wartime.

A reporter's news judgment did not vanish because he was a Marine, but official censorship and the public relations aspects of their work almost certainly contributed to self-censorship. In his 1999 memoir *Combat Correspondent*, Samuel E. Stavisky asserted that CCs were not permitted to send "bad news" back to the States and that he came to regard the censors as much an adversary as the Japanese. In one example, Stavisky wrote that several Marines had given him their account of a highly publicized action that was contrary to the heroic tale that civilian reporters had already published. "I didn't give the censors a chance to kill this incredible story. I killed the story myself. Why get another reprimand?"

The first line of defense against problematic material was, in actuality, the CC himself. The Marine combat correspondent Dan Levin made this point in his 1995 memoir *From the Battlefield*. He described a truck on Iwo Jima piled high with the bodies of Marines and explained why he decided not to attempt to include the scene in a story. "Our dispatches avoided such raw and close-up scenes," he wrote. "This was not due merely to censorship. We accepted the war as a just war. So our restraint came from within. We had to report truth, but total battlefield truth could injure morale. That was understood by civilians as well, and we had to understand it even better."

Self-censorship may also have been a reaction to a system that did not allow for discussion and argument over content. It would have been impractical to seek or receive an explanation for censorship or any other changes or to argue about them given the distances, time constraints, and multiple people in the copy chain, not to mention that the changes were being made by a person of higher rank. Undoubtedly mindful of the Marine image, some of the combat correspondents still believed there were stories about the war that readers should read. They may have written a story knowing it would be killed by their editors but tested the boundaries anyway—an act of defiance not unfamiliar to civilian reporters covering their beats back home.

Reflecting on censorship sixty years after he had served as a public relations officer, Millard Kaufman recalled trying to retain the writer's voice and to "let the guy write" as he edited stories. Kaufman was a young but experienced journalist, having worked in New York for the *Mount Vernon Daily Argus* and the *New York Daily News* before joining the Marines in his mid-twenties. He later accompanied landing forces at Guam and Okinawa. He recalled leaving censorship decisions to those in higher command. However, Kaufman noted that reporting such incidents as shell shock and friendly fire would not have been in keeping with the public relations mission. "All this stuff was done to recruit Marines. They didn't want any situation where a guy was going to go off his rocker. That didn't encourage enlistment," he said. "Marines were perfect, immortal human beings. They didn't shoot at each other. Nobody was reporting grisly deaths, and they certainly weren't being reported as shooting at each other. I think all that was done from higher up."

Whether civilian journalism or Marine Corps public relations, stories from the battlefield were subject to many of the same limitations in pursuit of the shared goal of an American victory over its enemies. For the Marine combat correspondents, the goal of advocating for the Marine Corps provided an additional rationale not to acknowledge all the uncomfortable truths of war. Tugging at the CCs, though, was the journalistic desire to find a good story and report it.

Though framed as a publicity campaign, the effort would prove to be uniquely dangerous. By May 1944, twenty-five noncommissioned Marines assigned to the Division of Public Relations, either as writers or photographers, and eight PROs were listed as casualties and were not expected to return to front-line assignments. With the number of enlisted men allowed in the DPR frozen at 179, their casualty rate was nearly 14 percent. One-third of the commissioned and noncommissioned officers listed as casualties had been felled by malaria and five others by battle wounds. Five additional men, not among those nearly three dozen casualties, had died by May 1944, before the bloody battles for Saipan, Guam, Tinian, Peleliu, Iwo Jima, and Okinawa added to the ranks of the DPR dead and wounded. Before the war ended, at least thirteen men working in the public relations division would be killed—some estimates placed the number closer to twenty—as they pursued stories designed to enhance the Marine Corps' image, record its history, and inform the public.

As the summer of 1942 ended, the Division of Public Relations was moving into high gear. Combat correspondents and other personnel were dispatched to Marine operations in Alaska, British Guinea, Trinidad, Cuba, Iceland, England, and Ireland as well as Hawaii's Pearl Harbor, the latter the most likely stopover for a CC destined to accompany a Marine division heading to the Pacific theater. With their early assignment to the First Marine Division, the public relations officer Second Lieutenant Herbert L. Merillat and combat correspondent Sergeant James W. Hurlbut were destined to become the first DPR personnel in combat. Soon, General Denig's unique proposal would undergo a literal trial by fire.

2

In the Jungles of Guadalcanal

The sun had not yet risen when the first Marine combat correspondent in the field, Sergeant James W. Hurlbut, went topside on the transport ship *Hunter Liggett* to gaze at their objective. To him Guadalcanal appeared to be like any other tropical island in the South Pacific. For the last three days a massive US Navy convoy had crossed the ocean under thick gray clouds that apparently had allowed them to close in on the largest of the Solomon Islands without being detected by Japanese defenses. Shortly after six o'clock on August 7, 1942, American naval vessels began firing a barrage of shells that ended the peace and quiet on Guadalcanal and the neighboring island of Tulagi. The Americans were on offense at last.

The initial wave of Marines headed toward Guadalcanal's northern shores two hours later. Hurlbut accompanied the second wave at about nine o'clock. The sergeant who had been a Washington-based newsman just three months earlier found himself crouching inside a landing craft with other Marines. "We were all green troops, had never been under fire before," Hurlbut later recalled, "and I think all of us were spending some time thinking about what it meant in terms of personal action. I think we all made the same mental resolutions to do the best job possible and give it our best." For the Marine combat correspondent, that meant observing the action and writing a story as soon as possible for distribution to American readers by the Division of Public Relations.

The first bylined story from a DPR writer in a battle theater came from a public relations officer, Second Lieutenant Herbert L. Merillat, who had accompanied Hurlbut to join the First Marine Division. Merillat had been in a landing group an hour after his CC. His story, dated a week later, on August 14, provided an eyewitness report from his transport ship and gave an overall account of the operation's opening days. "To the Japs on Guadalcanal and Tulagi it must have seemed that all hell had broken loose," Merillat wrote, later adding: "Salvo after salvo ripped into their midst. Navy planes unloaded high explosive and strafed the ground. The red trails of tracer bullets and shells cut the black coast of Guadalcanal."

Two weeks would pass before Merillat's story appeared in newspapers, both because of the time it took to send copy to Washington and out of the Navy's concern about releasing too much information too early. Still, his story provided the kind of color and drama that the bare-bones Navy communiqués had lacked about the unfolding operations in the Solomon Islands. The *Los Angeles Times*, for example, had given the terse Navy announcement on August 8 of the operation a half-dozen column inches on page 2 the following day and said it "may be of considerable significance." Merillat's story, even though it described events three weeks old, ended up on the front pages of the *Chicago Tribune* and the *Washington Evening Star* and inside the *New York Times*, *Boston Globe*, and *Washington Post*. Just as General Denig and Major Van der Hoef had envisioned at DPR headquarters, placing writing Marines on the scene delivered headlines about Marine Corps actions in stark contrast to the relative silence that had marked news about the siege at Wake Island.

Surprisingly, the Marines encountered little resistance on Guadalcanal in the assault's opening hours, but they took heavy fire on Tulagi and nearby Gavutu and Tanambogo. A serious response from the Japanese on Guadalcanal would come soon enough; aerial bombings began that first afternoon. Hurlbut was eager to get to work but had only a fountain pen for his correspondent duties. He had left Washington so quickly in the rush to join the First Marine Division that he had not had a chance to draw all his DPR equipment. Once on the island, he traded his pen for a mediocre portable typewriter belonging to a sergeant in a combat battalion who, because of his poor penmanship, was using it to type letters to send back home. "He was willing to sacrifice his own letters for the good of the service," Hurlbut said.

His own account of the lead-up to the landings at Guadalcanal came in a story that appeared in newspapers the day after Merillat's and offered additional details from the first week of the operation. Most of the piece focused on the experience of being aboard the transport ship as it met up with other vessels for the convoy to Guadalcanal. "Eight months after the treacherous assault on Pearl Harbor the Allies struck a powerful initial blow in an action that is a forerunner to someday clearing up the Pacific," Hurlbut wrote. The final sentence—"'See you in Tokio!' is the watchword of the Marines"—was likely not only meant to be uplifting for readers but a pitch for the Marine Corps as the service to watch. Banned by Navy decree from both civilian and military reports was the first clash of the American and Japanese navies, which had cost nearly 1,100 American lives and three heavy cruisers. The delay in publication of Merillat's and Hurlbut's stories also allowed for their optimistic perspectives.

The battle for Guadalcanal would stretch over six months before the Americans secured a victory that had been in doubt more than once. The main prize may have seemed small, just an airfield under construction by the Japanese, yet it posed a threat to the shipping lanes that brought troops and supplies to Australia. A seaplane base and port on Tulagi would be part of the spoils that went to the winner. The Americans initially poured 19,000 troops into Guadalcanal, and the Japanese responded by reinforcing their 2,500 and tried to prevent the enemy from doing the same. If seizing and holding the airfield was a primary objective for the Marines, Japanese forces turned that effort into a siege. At the same time, battles in the sea and sky raged between the Japanese and American forces. Both sides also faced common foes: a tremendously hot and humid climate, malaria and other jungle diseases, plus insects, scorpions, and spiders. Vicious fighting in a hostile natural environment would play out in other operations in the Pacific.

For the first two months of the fight, Hurlbut was the only Marine combat correspondent on Guadalcanal as the Division of Public Relations prepared to add CCs to the reinforcements heading there. "Guadalcanal was a pretty big beat to cover singlehanded, but I made it a practice to go on as many patrols as I could and take part in as many actions as I could," Hurlbut said later. In a September dispatch from Guadalcanal that again gained widespread publication in American newspapers, Hurlbut described a patrol operation against the Japanese:

> Enemy forces were well dug in. They had trenches and machine gun nests and many snipers in trees. Here again their uncanny ability at concealment was demonstrated. Lieut. John E. Flaherty of Wilmington, Del., reports that while leading a platoon he was fired upon at least 50 times during the day by snipers without actually seeing one.
>
> One of our lieutenants and his runner, a private, were active in reconnaissance work, going well ahead to scout enemy positions. While they were moving in the open, our observers saw the private shot and killed by a sniper. The lieutenant bent over the private to give aid and was also hit.
>
> Marine Gunner Edward S. Rust, of Detroit, Mich., said he saw the lieutenant, although mortally wounded, fire on the Jap sniper with his pistol. The Jap was found dead a few feet away with two slugs in his body.

To get additional information on his "beat," Hurlbut spoke with officers in the various units of the First Marine Division and checked in regularly with its headquarters, the field hospital, and other places where he found good sources of stories and information.

With civilian correspondents covering the battle and Hurlbut concentrating on Marine activities, Merillat spent most of his time recording a history of the operation, based on interviews and observation, which had been his assignment from Denig. The focus on "Joe Blow" stories for hometown newspapers had yet to be developed when Merillat and Hurlbut left Washington. Still, as the only public relations officer on Guadalcanal, Merillat was intent on the news getting out regardless of who wrote it. Transmission of news stories, military and civilian, was problematic. Stories were cleared for security by the chief of staff on the island, then, if sent by radio to Pearl Harbor, enciphered. Airplane or ship became the more common way news stories reached the Navy censors at Pearl Harbor, who then sent the Marines' copy by air mail to DPR headquarters for editing and distribution to news media.

Delays were common, even for stories Merillat and Hurlbut thought were important. One night in October, after a period of heavy fighting but with no planes taking off for days, Merillat was desperate to get a thick envelope of dispatches off the island. Enlisting a nervous driver, Merillat took a jeep across the western end of the recently renamed Henderson Field, the section favored by Japanese gunners waiting for landing aircraft. "We made a mad dash across the airfield, got to a transport plane just as it was taking off," Merillat later recalled. Someone on the plane was turned into a courier. "I shoved an envelope into his hand and told him please to get this out, it is the only news that the world will have of us on this past week."

Although Hurlbut and Merillat led the way for "Denig's Demons," their files held by the National Archives and Records Administration include relatively little of their edited copy—none in Merillat's case. There are carbon copies of stories, the originals probably sent along the copy chain to DPR headquarters for editing. It may be that in the infancy of the public relations operation the edited dispatches were simply not kept or that over the years they were separated from the others. This appears to be true for the Marine writers in general; files in the archives are far from complete, and some combat correspondents are not represented at all.

Hurlbut's archived files show edited stories that carry typical changes expected in the copy flow: Words are trimmed, sentences are shortened or cut, and paragraphs are shifted or deleted. Occasionally information relating to sensitive subjects, such as assistance from island natives and a decoy tactic to draw Japanese naval fire, were struck. None of Hurlbut's archived stories carries a Navy censor's red-pencil verdict "kill" or "do not release." If stories by the two men were rejected, those edited versions may have been discarded at some point. Their files do not include all the official versions of their reports, the "press releases" that were sent out to civilian media. Thus, it would be difficult to ascertain differences between what Hurlbut and Merillat wrote and what the division distributed in those early months of the DPR operation. What they wrote that was rejected in whole is impossible to determine. However, as more Marine writers spread across the battle theater, a system that saved original dispatches apparently developed.

One Marine combat correspondent, Sergeant Edward J. Burman, a news announcer for a San Francisco radio station as well as a Marine reservist before the war, arrived with relief troops in October. Only two civilian journalists were on the island then, but Hurlbut contended that "ten men, pooling their activities, couldn't possibly keep adequate track of the events of the past week." Four additional CCs would arrive in November, and more would follow. Once the island was secure, Marine writers scrounged to find interesting subjects. Stories about Guadalcanal also came from interviews with Marines recovering from their wounds or enjoying a rest on a base in the region. Interviews in sick bay or a hospital ward would become a mainstay of the DPR coverage of Joe Blow's war. Those stories too would be cast aside if they crossed the lines drawn and patrolled by Navy censors and Marine Corps editors.

The following censored or otherwise rejected stories and story segments were written from the autumn of 1942 through 1943. Italics are used in stories that were released to indicate deletions. If an entire story was withheld, it is presented in full in regular typeface. To aid the narrative flow, stories have been placed to follow a general timeline of the events described, not the dates on which the stories were written or distributed. The CCs gathered much of their information in interviews days and weeks after a battle. For those reasons, bylines and datelines appear at the end of a story and dates in endnotes. If a date on a dispatch is unclear, it is placed in brackets. The headlines are usually the author's, though taken from or inspired by the stories themselves.

"They were pleased with the power of their new weapon"

Germany developed the modern flamethrower at the turn of the century. Japan as well as the United States found such weapons effective in clearing the enemy from jungles, caves, and fortifications on Pacific islands. The Navy recommended against the release of this account of a Marine unit employing the weapon for the first time. A Navy censor told the Division of Public Relations that the flamethrower was not a weapon it wanted publicized. Whether the request was an attempt to avoid possible controversy or driven by tactical considerations alone was not stated by a censor's note attached

In the Jungles of Guadalcanal

to the heavily edited copy of the story and its original version, which follows. This dispatch was unusual in that it was presented as a quoted statement from the subject.

"I gave 'em a squirt of flame and somebody yelled, 'How d'ya like it, Tojo?'"

Corporal Frank W. Menane of Spokane, Washington, a husky young giant with a stubble of black beard, was describing the first action in which he participated as a flame thrower.

"Just the sight of the flames scared those Japs to death. They were panic stricken.

"Our officers say we're the first Marines to use flame throwers in this war. We are a Combat Engineer outfit under the command of Colonel Elmer E. Hall, from Oregon. The Colonel is an old Marine football player and coach. He's a regular guy.

"Combat Engineers work as road builders, construction workers, and demolition men. We do any kind of a job of construction or destruction. But being 'fire-bugs' or 'fire-eaters' was something new to us.

"When we arrived on Guadalcanal we didn't have any flame throwers. The Army had some which they hadn't used. An Army Colonel turned them over to us, and a sergeant showed us how they worked. We practiced for an hour and a half or so, and the boys were ready to try them out on the Japs. Eleven Combat Engineers had volunteered to be the first Marine flame throwers. They took to the job like ducks to water.

"The detail went up to the front and I was NCO in charge. We were to go to work on a pocket of opposition holding up the Marine advance through a wooded ravine. The Japs had two machine guns well dug in and hidden from sight. The guns were protected by at least ten deep fox holes with one or two snipers in each. They commanded a field of fire which would have cost many men if taken by direct assault. That's why we were called in. To burn 'em out so the advance could continue without heavy losses. Flame throwers are used only as a last resort.

"The Marines were in fox holes just taken from Japs, and we found 'em sitting on Jap bodies. We moved up carrying the 75 pound weight of the apparatus. The other men in the detail acted as refuelers and furnished protecting fire. By this time we knew how to hold our breath while firing, and how to judge wind direction, and avoid the terrific heat. The flames shoot 35 to 40 yards. We usually fire a three second burst or 'squirt'. A 15 second burst can melt a rifle barrel.

"Covered by the protecting fire of automatic weapons and rifles, we went 10 yards in advance of our infantry, to keep the flames in advance of them.

"Corporal Russell M. Rowland, Forrest City, Arkansas, moved out with me. We couldn't see the fox holes till we were almost on top of 'em. I came onto a hole and gave it a squirt. The Japs in that hole must have inhaled the flames. They were dead before they had a chance to move. I was firing a burst on another hole when Rowland saw a Jap pop up and take aim at us. Before he could fire Rowland gave him a squirt and hit him in the leg. I turned and saw the Jap drop his rifle and scramble for a hilly path. I caught him with a sheet of flame right in the seat of his pants. Instantly he became a ball of flame rolling down hill. He must have died instantly. Another Marine used a grenade and got the other Jap in the hole. I saw a Jap behind a tree going after his rifle. Their snipers have a trick of propping a bunch of rifles around in different spots behind trees and natural cover. Then they run to the nearest one and fire. I saw this guy and yelled for somebody to get him. Nobody saw him, and I was unarmed, so I grabbed a Reising gun from another Marine and got the Jap before he could fire on the 'fire-bugs'.

"Then Rowland and I went back to refuel. The next move was to get the machine gun nest. It was in a good spot with natural cover. They had an L shaped dugout backed up by a huge tree. As the automatic weapons were knocking out the snipers, I got close to the dugout and gave it a squirt. After that the gun didn't fire again. Later we found the barrel was melted. The heat was so great the little yellow monkeys scrambled out to make a run for it. At least eight of 'em came rushing out to be cut down by the hail of fire from our infantry.

"Our job was done. The machine gun nest was knocked out and ten fox holes were cleaned up. So the Marine advance continued.

"There were no casualties among the Combat Engineers. This was due to the great support of the infantry. Our detail was complimented by the officers for doing a good job. The advance was able to continue with a minimum of opposition, thus saving the lives of many Marines. Between 20 and 35 Japs were killed in the action by either the 'fire-bugs' or by rifle fire. The rifles of the Jap snipers were badly burned up.

"The men who took care of the refueling did a good job, too. 'Fire-bugs', Private Ralph Roden, Madera, California, and Private First Class Denver H. Cox of Fresno, California did a swell piece of work. Private Howard C. Foreman of Glendive, Montana, gave us protection when it was needed, by his accurate sniping.

"The Combat Engineers were pleased with the power of their new weapon. The boys have been under fire a lot, but now they can do some attacking on their own.

"I've seen our boys operating steam shovels and bulldozers on roads to the front lines, while Jap snipers blaze away at 'em and shoot holes in the equipment. But after the fireworks, these boys climb up on the driver's seat and get on with their work.

"The only trouble with being a 'fire-bug' is that we never get any Jap souvenirs. After we work on 'em you never can find any."

Sgt. E. J. Burman
Guadalcanal

"The great mistake of coming in contact with a Marine"

International agreements and individual nations' military regulations required that the remains of enemy dead be treated with respect. Putting aside this story's tone of enthusiasm mixed with barbarity, Navy censorship regulations deemed "the taking of any part of the body" as a prohibited subject.

In the tent of Marine Private First Class Leroy J. Weathers is a Japanese soldier's skull. Perched on top of the skull is a battered Japanese helmet.

Private First Class Weathers keeps the skull in a prominent place in his tent just as a daily reminder that many more skulls must be collected before the war is won.

Working with a survey section along the sandy and once bloody beaches of this tropical island, Private First Class Weathers stumbled across the skeleton of a Japanese soldier. Shoes and shreds of clothing remained on the bones of the Japanese who had made the great mistake of coming in contact with a Marine.

In the vicinity were other skeletons. Private First Class Weathers covered them with sand. He decided to keep this one particular skull because he says "the guy looks as if he is about to say, 'so sorry, please'."

Private First Class Weathers, 22, USMC, enlisted in the Marine Corps in September, 1942, in Chicago, Illinois. He is the son of Mr. and Mrs. Tracy Weathers, of 5719 North Melvina Avenue, Chicago, Illinois. In addition to currently being on this island outpost, he has seen service at Camps Dunlap and Pendleton in California and at the Marine Corps Base, San Diego, California.

Sgt. Francis H. Barr
Guadalcanal

"We seldom see 'em in Brooklyn"

Rank with stereotypes and taking a swipe at the Army, this story sought to show a touch of humor and irony. It was rejected for wholly other reasons. The title is the Marine writer's.

Marine Pfc. John Brown Jr., of Fort Defiance, Arizona, realizes today, with justifiable humiliation and no small measure of chagrin, that he faces more than his expected allotment of danger in this war. His buddies in a communications outfit, however, have one more incident about which to rib army newcomers to the island.

John Brown Jr. has been faithfully performing his task of carrying confidential messages from the front lines to headquarters at the rear. He has gone about his job with spirited stride, proud carriage and a satisfactory sense that his service befits a true and patriotic American. All of which has been fine, until this morning John Brown Jr. encountered a freshly-arrived army MP, whose assignment it was to patrol the road along which the messenger was making a routine trip.

"Halt!", barked the MP, as John Brown Jr. approached. Then, in unmistakable Brooklynese, and with leveled revolver, "Where the hell do ya' think you're going?"

"Over there," came the challenged one's reply. He indicated a headquarters tent.

"Yeah—for what?", growled the MP, flexing his trigger finger.

"Got a message."

"Message, eh?—What's your name?" The finger stiffened.

"Brown," was the prompt reply.

"Brown, indeed," snickered the MP.

He lunged toward John, prodding him roughly with his weapon. The triumphant captor hustled his quarry ahead to the officers' tent, to be met at its entrance by the Marine captain in charge.

"What's this?", asked the captain, recognizing at once the daily message-bearer.

"This %**!#/! Jap says he's got a message," answered the MP, shaking John Brown Jr. for emphasis.

"Better go easy on that boy," chuckled the captain. "And I'd advise you to insure your scalp. This lad's a full-blooded Navajo. Come in, Brown."

Sgt. Dick Hannah
Guadalcanal

A revised version of the story trimmed it by nearly half, mostly by removing the opening sentences describing Brown's treatment. A Navy censor's stated reason for withholding even a shorter version—"kill because of Navajos"—reflected not the insults or the stereotypes but the fact that the military was trying to keep secret its use of the unique Navajo language as an effective code.

"He looks like the freckle-faced kid next door"

A Marine combat correspondent, like any journalist, had to be wary of stories that sounded too good to be true. Division editors were skeptical of this young Marine's tale because it lacked any supporting information—a flaw that they believed the writer should have recognized. In killing the unverified story, an editor noted that the reputation of the DPR was at stake.

> Private Darrell F. Blake, U.S.M.C., 17, of 530 2nd Ave., Powderly, Ala., killed at least 20 Japs and captured a light enemy machine gun and a mortar during recent fighting in the Matanikau River section.
>
> Blake, who looks like the freckle-faced kid next door, became separated from his unit while deep in enemy territory. He spotted the enemy machine gun nest while advancing down a wooded slope.
>
> Blake shot the gunner, then advanced forward. He reloaded his rifle as he neared the machine gun emplacement. Suddenly eight Japs rose from the position. One of them, an officer, raised his pistol. Blake opened fire, killing the officer and his companions.
>
> Several yards away, Blake heard thrashing in the grass. He threw two hand grenades in that direction. Japs ran for cover. Blake blasted away, killing nine.
>
> He continued on and, from a vantage point, observed two Nipponese operating a mortar. He crept to the left and took aim, killing both of them. The mortar, too hot from recent firing, could not be moved, so he smashed it.
>
> Returning to the machine gun nest, he discovered that the gun weighed only about 22 pounds. He carried it back to camp, arriving there an hour later without injury.
>
> His mother lives at Route One, Bessemer, Ala.
>
> Sgt. Norman A. Miller
Guadalcanal

"He was picked up and dropped before being buried alive"

Judging from the notations on the story—"killed Navy" and "doubtful story"—this young Marine's tale of survival also strained credulity.

Four 100 pound bombs fell within a five foot radius killing six Seabees and wounding Corporal Lester C. Aiken, U.S.M.C., 19, son of Mr. and Mrs. Jeff Aiken of Crossett, Arkansas, who lived to tell the story.

He was picked up and dropped three times by the concussion before being buried alive.

The incident occurred on August 21st while Corporal Aiken was assisting in the landing of heavy artillery at Vella Lavella.

Suddenly several Jap planes dived toward the beach chasing Corporal Aiken and the Seabees into a nearby palm grove where they dived into foxholes arranged in an imperfect circle.

The Japs aimed for the landing boats and missed—their bombs crashing into the center of the fox hole circle. The Seabees were killed immediately; Corporal Aiken, hit by shrapnel, bounced around before the side of the foxhole caved in on top of him. He managed to call for help and buddies nearby dug him out within a minute and a half. "I never lost consciousness," the slim, brown, Arkansas Marine said, "though the only air I had seemed to be that in my helmet."

Gangrene developed in the lower part of his left leg and it had to be amputated. But Corporal Aiken has the satisfaction of knowing that none of the planes that wounded him got away.

Staff Sgt. Solomon I. Blechman
Guadalcanal

"The elements were in control"

Rarely were the effects of tropical storms reported in CC dispatches. This detailed account drew an emphatic "No!" from a Navy censor likely concerned that the impact of a heavy storm on every aspect of Marine operations was too much information to publicize.

Sea and sky conspired May 9 to ravish this island with the most vicious storm experienced here since the Marines first landed.

Huge waves battered the beach areas, ripping landing boats loose from their anchors and grinding them into tragic, battered hulks. Twenty-two ton tank lighters were tossed ashore like broken toys.

Torrential rains turned tiny streams into raging rivers. The Ilu, the Lunga, the Teneru and all the rest roared out of their narrow channels. Bridges were swept away, or the approaches washed out and the span left standing, useless.

The backwaters and the five-inch rainfall turned lowlands into lakes. Some camp areas were inundated, the men retreating to higher ground as the flash flood filled their tents.

Patients were moved from their beds to temporary quarters as the rising tide spilled over into one hospital sector.

Roads were blocked when drainage ditches proved inadequate to carry off the deluge. Trucks and jeeps bogged down in the middle of washed out roadbeds, or slid into the sticky morass alongside. Some vehicles drowned out and were abandoned, and the water swept over their tops.

Traffic was at a standstill except within isolated areas, and communication lines were broken. Telephone wires were ripped down by falling tree limbs, broken by the force of the rain and the accompanying 30-knot wind. The power system failed in one camp.

With the lighters and landing barges wrecked, sunk or beached; with the bridges washed out and lakes where roads had been; and with telephone communications broken, the various forces here were segregated into many little islands of camps. Overall contact was impossible.

The war was detoured, and not a fighting flight left the ground all day. The elements were in control.

Incidental to the storm itself was the heroic work done on every hand to minimize its destructive force. Navy SeaBee Battalions, Marine Aviation Engineers and Army Engineer Battalions worked without respite.

The main Lunga River bridge was saved by men who dynamited the heavy flow of debris before it could smash the span. All through the day and until early morning on the 10th, charge after charge of explosives were fired to break up whole trees and heavy logs being borne by the current toward the pilings.

The bridge, though saved and now easily repairable, was put out of use when the approaches caved in.

A few landing barges were saved from serious damage by men who operated their heavy lifts right down to the breaker-swept beach and pulled the boats inland and out of reach of the waves.

As many as six breakers at a time were rolling in toward the littered beach. The "General's barge" was crushed against a small dock and sunk. The docks were demolished.

Before the storm subsided here, one man was dead and several injured. The damage, while not detailed as to places and organizations, was considerable.

Actually the storm had started here with heavy rains on May 8, but it didn't reach its full fury until the 9th.

Almost as rapidly as they had overflowed their banks, the rivers were running back toward normal on the 10th. The surf was only moderately rough along the beach. The roads still were muddy, but drying. Construction sections already are well along on temporary repair of the bridges. War planes are flying again.

1st Lt. Henry F. Childress Jr.
Guadalcanal

"To have died would have been better"

Navy officials categorized as secret the interrogation of prisoners of war and how they were treated. They were not won over by stories that presented the Japanese in a sympathetic light or provided insight into their perspective.

To their families, country and Mikado, the Japanese captured at Guadalcanal and brought to this prison camp are as dead as the soldiers who fell on Bloody Ridge, as the sailors who drowned at Santa Cruz, as the pilots shot down over Henderson Field.

These prisoners are well aware they are "dead", and accept their status with fatalistic resignation.

"Shikata ga nai"—they say—"So let it be."

The Japanese attitude of "death" is no pretense. It springs from a deep tradition that the Nipponese warrior can return to his homeland and to his home only as the victor—alive or dead, as a conquering hero or as revered ashes. There is no return for the defeated. Capture by the enemy, so far as the Japanese code is concerned, is akin to ignominious death.

That is why the Jap soldier fought so fiercely, neither giving nor seeking quarter in Guadalcanal. That is what makes the numerous reports of trapped Japs committing mass hara-kiri credible and the action understandable. That is why, aside from the bloody and bitter fighting, so few Jap prisoners were taken in the Solomons campaign.

Most of the prisoners here did not give themselves up voluntarily. Some did. But most of them were captured while they were unconscious, or dazed by injury, weakened by hunger and disease and privation.

Many can not understand why they were taken alive. They bring this up with the interpreters. It puzzles them that they were not killed. That, they argue, is the only honorable end for the vanquished warrior.

Sometimes, as if pleading their case to the world, they ask for paper and ink, and meticulously explain how it came about that they were taken alive, and why they did not commit hara-kiri.

"I was out of my head from the loss of blood," writes a soldier. "I was numbed from long immersion in the sea," protests a sailor. "I lost my wits in the crash," explains a pilot.

With some of the prisoners the excuses they offer for being captured alive are a matter of Oriental face-saving. With others, though, the protestations are sincere.

"Shinda ho ga ii"—"To have died would have been better."

But the mysterious hand of fate intervened, and now, though "dead" to family and country, they are actually still alive, their past severed, their future dubious. How wrestle with the maneuverings of the gods? Shikata ga nai—they say—so let it be.

The prisoners won't discuss their past. They give false names on being questioned, lest somehow word of their capture get back to Japan and bring disgrace to their family. For the same reason they avoid being photographed.

Rare is the Jap prisoner who requests the opportunity to write a letter to his people in Japan.

About their future, the Japs are less reticent, but necessarily vague.

Perhaps—whichever side wins—they will be able to start life anew in some other part of the world? Some naively express the hope they may be permitted to immigrate to the United States. Whatever happens, happens.

Resigned to their paradoxical "death", the Jap prisoners accept what follows as a matter of course. As a result, they are model prisoners—disciplined, courteous, and obedient.

Their past gone, their future uncertain, they live for the present. They work, they play, they gamble for their daily cigarette ration, they sing, they joke.

Shinda ho ga ii . . . Shikata ga nai.

Staff Sgt. Samuel E. Stavisky
A prison camp in the South Pacific

The Japanese-to-English translations reflect the military translator's level of expertise and thus could be interpreted differently, and perhaps more accurately, by others. Rather than "So let it be," the phrase "Shikata ga nai" may be better understood as "There's nothing to be done" or "It can't be helped." Similarly, the phrase "Shinda ho ga ii" could be more directly stated in English as "I prefer to die" or "It's better to die," rather than "To have died would have been better."

"Better to kill fish with dynamite or hand grenades?"

A jibe at the Army was cut during editing of this feature story. However, since the supply of explosives was not unlimited, using them for recreation likely led to the story's rejection.

Fish on Guadalcanal are slow to nibble at the Marine angler's hook but they yield to the less gentle methods of persuasion—hand grenades and dynamite.

Scores of Leathernecks have gone out with tackle borrowed from the Red Cross or with simple lines attached to bamboo poles and returned empty-handed. *They have offered such excuses as: "I fished for hours without getting a bite and then discovered the Army was bathing up stream," or "There just weren't any fish."*

Sergeant John F. Carlson, U.S.M.C., 23, of Yakima and Kirkland, Washington, who went with the only fishing party to catch anything with fins, recently, said that after accepting native hospitality of cooked bread fruit, the party was led to a "slow stream" full of fish.

Marines caught a nine inch trout with worm bait and a "flat shaped fish, like a flounder, which the native boy called 'Galsoki.'"

"Later they took us into the jungle, gave us a new sort of bait—snails which they picked from the undersides of leaves, crushed in their teeth and extracted the meat—and pointed to a better fishing hole. We caught over 17 fish which the natives cleaned (leaving the head and lungs) and fried for us in lard. The fish were sweet and tender and we ate them to the tune of Christmas Carols which the natives were singing as Sunday hymns," Carlson said.

Controversy exists as to whether it is better to kill fish with dynamite or hand grenades. Sergeant Hopewell A. Reif, U.S.M.C., 26, of Highland Park, St. Paul, Minnesota, related that he killed over 100 fish by tossing a block of T.N.T., into the water. After the blast he and his companions waded into the water and speared the fish with their knives.

Private First Class Raymond E. Fernwood, U.S.M.C., 23, of 2900 Coosgrave Avenue, Oakland, California, prefers grenades because they are handy to use. He recalled how, during a recent trip to the west coast of Guadalcanal, he solved the food problem. Native guides would tear chunks of red ant's nests from the trees, drop them into streams to attract fish and then call to him to "grenade" the mass.

"After the muffled explosion sea bass and tuna that had come up the river from the ocean came to the surface. Our boys had to battle the stream of natives who came from the jungle in order to gather our fish.

"They partly cleaned them and roasted them over hot coals. We ate the white meat after peeling the fish skin like one does an orange.

"We also gathered turtle eggs on the beach, driving the mother from the nest. Roasted they tasted like duck eggs," he said.

Some fish have been caught by Marines and natives by seining the river with old mosquito nets. No one reports having shot fish.

Ocean fishing, done from sand bars off shore, is poor as the fish refuse to strike at bits of beef and sand crabs.

Staff Sgt. Solomon I. Blechman
Guadalcanal

"It's a heck of a note"

This rejected story touched on more than one troublesome topic: disobeying orders, leaving one's post without permission, dangerous souvenir hunting, treatment of prisoners, and native cooperation.

Private Louis J. Zib of 2722 S. Lombard Avenue, Berwyn, Illinois, wanted some Jap souvenirs to take home with him . . . whenever he goes home.

So one recent day Private Zib left his Marine aviation squadron area without permission and went toward the hills of Cape Esperance, where the Japs made their last stand in February.

He didn't have a pass to go into that zone, but managed to get there by devious routes, hitch-hiking and walking the whole distance. He turned from the beach finally, and started following a small stream back into the hills.

Souvenirs were plentiful and Private Zib collected a Jap skull, helmet, bayonets and rifles. But then he noticed it was getting late, so he cached his find and started back toward the beach and his own camp.

He still was in the hills, however, when his journey was interrupted by a native running out into his path and shouting, "Jap! Jap!" Zib loaded and cocked the rifle he was carrying, and followed the native into the bushes.

Sure enough, he found there that the natives had captured a Jap soldier, disarming him of the bayonet he had carried as his only weapon. Apparently he had lost his other equipment in two months he had been hiding out on the island.

Zib started to shoot the Jap, but the chief of the natives stepped between the American and the Nip and said "don't shoot, take prisoner." All the time the Jap was squalling what apparently was his entire vocabulary. It was "No, No, No."

Private Zib then consented to take the unhappy foe a prisoner, so he marched him at rifle point and with an escort of the curious natives, back to a nearby Army camp area. Finally he turned the Nip over to Army custody, then went home.

The story didn't end there, however, as the next day Private Zib again went out of his own area without permission and returned to the place he had left his souvenirs. He brought them back this time, but in doing so he had missed a muster of his squadron.

Now, for the sake of discipline, Private Zib is working on his squadron's "bull gang," the heavy labor crew of men who broke the rules. He isn't very happy, really, but he does say "It's a heck of a note when I bring in a Jap prisoner and turn him over to the Army and they'll get the credit for that and I wind up on the bull gang."

His squadron commander smiled at that, proud of his Private Zib but demanding discipline at the same time.

1st Lt. Henry F. Childress Jr.
Guadalcanal

"He had found his niche at last"

Trained as storytellers, the CCs naturally saw appeal in the subject of a negative act that had a positive outcome. However, the Navy censor had a different focus and clearly was not impressed with desertion, marking this item "kill" and adding a big red X for emphasis. The blank suggested the writer did not know the subject's hometown.

A deserter—to the Marine Corps—has gained fame as a sniper on Vella Lavella.

He is Machinist Mate First Class Clarence J. Weitan, U.S.N., of _____, who disappeared from his Seabee outfit almost as soon as it landed on Vella Lavella carrying his Springfield rifle and ammunition.

After two days in the jungle, about which he remained discretely mum, he returned to a Marine outfit, which he made his base of operations, and stood guard duty with the Leathernecks in gun emplacements.

Jap hungry, Machinist Mate Weitan loaded up again and took off for the jungle. He returned after two days, still silent, but contented. "I love it here," he said.

Stories of Machinist Mate Weitan's sniping activities were brought from the jungle by Marines and eventually reached the ears of Lieutenant Arthur J. Benoit, U.S.N., Executive Officer of the Seabee outfit. "We weren't worried about him," he said, "because we were glad he had found his niche at last. He was the 'bad boy' of the outfit, always getting into trouble. And now if he wants to trouble the Japs, that is all right with us."

Staff Sgt. Solomon I. Blechman
Guadalcanal

"A future blurred by a shattering Jap bullet"

This story of a Marine wounded in action was not rejected for being routine. Applying the label "bad taste" to the account, an editor suggested a rewrite and remarked: "I don't like sympathy angle. A Marine goes in the fight and is fully aware of its consequences."

Marine Private George Arthur Finger, a Buffalo, New York, youth of 24, was formerly an amateur baseball player and had visions of the day when he could return from the war and again take up his favorite sport.

Today his visions are only a memory, blurred by a shattering Jap bullet which pierced the muscle in his right arm.

Recovering here from his wound, Pvt. Finger is happy over the fact that he got his share of Japs on Guadalcanal and volunteered to bring back ammunition to the firing line through a mile of jungle infested with Nipponese snipers.

A doctor told the Marine that his right arm might remain stiff for several years as a result of the wound.

The morning of 21 August found Pvt. Finger walking up and down the bank of Tenaru River on Guadalcanal. Although he was a member of a machine-gun section he had been chosen during the night for patrol duty and was far away from his crew buddies when hordes of Japs started pouring across the river from the opposite bank.

"We went into action immediately," Finger said. "It wasn't long before I had used up the 100 rounds of ammunition I carried. I don't know how many Japs I killed. I didn't waste any bullets. The Lieutenant in charge of our patrol said someone would have to go back of the firing line and bring up more cartridges.

"The bullets were coming out thick and fast but I volunteered to go after the fresh supply of ammunition."

The Marine crawled out of his foxhole. A volley of Jap bullets splattered the trees around him but fortunately he was not hit. He made his way cautiously in the underbrush and back for a distance of a mile to the ammunition dump.

There, a small cart with rubber wheels was loaded with ammunition.

"I don't know how many rounds of ammunition were there but the load must have weighed at least 300 pounds. With the aid of a guard we set out for the return trip. It was tough going in that underbrush. Coconuts on the ground impeded our progress and we had to be on the lookout for Jap snipers who kept banging away at our men.

"About 150 yards from the firing line we halted and I proceeded ahead to the firing line to let the Lieutenant know the position of the ammunition. I stuffed every pocket with cartridges."

Upon arrival at the firing line Finger reported to the officer and started distributing the ammunition he had brought. A Jap bullet struck him while he was throwing ammunition to a B.A.R. man. He staggered and fell back of a coconut tree. His right arm was painfully wounded and he knew he was losing blood fast.

Making his way back of the lines, Pvt. Finger crawled weakly forward. He was losing strength and he knew he could not struggle far. Finally he came upon a Navy corpsman who was treating a badly-wounded Marine.

"Come alongside, Mac. I'll help you in a minute," the Marine quoted the corpsman as saying.

"I have seen a bright, silvery cloud unfold from darkened skies," the Leatherneck said philosophically. "That corpsman looked just like that cloud."

The Marine praised Private A. A. Schmidt, machine-gunner who was responsible for killing more than 200 Japs attempting to cross the river. Schmidt is now recovering in a Naval Hospital.

"If it had not been for Smitty," Finger said, "the Japs might have succeeded in their raid and I might not be here today."

Pvt. Finger, who enlisted 3 January, is the son of Mr. and Mrs. George W. Finger, 196 Geary St., Buffalo, N.Y.

Sgt. Earle W. Johnson
Naval Hospital, San Diego, California

"A medal for guys who don't do a damn thing"

Technical Sergeant Jim G. Lucas was drawn to human interest stories that combined sentiment with irony while acknowledging the Marine commitment to duty. He likely felt an affinity for a fellow Oklahoman with a religious streak. In marking this story "not used," a division editor may have found it mawkish and the question it posed—what makes a hero?—outside the CC's range of inquiry.

The [redacted] at this Pacific base had come in just before dusk from a 20-mile hike back in the mountains, and were sitting around the sergeant major's tent "shooting the breeze."

The talk was of the Solomon Island campaign, and heroes were a dime a dozen. A lot of those present had qualified for medals.

That's why it was a surprise when Platoon Sergeant Ewers White of 710 East Sixteenth Street, Oklahoma City, spoke up and said:

"I'd say our biggest hero was Charley Perry."

Perry was a new one, but every man there nodded his head in solemn agreement, so I asked to hear Charley Perry's story.

"He didn't do anything, except that he's dead now, like a lot of other good Marines," Sergeant White said slowly. "And that's why I say he's a hero."

"Charley Perry was a sergeant, and a cook. He came from Enid, Okla., and had studied to be a minister. Even when we were training at New River, he'd take Sunday off and preach in some of the little churches around there. None of us ever kidded him about it, because we knew Charley was a real Christian.

"When we came out here, he was our chief cook, and a good one. But when we went into action, we learned what a real Marine he was.

"Not that he ever did anything spectacular. Charley was always too busy for that. He carried his gun, and shot his share of Japs, but he never said anything about it. While the [rest] of us would be resting—and the Lord knows we needed it—Perry would be busy. I don't think he ever missed a meal, though how he ever did it only Charley and the Lord know. He didn't have a thing to work with, but he fixed up a range and he made some pots and pans out of discarded oil tins, so that every meal he brought us out a cake or a pie or something a man in battle has no right to expect. We got so we got a lot of comfort out of seeing Charley dashing around, but I think we got more good out of his grin than we did out of his chow, good as it was. While we were on Tulagi, I think he did more than any one man to keep our morale up. I'd hate to think what it would have been like without him.

"Then we went over to Guadalcanal, and Perry was killed. It wasn't spectacular. He was working about his galley one morning, and a Jap sniper put one through his head. We got another cook, and buried him where he fell. But that guy was a hero, and we know the Lord won't forget him."

I didn't feel like saying anything, nor did anyone else.

It was First Sergeant John Daskalakis, 515 S. Beaver Av., Freeport, Ill., Charley's platoon leader, who broke the ice.

"I sometimes wonder," Daskalakis said, "why they don't have a medal for guys who don't do a damn thing—guys like Charley Perry."

Technical Sgt. Jim G. Lucas
A South Pacific Marine Base

American forces won the battle for Guadalcanal in February 1943 with an estimated 1,300 Marines killed in land and air engagements over six months;

the number of wounded was close to 3,000. Nearly 450 more Americans in the other services were killed, with 2,000 or more casualties reported. Yet the Japanese were no longer advancing in the South Pacific after Guadalcanal. Their losses were staggering in comparison: Nearly 25,000 died in the failed effort to secure the island. Operations to come in the Solomon Islands—notably the battles for New Georgia and Bougainville—and on the New Guinea island of New Britain would bring home the challenges the Marine Corps faced in the effort to drive Japanese forces out of the South Pacific.

Similarly, the Division of Public Relations learned during those first eighteen months that its goal to deliver stories of Marines at war to American readers would be far from easy. Sergeant Samuel E. Stavisky, who joined a half-dozen Marine combat correspondents on Guadalcanal in January 1943, recalled that those early months had been difficult for the CCs because the field command officers had not been informed of their functions and did not know what to do with them. Those problems eased as word of their unique duties reached commanders and the impact of their stories became clear in newspaper clippings.

Censorship for security reasons remained a hurdle that occasionally tripped up the writers, who also were learning that stories that would grab headlines in a peacetime civilian setting would be rejected if they reflected poorly on the Marine Corps. This included not just funny bits about wayward Marines but incidents such as artillery shells falling short and killing their own men or blowing up their own ammo dump. "That's a 'normal' happening in war," Stavisky recounted in a memoir, "but, of course, I didn't write about the 'bad' incidents. I knew such fatal mishaps would never clear censorship." His statement was in hindsight, however, because he'd had his share of stories held back. Other Marine writers would learn that lesson when their stories drew the slashing red pencil of censors or heavy lead markings of editors for straying from the public relations mission. Or would they? It is doubtful whether the writers in the field saw the edited copy. Weeks if not months might pass before the published versions reached them, if they did at all.

Getting stories past the Navy censors and through channels to Washington paled in comparison with the day-to-day dangers of combat and illness. As a newly arrived CC, Sergeant Edward J. Burman thought his first night on Guadalcanal might be his last. A severe naval shelling woke Burman and other Marines sleeping in the open near Henderson Field. In the pitch of darkness, eight to ten of them crawled under a truck for safety. Burman's knees began to shake uncontrollably, and several of the men prayed out loud. "There's something pretty terrifying in the sound of those shells whistling over and landing not far away, and then another one landing just a certain measured distance away," he told a fellow Marine combat correspondent for a profile. "The pattern of the shelling was so calculated that I kept thinking of myself as being on a huge checkerboard, and hoping I wasn't one of the black squares." Experience in combat had its advantages. For Burman the next night of bombings and those that followed did not seem so bad.

Burman spent Christmas Eve in 1942 in a dugout carved in coral rock on a Guadalcanal hillside. To avoid giving Japanese bombers a target, commanders had ordered a blackout for the area at sundown. "As a Combat Correspondent, I must work by night as well as by day," he wrote in a dispatch describing his activities. "It is impossible to work during the blacked-out jungle night, unless one finds a dugout, uses a small lamp and seals in the light." The tiny flame shook from the concussion of the Marines' big guns on the island. Sweltering in the covered shelter, Burman occasionally mopped his face while working on assignments. As a radio newsman he had grown accustomed to writing under deadline for a broadcast. Those nights on Guadalcanal, he wrote his stories as quickly as possible just to finish before the lamp burned out.

3 Somewhere in the South Pacific

Americans following the war news would read more and more about faraway places as Marines, soldiers, and sailors engaged Japanese forces. Pearl Harbor, Wake Island, and Guadalcanal were only the beginning of the nation's crash course in Pacific geography. To the northwest of Guadalcanal lay other islands in the Solomon archipelago, and names like New Georgia, Rendova, and Bougainville would be on the lips of Marines and civilian readers alike throughout 1943. Marine combat correspondents and other Division of Public Relations personnel joined civilian reporters in covering the advance. For security reasons, the preferred dateline for stories coming out of active combat areas was "Somewhere in the South Pacific" or a variation depending on their location in the vast region. Each story reproduced here carries the actual location whenever it was included in a typed report—if legible in spite of being marked through with pencils by censors or editors and replaced with a "Somewhere" dateline.

The strategy of American forces moving across the Solomons toward New Guinea and beyond mirrored that employed in the Marines' successful if hard-fought battle for Guadalcanal. Guided by the modern maxim that those who ruled the air ruled the land and sea, Americans and their allies sought to take over Japanese airfields and harbors on key islands and establish their own bases. Planes would fend off air and sea attacks and batter the next island in advance of naval shelling and amphibious landings by ground troops as the process repeated itself. Critical to the Solomons strategy was securing the island of New Georgia, with its Munda Point airfield, Bairoko harbor, and Enogai port, and later the island of Bougainville, the northernmost in the Solomons chain. In between were the island of Rendova and numerous others defended by a relatively small number of Japanese troops determined to die rather than surrender.

Putting truth to Marine Corps General Robert L. Denig's claim that each one of his public relations recruits was a "fighter-writer," several Marine combat correspondents were distinguishing themselves when not writing. For example, Master Technical Sergeant Frank McDevitt participated in the attack on Bairoko, New Georgia, and administered first aid to the wounded at his own peril, including to a corporal badly wounded by mortar fire, likely saving the man's life. Technical Sergeant Murrey Marder was in the same campaign and volunteered again and again to help rescue and treat wounded Marines, then carry them on stretchers to safety. Months later in Bougainville, Marder volunteered to join a raiding party behind enemy lines. Both McDevitt and Marder, once newspapermen in Philadelphia, received letters of commendation for heroism in combat.

"When we were enlisted, we were told we were Marines first, correspondents second," Technical Sergeant Jim G. Lucas wrote in a dispatch from New Georgia that heralded his fellow CCs. "In the thick of the battle, the credo of the combat correspondents requires us to drop his typewriter and grab up a gun. The record of the boys on New Georgia proved that they had learned their lessons well."

Marine combat photographers shared in the danger as well as the action they sought to capture on film. On New Georgia, Corporal Cyrus P. Collings, forty feet high in a mahogany tree, used the last frame in his camera to photograph a Japanese soldier swimming across a river toward Marine lines. He then unslung his carbine and shot the advancing enemy, by his count his fourth kill in combat. But firing on the soldier revealed Collings's location. Gunfire from other Japanese soldiers splintered the bark near him, and then a mortar shell blasted him out of the tree. While his injuries turned out to be minor, what really hurt Collings as he recovered in a medical unit was the loss of his film—it was waterlogged and ruined.

Routine newsgathering in the Pacific theater carried its own dangers. Among the Marine writers with tales of close calls was Technical Sergeant Harold Azine. He and the Marine combat artist Technical Sergeant Elmer Wexler were returning from Bougainville to Guadalcanal when a Japanese torpedo struck their PT boat. It punched through the craft but did not explode. Sergeant Charles P. Evans accompanied a platoon of Marines as they marched through knee-deep mud and thick jungle on Bougainville, always on the alert for snipers. "No one needs to tell you as you approach the front lines for there is a steady 'ping' of the enemy sniper fire and occasional return fire from our own troops," he wrote. Reaching a command post, they soon received their orders to engage the enemy near a river. "At the front, we took cover and awaited the time for attack."

Sergeant Bob Stinson often covered Marine and Navy air operations in the Pacific. For one story the CC joined the crew of a Navy observation plane that flew over friendly antiaircraft batteries during target practice and radioed feedback on the guns' accuracy. Stinson watched nervously from the "fish bowl" in the nose of the plane as the shells exploded below. He donned an oxygen mask when the plane climbed higher—and passed out. Stinson had turned the oxygen switch off instead of on, a self-effacing detail he included in a first-person account that probably resonated with stateside readers who, like Stinson, had never experienced such a ride.

Allied forces invaded New Georgia on June 30, 1943, and captured Munda Point about six weeks later. Two more months of fighting pushed the Japanese completely out in early October. The Japanese on Bougainville saw their defenses challenged beginning November 1, and the battle would continue into the following year. More than two dozen civilian and Marine writers were on hand for the initial invasion to provide reports. The Division of Public Relations also deployed about fifteen combat photographers for still photos and another ten combat cameramen for moving pictures. The following censored or otherwise unreleased stories were written about events that occurred during the Solomons campaign.

"First they bomb our wounded and now they strafe them!"

A censor's stamp indicated that this story from New Georgia's Enogai Point was reviewed ten days after it was written, and a handwritten note suggested it was evaluated by editors nearly a month later. Although the story was marked "not used" and "too late," some sections detailing the damage and chaos from a Japanese attack were deleted with a razor blade, literally cut from the copy.

Yesterday we began to move our wounded, the men who fell at the short but bloody battle of Enogai July 9–10, together with casualties suffered during the taking of Jap outposts at Triri and Maramusa.

The capture of Enogai, on Kula Gulf, opened a wedge in the Japanese defenses which we knew could not pass unnoticed. It didn't.

At noon yesterday enemy bombers broke through our air defenses, bombing and strafing what had been one of their most impregnable outposts only two days before.

It was not difficult for their bombers to find the target; they knew the ground only too well, sighting in on the small coral causeway connecting the mainland and Enogai Point.

Casualties in the first air attack were small, *five men wounded, none seriously, and we soon heard the cheering sound of our own fighters pouncing on the enemy bombers.*

But three hours later the bombers returned, this time more successfully.

One bomb fell right next to the sick bay, set up in two adjoining Japanese thatched shacks, killing three men and wounding nine other Marines. Two of the men killed were Marines already wounded.

The bomb blast spread momentary confusion among the patients, who frantically attempted to drag their injured bodies to safety, but they were soon calmed by the hospital attendants. After a few moments, when no other bombs dropped close, the damaged field hospital was propped up to shelter those hurt in the recent bombing.

It was impossible to tell what was happening in the air but apparently the bombers were once again driven away by our fighters, for the bombing ceased abruptly.

But the day was not over, we were yet to undergo our most maddening experience.

[two lines cut]

(The Marine) commander asked the Allied command to send flying boats to evacuate casualties.

Three flying boats arrived soon after the second bombing, *landing in the inlet off Enogai Point*. The wounded were ferried out to the waiting planes in rubber boats and all were safely aboard by 4:30 p.m. and the flying boats prepared to take off.

Suddenly, two twin-engined Japanese float planes swooped out of the sky, diving on the flying boats with their loads of casualties.

Motionless on the water the evacuation planes looked like easy victims for the diving attackers.

With the first crackling of strafing fire, the Marines sprang into action.

"All automatic weapons down on the beach," went the cry. "B.A.R. and machine gunners get your weapons down here on the double!"

With machine guns, rifles, and even pistols, the Marines rushed to the beach and opened up with a curtain of small arms fire. Meanwhile, two other Marines sped to man two Japanese anti-aircraft guns set up on the beach.

The top turret gunners in the PBY's now had their weapons operating, and heavy fire from the beach and the flying boats poured at the attacking Jap planes.

This new attack on the wounded, most of them his men, had aroused [two lines deleted] (a Marine) *commander into a blaze of emotional fury.*

"My God! Those dirty ___ ___" he shouted between roars of orders at his machine gunners, "first they bomb our wounded and now they strafe them!"

However, the tables were turned now. The Japanese planes were seeking protection from the heavy beach fire by climbing skyward. Their strafing runs on the flying boats had been close enough, but not effective. One bomb dropped close by a PBY had sent a shower of water over the plane, but had caused no damage *visible from the shore.*

With the Jap planes driven off, the flying boats were free to take off over the reef-studded inlet.

We held our breaths as one by one they taxied across the water into the setting sun and slowly, with every man on the beach almost giving them added power with his eagerness for a safe takeoff, they rose quietly, airborne.

You could hear a sigh of relief pass along the beach as the flying boats disappeared in the distance. At least the wounded were safe.

Technical Sgt. Murrey Marder
New Georgia

"A Marine who thinks he's a Seabee"

Technical Sergeant Murrey Marder had been a reporter for the Philadelphia Evening Public Ledger and knew a good story when he saw one. He ran afoul of Navy policy with subjects that officials did not want publicized—how native islanders on New Georgia were organized and trained to assist Americans, for example, and how a Seabee had joined the ranks of Marine Raiders, a relatively new elite force using guerilla tactics in occupied territory.

He had been a Marine before but when he tried to re-enlist in 1942 the doctors discovered he was color-blind, so he decided that the next best thing was to join a Naval Construction Battalion, where men with limited eye deficiencies were still acceptable.

He liked the men in the Seabees, they were all regular fellows, most of them trained specialists, and they had an important job to do.

But when he stood on the beach at Guadalcanal watching the Marine Raiders prepare to embark aboard destroyers—that old attachment returned, and this time he couldn't resist it. Where the Marines went there was going to be action, and in this man's war you don't just take off with whatever outfit strikes your fancy, but—

In the improvised field hospital here at Enogai yesterday, the medical attendants were checking casualties from the bitter fighting at Bairoko the day before. The wounded were lying in a former Japanese thatched hut, privates, sergeants, lieutenants, men of all Marine ranks resting from their battle injuries.

A hospital corpsman walked to the husky youth, lying quietly in a corner.

"Can you give me your name, age, and rank," asked the corpsman.

"Richard H. Maurer," was the reply, "age 22, Seaman First Class."

"Seaman First Class!" said the surprised attendant. "What outfit are you in?"

Maurer looked up with a 'well, here-we-go' expression and answered: "63rd Naval Construction Battalion."

That was enough for the attendant, who well knew there were no Seabees as yet participating in operations in this area, and he went to the doctor-in-charge, convinced that here was a mental case.

"I've got a Marine over here who thinks he's a Seabee. He was brought in as a heat exhaustion case, but he must be cracking up—" and the corpsman walked away muttering.

Half-an-hour later Maurer, beset by visions of a court-martial and firing squad, had convinced the medicos that he was a Seabee and was telling his story to a group of sympathetic Marine officers.

Maurer, who lives at 730 Orcas Street, Seattle, Washington, had served a cruise in the Marine Corps, from 1937 to 1941, completing his service with the rank of Corporal. In November, 1942, he joined a Naval Construction Battalion after he was unable to gain reenlistment in the Marine Corps because of color-blindness, and rose to the rank of Seaman First Class.

Sent to the South Pacific, his unit was encamped near the Marine Raiders bivouac area on Guadalcanal where the Marines were completing preparations for their part in the New Georgia campaign.

"The Seabees always admired the Marines," said Maurer, "and we would go over to give them knives or anything else we had which we thought the Marines could use in action."

Being a former Marine, Maurer soon became friendly with the Raiders, spending as much time at their camp as possible.

"I like the Seabees," said Maurer, "but I wanted to go into action with the Marines. With the Seabees I had been doing mosquito control work, which is important enough, but it seemed odd for a big guy like me (he is six-feet-two and weighs almost 200 pounds) to be chasing mosquitoes instead of Japs."

Familiar with Marine procedure, Maurer had little difficulty obtaining a Marine field uniform and when the 4th Marine Raider Battalion sailed from Guadalcanal July 18 to reinforce Marine forces already in the Northern sector of New Georgia, Maurer unobtrusively slipped aboard with them.

When the Marines landed, Maurer disclosed his presence to Captain Anthony Walker of 2009 Belmont Rd., Washington D.C., a company commander (Captain Walker, leading his men in the attack on Bairoko July 20, was wounded in the right thigh but refused to leave the field until all of his wounded men were evacuated).

Maurer asked for a chance to fight and Captain Walker assigned him to a platoon led by First Lieutenant Bud Tinker, 26, whose wife lives at 2940 Pacific Ave., Stockton, Cal. Lieut. Tinker's platoon was short-handed due to casualties suffered in an earlier attack on Viru Harbor in the Southern area of New Georgia, and he was eager to have an able-bodied man, especially when he learned Maurer was a former Marine.

From here on, Maurer's activities can best be described by Lieut. Tinker.

"When the attack on Bairoko began, the morning of July 20," said Tinker, "I assigned Maurer to a machine-gun squad that didn't have its full complement of men. Dick's a big fellow, so he was made an ammunition carrier. And he turned out to be one of the best damned ammunition carriers I've ever seen."

Maurer made more treks through the jungle for ammunition than he can possibly remember. During that full day of contentious action, one of the fiercest fire-fights ever held in the Solomon Islands area, the machine-guns spat cartridges until the barrels melted into uselessness, and there were more guns and more calls for ammunition.

An assistant machine-gunner in-between trips for ammunition, Maurer stayed with one squad until he was the only man left in action. The machine-gunner, assistant gunners and leaders were casualties, the gun barrel "burned out" before he reported back to Lieut. Tinker asking if "there is anything else I can do."

There was, he was sent to another machine-gun squad. When their supply of ammunition was gone, one man was sent to the rear, through a curtain of mortar fire, for more. He didn't return. But Maurer managed to get through and back with two boxes of cartridges.

When darkness came, and the firing ended, he carried wounded until he was ordered to the rear and collapsed on the trail, exhausted.

He told his story to the Marine Commander today when he was discharged from the hospital, and pleaded to remain with the Marines, at least until the end of the present campaign.

"If you send me back now I'll be taking up space that could be used to evacuate a wounded man," he argued convincingly.

And when he was told he could stay he whispered a breathless "Thank you, Sir," and hurried to give the news to his buddies in the machine-gun squad.

When he returns to his own unit Maurer will be subject to disciplinary action. He realized that when he left. When he is sent back to the Seabees, tho, he will go back with as fine a recommendation as Lieut. Tinker and the Battalion Commander, Lt. Colonel Michael S. Currin, can give him.

"And maybe, just maybe," sighed Maurer optimistically, "somehow I can get a transfer back to this outfit."

Technical Sgt. Murrey Marder
New Georgia

The story carries the markings "Kill" and "no release." Yet Maurer's heroic actions on behalf of the Marines did not pass without notice. In spite of disciplinary action against the young Seabee, the Navy awarded him a Silver Star.

"A report from aboard 'The Slave Ship'"

Stories written aboard transport ships heading to an island landing commonly described Marines as calm and courageous, exchanging stories and wise-cracks, while conscious of the dangers that lie ahead. Not so this rejected account. Criticism of the Marine Corps or the US Navy was rare from Marine combat correspondents, given censorship prohibitions. While passed by a Navy censor, the story was nonetheless marked "doubtful taste!" and "needs rewriting!" as well as "not used."

The discomforts of going to battle are probably exceeded only by the discomforts of battle itself.

Take this transport, for instance, overflowing with U.S. Marines enroute to invade the Jap island of Bougainville. These jungle fighters are so hot, dirty, crowded, and generally harassed with living that they rarely think of their impending battle. They're much too concerned with their present discomforts.

They don't blame anyone in particular, of course, for all realize the Navy has only so many ships in this area for such an operation.

But that hasn't kept them from nicknaming this vessel "The Slave Ship." On "The Slave Ship" there are bunks for only 70 percent of the troops aboard. The rest must find a place to sleep, and to store their gear, as best they can.

None of the troops' bunks, all of them down in the holds, is bearable anyway. With no ventilation here in torrid seas, these holds are humid dungeons reeking with foul odors of human perspiration and jungle fighting gear. Most men simply use their bunk (if they're lucky enough to get one) as a place to pile their equipment.

This means that practically everyone sleeps on deck at night. They sprawl out on the quarterdeck, under Higgins boats, in passageways, literally all over the ship. Deck sleeping space is at such a premium that right after supper (which is around 5) men rush to get a place for the night.

Some men attempt to soften their berth by laying down a "shelter-half" (half of a pup-tent) or a blanket. But most simply lie on the plank deck, resting their heads on life-jackets that countless other men have used for the same purpose before.

Hardly a square foot of the deck is left uncovered by human bodies at night, and one can't take even a few steps without stumbling on a sleeping form in the darkness.

As it rains every night in these waters, the men awake in the morning covered with dampness, as well as deck filth.

The eating problem for the troops is equally intolerable. "Chow" is served far below, and one had to stand in line for half an hour, passing through sweltering passageways, before arriving at the mess hall, which men call "The Torture Room of the Slave Ship."

Everyone eats standing up, stripped to the waist, and a man can't finish a meal before part of it is spoiled by his own salty perspiration dripping into his mess tray.

The Marines have to supply their own canteen cups and spoons when they eat, and, dreading trips to their bunks, they carry these utensils around all day. The cups and spoons gather a fresh coat of rust between each meal, and about the only thing to do is try to wipe them off on the dungarees slept in the two previous nights.

"You can't keep all the rust off," remarked one Marine, "but it probably doesn't hurt that hot coffee they always serve us."

There are fountains aboard that are supposed to produce ice water, but the overcrowded, thirsty troops drink the water so fast it comes out at boiler room temperature. The ship's store doesn't dare open, for the crew's supplies would be bought out in ten minutes. So there's no candy, gum, or cigarettes for these Marines going to war, except what they've brought along.

Yesterday, one Leatherneck appeared on deck with a whole box of Baby Ruths which he had magically produced from somewhere. He was offered $20, $30, then $50 for the box, but he didn't even consider the sale. He and three buddies sat down, divided the Baby Ruths, and ate them all.

A trip to the troops' lavoratory is a major effort. There is always a line waiting for the salt water showers, for the basins, and for the "heads." The only way to get a fresh water shower is to wait one's turn for one of the few wash pans, fill it with fresh water from one of the basins, and pour it over yourself in the salt water shower.

The toilet paper frequently runs out, but Marines are wise enough to carry their own individual supply. Troops can't go into the lavatory at all between 8:30 and 11 in the morning—because the place is being cleaned during those hours.

But a Marine's proclivity for keeping himself and his clothes clean is surpassed only by his efforts to keep his rifle spotless. All day long, except when the lavatory is closed, sweating Leathernecks can be found there shaving, bathing, and scrubbing their clothes.

During most of the rest of the time they busily prepare their fighting gear for the Japs they expect to find at Bougainville.

The men grouse a lot about their traveling discomforts, but they take them with a philosophical good humor. "It's the old Marine Corps system," one man explained to me. "They make us so uncomfortable, they get us so mad, that we'll be happy to run off this ship fighting no matter where they land us—even if it's inside the Yokohoma harbor."

Nevertheless, after this experience, these Marines would hardly sympathize with any strikes back home which would hold up U.S. ship production, no matter what the cause. For they will have put up with these conditions aboard "The Slave Ship" for 12 days <u>before</u> risking their necks on the beaches at Bougainville.

Staff Sgt. Milburn McCarty Jr.
Aboard ship en route to Bougainville

"A sailor recognized the pilot as a Jap"

The word "kill" was underlined in red for this report on what appeared to be a violation of conventions governing prisoners of war. A Navy censor passed the dispatch, however, suggesting it presented no security problems. Others probably recognized the incident would prove to be controversial if publicized and could support enemy propaganda about mistreatment of prisoners.

The Jap pilot who torpedoed a destroyer-transport on November 17 near here was rescued from the water unwittingly by Second Lieutenant William T. Kosanovich, U.S.M.C., and shot by an infuriated sailor aboard a Higgins boat.

Shortly after the Jap plane had torpedoed the ship another ship in the convoy shot it down.

Lieutenant Kosanovich, the son of Mr. and Mrs. Theodore Kosanovich of 69 School Street, Universal, Pennsylvania, was in the water helping the wounded to a rescuing Higgins boat and then helping them aboard. The Jap pilot swam or floated in among a group of Marines and sailors and the lieutenant boosted him up where rescuing hands grabbed him and swung him inside.

A moment later a sailor recognized the pilot as a Jap, pulled his automatic and shot him.

Staff Sgt. Solomon I. Blechman
Bougainville

"Don't shoot, I'm a Jap..."

In the same week and locale as the incident described above there occurred another Marine encounter with a Japanese. This time the outcome did not end in death. In fact, the story was conveyed in a humorous or ironic vein. Its connection to intelligence operations likely resulted in the story's rejection, but highlighting a blunder would have been another reason.

They call him "Sergeant York of the Marine Corps" since his daring capture singlehanded of a "Japanese."

Sergeant Anthony Mizell, 31, USMC, of a Marine artillery unit on Bougainville, had just finished noon chow, when he looked up and saw a ferocious looking Jap not more than 15 feet from him.

Both were surprised. The sergeant gasped. The Jap gasped.

Doing a somersault into his foxhole, Sergeant Mizell reappeared in about 10 seconds armed to his teeth with rifle and knife. By this time the Jap had somewhat regained his composure and yelled, "Don't shoot, I'm a Jap..."

"I know you're a blankety blank Jap," shouted the sergeant. "Get moving."

Sergeant Mizell would have saved himself future embarrassment if he had allowed the Jap to finish explaining. But instead he hurriedly marched his prisoner to the commanding officer of the battery.

Already Sergeant Mizell was day dreaming. He could see himself decorated by the general.

His ego was soon deflated when the Jap explained he was with the U.S. Army intelligence.

Sergeant Mizell hails from 52 State Street, Hammond, Indiana. He is the son of Mr. and Mrs. Sam J. Mizell, route 31, Greenwood, Arkansas.

Sgt. Francis H. Barr
Bougainville

"If it wasn't for him, we wouldn't be here now"

Tales of deadly combat were not unusual in CC dispatches. This story may have been marked "killed" because of its unnerving details.

The heroism of a Philadelphia Marine sergeant who lost an arm as a result of a hand-to-hand foxhole fight with two Japanese on Bougainville was recounted by two Marines in the same action.

As the Marines pushed inland to secure their Empress Augusta Bay beachhead, one company of Marine Raiders was sent 200 yards beyond the main lines to act as security for a forward artillery observation post.

In one foxhole, after dark, were Sergeant Paul M. Rickert, 23, of 3243 North Sixth Street, Philadelphia, Pa.; Corporal Raymond R. Thornton, 20, of St. Andrews, Florida; and Private First Class Donald L. Konrick, 19, of 755 South Genois Street, New Orleans, Louisiana.

"Our sector was fairly quiet," said Corporal Thornton, "so we agreed that two men should sleep while the third stood watch until he became sleepy. Then he was to wake his relief."

About 11 p.m., Sergeant Rickert, on watch, was about to wake his relief, Private First Class Konrick, when two Japs slipped up and jumped into either end of the foxhole.

"One stabbed me in the stomach with a bayonet he had in his hand, before Rickert could reach him," said Konrick.

"Thornton reached out, grabbed the bare bayonet and broke it in half, but he was cut across the hand and leg," Konrick said.

With both Konrick and Thornton wounded, Sergeant Rickert wrestled with the two Japanese and finally stabbed one of them with a knife. Before the second bayonet-wielding Jap was driven off, he succeeded in slashing Sergeant Rickert's left arm in two places.

Mortally wounded, one of the enemy crawled off to die a few feet from the foxhole while the second fled.

Corporal Thornton tied up Sergeant Rickert's badly bleeding arm with thongs from his boots, until a hospital corpsman was able to reach him.

Sergeant Rickert and Private First Class Konrick were evacuated from Bougainville the next day, and Corporal Thornton five days later.

At a rear hospital it was necessary to amputate Sergeant Rickert's left arm. He is now recuperating successfully in a rear area. Both Konrick and Thornton have recovered and have been returned to duty.

"If it wasn't for Rickert," they agreed, "we wouldn't be here now."

Technical Sgt. Murrey Marder
Bougainville

"He jest throwed up his hands and began gibbering"

A paragraph crossed out from this battlefield account, probably by an editor, suggests that shooting an enemy soldier with his hands in the air might not be viewed as acceptable behavior. The use of dialect was rare in Marine stories and was mainly employed to convey humor or regional differences in attitudes.

Marine Sergeant Sam J. Justice, 26, former ranch hand of Farwell, Texas, meted out a bit of his [redacted] to at least one Jap rifleman during the first few minutes that Justice's unit went into its first combat here the other day.

The lanky, drawling Texan was with a five-man patrol proceeding ahead of his lines when they encountered a group of Japs. Sam saw a Jap pop up out of a fox-hole.

"Ah expected that itty bitty ole devil to come up a 'clawin' and a shootin'," Sam says, but instead "he jest throwed up his hands and began gibbering a mile a minnit. Ah cain't understand that Japanese stuff, and besides I was pretty busy just amoving fast."

Sam finished him off with one shot and then hurried on to catch up with the remainder of his group, which had meanwhile killed off a half dozen or more of the enemy.

Sgt. Peter Pavone Jr.
Bougainville

"We were all a little crazy for a while"

The original version of this stark description of men in battle, presented below, was heavily edited for distribution and cut by half. Among the details removed were the descriptions of the Marines' emotional state—angry, hysterical, weeping—during and after the encounter with Japanese soldiers.

For 11 days, a small garrison of Japs firmly entrenched in a series of knolls now known as Hellzapoppin Ridge held off Marine charges, resisting even heavy barrages of mortar and artillery. Three times, American planes had bombed the knoll in which they had dug in. Still they held out.

Finally it became evident that when the serial attacks were being made, the Japs left their holes and moved to the lee of the hill away from the side from which the planes came. When the bombings were over, they returned to their positions.

Today, a bit of counter strategy ousted them. The American planes came, and the Japs moved out to protection. But this time, a company of Marines was moving forward to forestall the Japs' return to their pillboxes even before echoes of the last bomb had died away.

Four volunteers were in the vanguard of this unit as scouts, and to them goes credit for some of the wildest maneuvering and certainly some of the loudest yelling of the campaign to date.

The four had crept silently some 50 yards ahead of their company and had reached a point deep within enemy territory when they surprised nearly a score of Japs sneaking back to their gun positions. It was here that war-painted Comanches of the early West were put to shame by the Marine scouts as they began their "war of nerves."

Screaming and yelling like zanies, they dodged from fox-hole to fox-hole, from bomb crater to bomb crater, throwing grenades in an almost continual stream, firing their weapons and in general creating such pandemonium that to the Japs it must have sounded like an army gone mad, and to their comrades behind them, like a slaughter.

Private Harold R. Gray, 18, of Ewing, Ky., whose handle-bar mustachios and long Mexican-like sideburns give him the appearance of a Wild West scout of the covered wagon days; Private First Class Vernon S. Harding, who will be 20 years old in three days, and who hails from Belmont, Mass.; Corporal Thomas F. Rice, 22, tall, broad-shouldered red-head from Niagara Falls, N.Y.; and Private George N. Benjamin Jr., 20, slim, black-haired and quiet, son of Framingham, Mass., came out of the hectic melee without a scratch to win from their commanding officer the tribute: "They're damn fools, but I wish I had a thousand more like them."

And what's more, the four were credited with holding the Japs at bay until bazookas and deadly flame throwers were brought in to rout the last of the Nips from the long fought for hill.

"It was just about dusk when the last aerial bomb was dropped," Private Gray, as spokesman for the quartet, said later. "We moved right on down the far slope of the knoll, going fast and as quietly as we could, trying to catch the Japs before they got back to their holes.

"I was on the left flank, Harding and Benjamin were in the center and Rice was on the right with a B.A.R. (Browning automatic rifle)."

In their path were two huge bomb craters, one before the other. Benjamin and Harding remained in the one at the rear, covering Gray as he dodged to the first hole, while Rice moved to the base of a banyan tree, hoping to catch a sniper that had been harassing them.

Corporal Rice, who sports a flaming Ulysses S. Grant beard, started the fireworks. The sniper, apparently spotting him first, fired a single shot which caromed off a tree and grazed Rice's head, knocking his helmet off and cutting a swath through his red hair about half an inch in width.

"Seems like Rice suddenly went nuts," Gray drawled. "He jumped up, cussing and swearing like a mule skinner, and with that B.A.R. just blazing away a mile a minute." With Rice's outburst, Private Gray, in his forward crater, saw three hand grenades sailing over the brim toward him.

He dodged back to the rear crater where all four of them began firing simultaneously, yelling meanwhile to others in their unit to bring up hand grenades. "It was like a production line in a defense plant," their captain, John C. Landrum of Tignall and Maysville, Ga., explained. "We had nearly everybody in the outfit crawling forward in single file carrying grenades in their helmets, in gunny sacks, and even in ration bags. Seems to me that we took up about 500 grenades before it was over."

Those grenades were left on the rim of the rear crater. The four Marines set up a grenade throwing barrage, which had its reaction the next day in sore arms. They'd load up and dodge forward to the first crater, and to holes on either side, yelling at the Japs and to each other, laughing and whooping and carrying on like men bereft of their senses.

Apparently referring to the one case where an American war bond receipt was found in the clothing of a dead Jap—taken apparently as a souvenir from a dead Marine—Gray raved with each grenade he threw: "Buy bonds with that, Tojo!", according to others of the company who heard their yells coming up through the jungle.

Harding, Rice and Benjamin were more versatile in their invective and wild humor. "Split this up among you . . . Take inventory now, Mr. Tojo . . . Here's a ticket to Hell, Hirohito" were among some of the phrases remembered afterward.

It was estimated later that the four threw nearly 200 grenades before word was passed to them that flame throwers were on the way down. At this point, the four gathered together once again in the same crater, and on the suggestion of Corporal Rice, they redoubled their shouting and screaming, but here their theme was: "Charge them, men. Bring up that other battalion, captain . . . and . . . Send reinforcements down the left flank." Meanwhile they were withdrawing to pick up the flame thrower squad, which they led down to their position.

The show was nearly over by that time, however, because when the deadly flame throwers arrived and began their work, Marines said they heard only one or two isolated screams from the Jap positions and the occasional sound of a Jap crashing in flight through the jungle underbrush.

Rice, Benjamin, Gray and Harding, who were more or less hysterical in their excitement, alternately laughed and wept for nearly an hour after the action was over, all of them trembling from head to foot from sheer nervous exhaustion.

"I've never heard or seen anything stranger than the actions of those four in my life," Captain Landrum said proudly afterward, revealing he had put all four up for the Silver Star medal.

Although they had exposed themselves time and time again in their reckless rampage, the four couldn't give a comprehensive account, had no idea how long their action lasted, and listened like strangers the next day when others of the company with ring-side seats recounted the story.

All four had sore arms, Rice's head hurt, and Benjamin was hoarse. "I've never laughed so hard in my life," Rice said. "I guess we were all a little crazy for a while."

The company moved unopposed onto the knoll after the flame throwers had mopped up, concluding the 11-days action for the strip of ground, which is only about 40 yards across and wide enough only for a small group of men to establish gun positions.

"They're fools, but I wish I had a thousand more like them . . ."

Sgt. Peter Pavone Jr.
Bougainville

"Complete with stockade, padlock, and turnkey"

Marines being punished for disobeying orders and committing other infractions would seem obviously out of bounds for publicity. The writer may have thought these examples suggested Marines acting on commendable if ill-advised impulses.

The always receptive Marine Corps brig follows the units of the Corps, no matter where they go.

Less than a week after the first camouflaged Marines hit the beach here, a Bougainville Brig had been set up by the headquarters' unit, complete with stockade, padlock, and turnkey.

First offenders to be locked up included two men who disobeyed orders in order to go to the front lines, several "trigger-happy" artillery men who fired on planes (our own) without orders, and one man who had to fill out a sentence for an infraction he committed before the invasion, back on Guadalcanal.

Somewhere in the South Pacific | 61

The men who "took off" for the front lines had been ordered to join a working party on the beach. They were given five days bread and water, then sent to line, or combat, duty, which was just what they wanted.

The Marine who had been sentenced on Guadalcanal pleaded with the Brig officers to be allowed to come along with his buddies making the invasion. This he was allowed to do, with the provision he serve out his time after he landed.

In charge of this Brig, which is the nearest to Japanese lines, is First Lieutenant Robert J. Newell, of Chicago. So far, the brig has had only six Jap prisoners to handle.

Staff Sgt. Milburn McCarty Jr.
Bougainville

"This method of fighting off sleep is <u>not</u> suggested"

Reckless behavior was among the red flags for DPR editors primed to reject stories that reflected poorly on the Marine Corps. A Navy censor had not viewed the story as a security issue and passed it.

A sure-fire but slightly dangerous method of keeping awake at night has been recommended by Marine Gunner Fred T. Roberts, of Washington, D.C., to all whose business demands they be alert during wee hours.

The warrant officer, who lives at 1040 Otis Street, North East, picks up a hand grenade, pulls the pin, and keeps the spoon depressed while he holds it. When he is ready to retire he puts the pin back in, releases the spoon and crawls into his foxhole.

This method of fighting off sleep is <u>not</u> suggested to other than those with healthy nerves.

Staff Sgt. Solomon I. Blechman
Bougainville

"He just got around the corner"

The composure of Marines under fire impressed the writer, but this story was rejected with little or no comment. It may be that the editors were concerned that the Marines appeared careless or even foolish.

If any proof were needed of Marine coolness under fire, an example was given by the Marine officer and enlisted man who, halted by machine gun fire 25 yards ahead of them and mortar fire about 50 yards to the right, whipped out a cribbage board and played a game before they continued their job of stringing artillery communication wire.

First Lieutenant Jack R. West, 24, of Ankeny, Iowa, former all Big Six center for Iowa State, and Corporal Allen W. Brennan, 29, son of Major (ret.) and Mrs. James Brennan, of 78 Robinson Street, Lynn, Massachusetts, were the under-fire cribbage players.

They had landed in the middle of the hot fighting near Cape Torekina, but their party had managed to get inland with only one minor casualty.

They were following an infantry company, laying wire so they could direct artillery fire. After they'd gone about 300 yards, they were halted by the machine gun and mortar fire.

Disregarding the bullets and the shells, Corporal Brennan got out his "crib" board and, as he says, "Mr. West pulled out a brand new deck of cards. I really trimmed him, too. I just missed skunking him. He just got around the corner."

A "skunk" is one of the worst fates which can befall a cribbage player. "Just getting around the corner" is missing that fate narrowly. After the one game, the two men went on with their business of fighting a war.

Sgt. James E. Hague
Bougainville

"A flourishing racket aimed at the gullible"

Dishonesty, stupidity, and carelessness were common qualities in stateside news stories eagerly published by newspaper editors. DPR editors turned down such stories when Marines were the focus. Civilian and military editors probably would have agreed that open wounds and toilet paper were subjects that readers would regard as in bad taste.

Veteran Marines returning to aviation units at the front have tipped off the newly arriving troops on this troopship on a more or less flourishing "racket."

Because the demand of newcomers for souvenirs cannot keep up with the supply, wise-acres in the Guadalcanal area have been converting torn and surveyed parachutes into Japanese flags with the free use of red paint.

The gullible have been paying as high as $25 for the highly regarded battle trophies.

Staff Sgt. Samuel E. Stavisky
Aboard a transport in the South Pacific

Two new medals—the "Coconut Heart" and the "Ration Cross"—have been suggested as additions to the list of service awards given for action on the field of battle.

The suggestion was made here yesterday by Lieutenant Joseph C. Humbert, of Stewartsville, N.J. and Philadelphia, Pa., Navy doctor attached to a Marine Raider unit which landed with the first assault troops at Bougainville.

"We should give the 'Coconut Heart' to men who carve themselves up with machetes while opening coconuts, and the 'Ration Cross' to those who get injured in tussling with tins of chow," remarked Doctor Humbert, as he observed the men lined up at this field hospital awaiting treatment for finger cuts.

"During the first few days of fighting we were called only in case of major battle wounds," said the doctor, "but now that the firing has slowed up, men are coming in from almost all the companies with various small wounds they carelessly inflicted on themselves.

"Maybe if we give them a booby medal, they'll be more careful."

Staff Sgt. Milburn McCarty Jr.
Bougainville

Marine Sergeant John A. Ross, 21, of 89 Fleet Place, Mineola, Long Island, N.Y., was proud of his new Garand rifle.

On Guadalcanal in 1942 he had used the old Springfield, and was unfamiliar with the more lethal current service model.

Elation turned to dismay when he discovered what seemed to be a pit in the bore of his new possession.

He scrubbed, cleaned and polished the barrel. The blemish remained.

In desperation he took his problem to a veteran Gunnery Sergeant. The oldtimer squinted down the barrel.

"Your troubles are over, son. That 'pit' is only the gas port."

Technical Sgt. John W. Black
Somewhere in the Southwest Pacific

Wounded on the Bougainville front and returned to a beach hospital here, Private First Class Lonnie J. Griffin now sits on the edge of his foxhole and amuses friends with his wound.

He blows smoke through a hole in his cheek made by a Jap bullet.

Doctors, busy with more serious cases, haven't yet gotten around to sewing up Griffin's wound, but the young Marine says it doesn't bother him a bit.

Private First Class Griffin, who is 19 and the son of Mrs. H.H. Griffin, Route 1, McGhee, Ark., received the injury the other day when his unit was engaging an enemy force.

"I felt something hit my left cheek," he explains, "but I didn't think much about it until a corpsman ran up with a bandage. Then I learned there was a hole right through the side of my mouth.

"But there was only the hole going in and none coming out. No sign of a bullet either. Then I remembered I was yelling at the Japs at the time I was hit. I musta had my mouth open, and it went right out, without even chipping my teeth. It was one time when cussing really paid dividends."

Griffin started blowing smoke out the wound purely by accident. He was smoking a cigarette when one of his hospital comrades suddenly stared, then explained: "My God, smoke's coming out your wound."

Griffin experimented, and, sure enough, found that he could blow smoke through the wound just as easily as out his mouth.

"I'm practicing on smoke rings now," he states, "but the bullet sorta went in from an angle and the hole isn't quite the right shape."

Staff Sgt. Milburn McCarty Jr.
Bougainville

Pay day being a week off, poker enthusiasts in one Marine outfit on this jungle island have been playing for sheets of toilet paper.

Nor are such stakes as silly as appears.

Toilet tissue is an important item in any jungle troop's pack.

One lad is reputed to have won 4480 sheets to date, the equivalent of 4½ rolls.

Technical Sgt. Samuel E. Stavisky
Goodenough Island

"There's a bit of strategy involved in this action"

Security issues had the potential for more serious consequences than embarrassment. In spite of their training at division headquarters and constant reminders in the division bulletin, Marine writers at times reported information that could be valuable to the enemy. Entire stories, some of which are excerpted below, could be devoted to such topics, the writers' time and effort wasted once their work reached the Navy censors.

If, by chance, the Japanese ever took the trouble to perform autopsies on the bodies of their battle casualties, they'd find that a good percentage of their losses resulted from being shot by their own weapons.

That may appear rather paradoxical at first but it is easily understood when you know of the unique job that Platoon Sergeant Joseph F. Meixner, of Berwind, West Virginia, is doing.

Meixner's duties include keeping in proper working order the varied weapons used by fellow Marines, as well as reconditioning arms captured from the enemy. The latter are restored to their original condition and go back into battle—this time for Uncle Sam.

There's a bit of strategy involved in this action. In the type of warfare peculiar to the jungles, adversaries rarely see each other, and firing is guided by the sound of each other's shots. When the Nips hear their own machine guns and other weapons, they think their fellow fighters have advanced to a forward position, and don't fire in that direction. The guns, actually, are being fired by American troops who captured them earlier during the fight and adapted them to their own use. The ruse has been very effective.

Technical Sgt. Frank J. McDevitt
New Georgia

Marine Raiders have made headlines many times by their unorthodox maneuvers and tactics. But here's one they use in self-defense which has been used by kids in neighborhood vacant lots during many years of "Cops and Robbers" games.

The Raiders, first let it be said, travel light and fast and more often than not are on lightning-like destructive thrusts behind enemy lines. As a result, they bivouac where they are when night falls and do not have the advantage of protection from other troops on their flanks or to their rears.

Here is where their simple trick fits in. They just string vines, wire or even shoelaces tied together into a rope about a foot off the ground all around their area and then fasten tin cans, mess gear, and other tin or metal paraphernalia capable of rattling onto them. Jap patrols whether walking or crawling have to be plenty cautious as a result to avoid hitting this crude "burglar alarm" and rousing the entire camp.

A single rattle and a cross-fire of machine gun and rifle bullets just tears up the ground for yards around the spot. "It's simple but very, very effective," a Raider Lieutenant explained with a grin.

Sgt. Peter Pavone Jr.
Bougainville

The harassed Japs on Bougainville are so confused they are firing on each other, it was indicated today by an enemy order found on a dead Jap officer.

Translation of the order revealed it to be a warning to all Jap soldiers to be extremely careful when shooting so as not to kill each other.

It pointed out that Jap and U.S. Marine uniforms often looked alike in the jungle, and suggested that Japs look closely at helmets before shooting to make certain the target was an American.

The order also suggested that Jap officers advise their men to wear red arm bands so that the confused shooting might be minimized.

Staff Sgt. Milburn McCarty Jr.
Bougainville

Apparently having an extreme shortage of land mines, the Japs depended almost entirely on a makeshift mine pattern of 77 mm shells detected by Marines east of the Numa-Numa Trail during heavy fighting November 25.

A cautious unit of Marine engineers led by First Lieutenant John T. McFadden, of 1340 Taylor Street, San Francisco, California, a senior demolition officer, dug up scores of the shells along trails before front lines advanced deeper into enemy territory.

The shells, according to Lieutenant McFadden, were buried in groups of three with detonators pointed upward and the pins of one or two pulled. Japs apparently intended for the projectiles to stop tanks of other heavy vehicles, he added.

"But demolition men could easily detect the shells, for the Japs left the shiny detonators sticking out of the ground, indicating their haste in evacuating the area," the Marine officer said. "The Nips, however, have been known to lay a more effective pattern. Sometimes, the mines are covered with boards over which dirt is spread and which sink under heavy weight, causing detonators to set off the deadly explosives."

Placed close to a few of the 77-mm shell groups were magnetic mines which the Japs had intended to intensify the explosions, but these, too, were detected by demolition men.

Booby traps were easily discovered because the Japs stretched vines across the trails and the vines led to freshly dug earth covering hand grenades.

Technical Sgt. Earle W. Johnson
Bougainville

"Most have already gone through the hell of battle"

The Division of Public Relations rejected without comment this description of what happens to Marines wounded in a jungle battle. While reassuring that they receive the best medical care available, a story with examples of men suffering amputations and emotional breakdowns may have been deemed too distressing for readers.

One of the saddest things on Bougainville is the sight of wounded Marines being evacuated to rear bases.

New evacuations are made every few days. The men—wounded, maimed, shell-shocked, and sick—gather at the evacuation point on the beach. Some come on crutches, and a few come walking on both feet. But most of the patients are carried in stretchers. Some are still wearing their camouflaged battle suits, some hospital pajamas, while others are simply wrapped, with their wounds, in blankets.

Emergency foxholes have been dug at the evacuation point for protection while the men are awaiting transportation out to the ships. Several of the evacuations had to be made under Jap bombing and strafing. When this happens, the men—most of whom have already gone through the hell of battle—cower in the foxholes while dog fights rage overhead and our own ack-ack fills the air with thunderous terror.

It's worst when the men are already in the landing boats, going out to the ships which will take them away from this battle-scarred beachhead. When a Jap plane dives on them then, they can only lie in dread apprehension, realizing they might be shot or drowned without being able to do a thing about it.

There is another problem of lifting the wounded from the landing boats into the ships. This correspondent helped on one of these jobs the other morning, and saw the fear on the faces of the injured as they were hoisted precariously over the bobbing water.

Talking with the men reveals all sorts of trouble. On one trip to an evacuation ship I spoke with a former Railway Express worker from New York City who had lost his left foot; a private first class from Niagara Falls who had gone beyond the front lines to save his sergeant and who had his own left eye shot out; to a Nebraska farmer who had had both feet amputated; to a Massachusetts Marine who had come down with appendicitis; to an Oregon butcher who was dragging his shrapnel-shattered leg with the aid of a crutch.

In charge of this important job of getting Bougainville wounded back for better treatment is a young Harvard Medical School graduate who practiced surgery in Beverly, Mass., near Boston, before the war—Lieutenant Commander Richard E. Alt, U.S.N. The evacuation set-up under Doctor Alt is a new system worked out from the experience gained in getting wounded men off Guadalcanal, New Georgia, and other South Pacific battle islands. Wounded from the front are fed back through the advance hospitals to the evacuation point on the beach, where they are dispatched with all possible care and speed to rear hospitals free from firing and bombing.

During the first month on Bougainville Doctor Alt and his staff handled more than 1,500 evacuees. Wounded men made up a majority of the cases, but there were also a number of non-combat illnesses—malaria and filariasis contracted at other islands, physical and psychological sickness, and advanced fungus infections.

Doctor Alt told me that the main objective of modern war surgery was to get the treatment as close to the point of injury as possible. "We've established field hospitals so close to the front line that some of our tents and surgical instruments have been shot up by Jap bullets," he said, "but still a man wounded in the middle of jungle fighting may not be brought in for 12 hours or more."

Blood plasma and the sulfa drugs—and tetanus anti-toxin—have been the greatest advancements in war medicine since the last war. "The plasma gives new life to the patient," pointed out Doctor Alt, "and sulfa stops the infection."

Seventy percent of the wounds treated here have been arm or leg injuries. Doctor Alt believes that 99 percent of the men evacuated will be saved. "With recent medical improvements we are able to save cases which a few years ago we would have considered hopeless," he said.

So far, no epidemics have broken out on Bougainville. Considering the treacherous climate here, and the danger of insect and other tropical diseases, that is a record for the medical men in the service to be proud of.

There have been psychological cases, as was expected, for not all men can go through the sort of war that's fought out here. One Seabee, cowering in his foxhole through repeated bombings, put his carbine in his mouth and blew the top of his head off. A Navy lieutenant, who came in with assault waves and performed brilliantly through several actions, collapsed completely when an unfounded rumor reached him that a friend had been killed by a bomb. Three Marines back from the front, resting in the hospital from shell-shock, became uncontrollable when a Jap shell landed nearby and they disappeared into the jungle.

Doctor Alt says, however, that the number of such cases has been very small, and that the general morale of the men under their hardships has been remarkable.

One consoling fact is that these wounded evacuees, although a terribly depressing sight to the observer, are not in great pain. "Once a corpsman reaches an injured man," explains Doctor Alt, "drugs are administered, and from then on the patient has little suffering."

The men themselves seem to take the odds of war with the old American gambling spirit. "Some of us are going to get it," as one Marine private remarked, "and if I do that's just tough luck."

Doctor Alt told the story of two Marine buddies who met at the evacuation point and each had learned the other had lost a leg.

"Well, Bill," said one of them, "when we get back and get our wooden legs I bet you five bucks I can still beat you in a hundred yard dash."

"Let's make it $25," replied Bill, "then the winner will have enough to go on a real Liberty when we hit the West Coast."

Staff Sgt. Milburn McCarty Jr.
Bougainville

If being a Marine combat correspondent somewhere in the South Pacific sounded romantic to readers or like easy duty to fellow Marines, Staff Sergeant Solomon Blechman sought to tamp down the idea. Writing from Bougainville in a one-page account of a day in the life of a CC, Blechman described getting little sleep because of overnight bombings. In search of a story he might walk long distances on jungle trails, at times alone, through swamps, mud, and water, always on alert for Japanese snipers. Sometimes he would be without food and water.

Joining the Marines on the front lines, he tried to interview them, but no one had time to talk. He might not be able to see much of anything because of the dense growth. More information for a story came later from talking to wounded men. Walking back to the command post, he might find it had moved and that he had another mile or two to walk before digging a new foxhole to set up for the night. All the while both his carbine and his typewriter were rusting and his typing paper was turning moldy from the dampness and daily rain. "This isn't a Marine Combat Correspondent's paradise," he wrote.

Whether it took the romance out of the assignment, sounded like whining, or that DPR headquarters did not want to publicize its own personnel too much, Blechman's story, dated November 15, 1943, was marked "not used." It was just as well given the greater hardships to come—and the kind of publicity no combat correspondent desired.

Three days after Blechman wrote his story, a fellow CC who had been reporting from the Ellice Islands, Sergeant Bob Stinson, climbed aboard a Navy bomber to write about its mission. When the bomber failed to return, Stinson was among those reported missing in action. Nearly a month passed before the Navy announced that he had died in an airplane accident in the South Pacific. Only later would officials reveal that the bomber had crashed into the sea near Nui, an Ellice Island atoll. In a letter to Stinson's parents, a Marine officer explained that their son was not among the twelve crewmembers pulled into life rafts after the crash and that it was believed he did not escape the sinking wreckage. His body was never recovered.

Stinson had been a reporter for the *Philadelphia Inquirer* and a public relations man for the *Saturday Evening Post* before enlisting and bidding farewell to his wife in Wayne, Pennsylvania. At thirty-one he was among the older members of Denig's Demons. He was also the first to be killed in action. For weeks the dozen or so stories Stinson had submitted before his final assignment trickled into division headquarters in Washington; those that were distributed noted his fate.

The Marine writers had been relatively lucky up to that time. One combat correspondent, Sergeant Lee E. C. Baggett, twenty-three, died in November 1942 in an off-duty road accident while covering Marines at the American base at Guantanamo Bay, Cuba. Several Marine writers and photographers had been wounded in action, including the public relations officer Captain Patrick O'Sheel and combat correspondent Technical Sergeant Theodore C. Link. They were in a press tent on the night of November 7, 1943, a week into the battle for Bougainville, when a 550-pound bomb landed ten feet away, killing the *Newsweek* correspondent and Australian newspaperman Keith Palmer. Though in pain and shock from the blast, O'Sheel directed rescue operations, searched for other wounded in the darkness, and oversaw medical aid for those in danger of losing their lives. The PRO was awarded the Bronze Star for his actions.

Stinson's death later that month shook the Division of Public Relations and foreshadowed more losses among its personnel. But then injury and death were part of the ongoing story of the Marines in the Pacific. Casualties in the New Georgia campaign reached nearly 640 men, including more than 220 dead; in the Bougainville campaign, casualties totaled nearly 2,000, with more than 730 dead. Worse was to come. Only a few days after Stinson was reported missing a dozen Marine writers and several still and motion picture cameramen were accompanying the Second Marine Division as its men landed at a Central Pacific atoll. On a blister of coral called Tarawa the Marine Corps would face the deadliest four days in its history.

4

Four Bloody Days on Tarawa

A heavy shell fired by a Japanese naval vessel whistled over the bow of the American landing craft. The shell exploded in the water with a shattering blast that rained sea water on the vessel and its eight passengers, one of them a Marine combat correspondent, Sergeant Pete Zurlinden. For the first time Zurlinden found himself ducking enemy fire. Much more was to come—bullets, mines, mortar rounds, grenades, bayonets—as he and several thousand other Marines set out for the main island of the Tarawa atoll. His craft would spend forty-eight hours bobbing in the ocean as brutal fire from Japanese defenders kept them from their beach landing. They watched the carnage play out 1,000 yards away.

"As the sky brightened, we had a ringside seat during the murderous bombing and shelling of Tarawa, the biggest Jap garrison in the Gilberts," Zurlinden wrote in an account sent to American newspapers. "Miles away we saw a continuous wall of fire flashing from the great battlewagons of one of the largest task forces ever assembled. Overhead roared more carrier-based planes than we could count." He added: "During the first hour Tarawa was a smoking hell."

The massive clash that took place on November 20–23, 1943, bespoke of Tarawa's strategic value among the atolls of the Gilbert Islands. Tarawa's airstrip was a key part of Japan's outer defenses—and was just as important to the US plan to move its forces ever closer to Tokyo. The Japanese had reinforced their defenses on Tarawa's main island, Betio, its flat coral surface only two miles long and no wider than a half mile. Coral reefs off the northern and southern sides of Betio offered a natural bulwark to invasion, and just offshore the Japanese had placed concrete pyramids and barbed wire to slow down any landing force. More than a dozen coastal defense guns and forty additional artillery guns awaited invaders, along with 100 machine gun nests and hundreds of pillboxes, blockhouses, and other emplacements dug into the island coral and reinforced with steel and concrete. Tunnels or trenches connected many of these positions. Japanese commanders had good reason to be confident their fortress was impregnable.

The American armada sent to Tarawa was equally impressive. To pound away at Betio before any Marines attempted to land there, three carriers would provide assistance with bomber and fighter planes, and even more firepower would come from the heavy guns of three battleships, five cruisers, and nine destroyers. The assault plan envisioned Japanese defenses all but destroyed by the bombing and shelling, paving the way for the Second Marine Division to execute an amphibious landing. Higgins boats, a type of landing craft nicknamed for their designer and manufacturer, would bring thousands of Marines to the shoreline while amphibious tractors, called Alligators, would cut through the water and crawl over reefs to bring men to the beaches.

Too little went according to plan on either side. Heavy Japanese fire threw off the Americans' timetable for the bombing runs and landing craft. Moreover, Japanese defenses held up despite the unprecedented shelling from air and sea. The unpredictable tides at Betio left some Higgins boats unable to get to shore in shallow water, and not enough Alligators were available to take up the slack. Through it all, the Japanese cut down Marines in their boats, in the water, and on the beach with withering fire from mortars, machine guns, and snipers. The biggest mistake made by the Japanese? It may have been underestimating the resolve of Marines to establish a beachhead and work their way toward the defenders no matter the cost.

The Division of Public Relations assigned ten Marine combat correspondents and two public relations officers to accompany the Second Marine Division and report on the Tarawa assault. With them were several of the DPR's still and motion picture photographers. Of the stories that came from Tarawa in the ensuing days and weeks, the longest and most widely published was Master Technical Sergeant Jim G. Lucas's powerful first-person account. It gained front-page headlines in the *New York Daily News*, the *Washington Post*, and the *Chicago Tribune* and appeared prominently in many other newspapers across the country on December 4, days after the civilian press reported the victory at Tarawa. His story began:

> Five minutes ago we wrested this strategic Gilbert Island outpost and its all-important air strip from the Japanese who seized it from a few harmless missionaries and natives weeks after they had attacked Pearl Harbor.
>
> Tarawa is ours, and the Rising Sun has set on another Pacific bastion. This is the first chance any of us have had to write, and our experiences of the past three days are so overwhelming that it is difficult to decide where to start.

Four Bloody Days on Tarawa | 73

It has been the bitterest, costliest, most sustained fighting on any front. It has cost us the lives of hundreds of United States Marines, but we have wiped out a force of 6,000 Imperial Japanese Marines, and we have seized a base which now brings us within *bombing* range of Truk, from which we can now force the enemy's fleet into the battle it has avoided for so long.

The original 7,400-word version took up eighteen double-spaced typewritten pages, but for public release it was scaled back by at least one-third. Editing marks suggest the Navy censor was concerned about revealing the name of a casualty, Marine public relations officer Second Lieutenant Ernest A. Matthews Jr., before his next of kin could be notified, per military policy. The version of the Lucas dispatch released by DPR headquarters may have been trimmed for length and to shift the focus from its own personnel to other Marines. Those changes remained in the version of the story that appeared in a collection of combat correspondent reporting published a few years after the war. Following are deleted sections of Lucas's story, then other examples of reporting from Tarawa that did not reach the public.

"I never expected to live to write this story"
Lucas's story continues from its three-paragraph opening.

A few minutes ago, we set up our news room in the ruins of a Jap hangar, which we share with the boys of the medical corps. A hospital is being set up 10 feet away under the direction of Lieutenant Commander Justin J. Stein, Chicago, Illinois, a veteran of the Guadalcanal campaign. In civil life, Lieutenant Commander Stein was a member of the staffs of three of Chicago's leading hospitals. Today, he runs his own. It isn't much, but it means a lot to the Marines who had laid wounded in the broiling sun for days, some of them with only a poncho to protect them from the Equatorial heat.

The rest of us have drifted in, until now only Staff Sergeant Richard Murphy, Washington, D.C., is unreported. We are confident Dick is safe. He landed on another part of the island. All of us have been reported dead at one time or another since Sunday.

I found Sergeant Pete Zurlinden, formerly of the Associated Press in Annapolis, Maryland, yesterday. I had given him up for dead. Pete left the ship three hours before I did, and had not reported in 48 hours later. Intelligence told me they held no hope for him. Pete spent 48 hours off the beach, his landing barge driven back every time it attempted to make the beach by murderous enemy shell and machine gun fire. Pete is safe, although his portable typewriter, slung over his side, was badly damaged by shrapnel. He has just succeeded in partially repairing it.

Pete and I found Technical Sgt. Gene Ward, formerly of the New York News, yesterday afternoon. Gene's landing barge was sunk out from under him 500 yards off shore. He, too, had spent more than 24 hours trying to make it to the beach. Gene and the Marines with him had to wade in past Japanese machine gun emplacements. Gene succeeded in reaching an undamaged pier extended far into the lagoon. Three Marines fell within two yards of him as he worked his way toward shore. Gene lost everything he had—his typewriter, his note book, his rifle.

This morning we found Technical Sergeant Mason Brunson, formerly of the Associated Press, in Baltimore, Maryland. Mason got ashore with his typewriter, but with his brief case gone. Like the rest of us, he underwent murderous shellfire before he reached the beach. He spent 36 hours at sea before his landing craft got in.

Sergeant Hy Hurwitz, formerly of the Boston Globe, and Sergeant Jack Pepper, formerly of the Daily Oklahoman, just got in. Hy spent 48 hours at sea, once reaching the pier only to be driven back by machine gun fire. He landing craft was shelled at the pier and destroyed as he stepped out of it. While at sea, his craft twice went back to the transports with wounded.

Jack landed on the far side of the island with the flame throwers, and has just worked his way to us—a distance of 800 yards. He might as well have been in New York City. He spent 18 hours pinned down by Jap machine gun fire and helped to wipe out a pill box of 18 Japanese, and capture 23 others. Jack looks like hell, but we're glad to see him.

Jack tells us that Technical Sergeant Sam Shaffer, formerly of the Washington Times-Herald, went down with a sun stroke yesterday afternoon, but is otherwise OK.

As far as we know, our photographers are still alive. Corporal Raymond Matjasic, 23, of 3047 East 126th Street, Cleveland, Ohio, formerly of the Cleveland Plain Dealer, landed with Matty and I. He was badly bruised and shocked by the Jap mortar which killed Lieutenant Matthews, and lost part of his film, but is still taking pictures.

I found Sergeant Ernest J. Diet, Hammond, Louisiana, 36 hours after we landed, after I had given him up for dead. I had even found a body I thought was Diet's, and wept like a baby when he staggered in. Diet's landing craft was sunk by Japanese shell fire, and most of its crew and Marine personnel were drowned or killed. Diet and Watertender Second Class J. L. Burton, Newton, Long Island, New York, a sailor, swam for seven hours in the bay before they were picked up by another boat. They were stark naked, and had lost all of their gear, but Diet somehow found another camera. It's enough to be alive.

Day before yesterday, I ducked in a shell hole to avoid a sniper and found Staff Sergeant Roy E. Olund, 21, of 1728 Burnett Way, Sacramento, California, another photographer. Roy didn't even have a pistol. His landing craft was sunk 500 yards off shore by two direct shell hits. Five men were killed, and 10 more were picked off by Jap machine gunners on the beach. Olund tried to swim ashore with his camera, but had to drop it in the bay. Only today, we got another for him. He's a sight, dressed in whatever we could find for him to put on.

The rest of the photographers, under Marine Gunner J. F. Leopold, are now ashore. They've all had experiences enough to write a book.

Only Matty is dead. Matty went through Guadalcanal and took some of the best pictures made there. He volunteered with me to go in with the assault wave. He didn't know what fear meant. It's hard to believe, but it's true. Two minutes before he died, Matty reached out and gave me a hand as I tried to get ashore with my gear. Matty went through the Spanish Civil War.

We continue to make startling discoveries. Pete's typewriter was hit by a bullet, not shrapnel. Two inches to the right and he would have been our second casualty. Gene just discovered his canteen and belt had been ripped by a stray bullet.

We saw the start of the Gilbert Islands campaign from the boat deck of our transport, a big vessel which had carried troops to North Africa a year ago and to Sicily in August. It began at 1 a.m. when our cruisers intercepted a Japanese patrol boat, and sent it to the bottom before it could give the alarm. Matty and I stood on the bridge and watched the fire works. We thought it was great fun.

We had expected trouble all day, but it hadn't come. At noon, there had been an alarm when our destroyers picked up two flights of planes 116 miles away. We were certain—jubilantly so—that we were in for trouble, but they were our own planes, headed for Tarawa to give it a preliminary pasting. We were disappointed and frightened. We suspected a trap.

Matty, Matjasic, Zurlinden and I slept on deck, fortified with passes granted by Major J. E. Mills, Norman, Oklahoma, commanding officer of troops on board our transport. We were hanging on the rail as we rounded the tip of Tarawa, out of range of a Jap searchlight which cut the sky.

At 5 a.m. our task force opened up. Three battleships—two of them all but destroyed at Pearl Harbor on Dec. 7, 1941—poured thousands of tons of shell fire into the tiny coral strip. Ten cruisers moved in closer and took up the bombardment. Our destroyers, too numerous to count, came within 600 yards of the beach. At sea lay five aircraft carriers, ready to begin bombing and strafing as soon as dawn broke.

The Japs replied, with six and eight inch guns. Within 10 minutes, two huge fires—we later learned they were ammunition dumps—had started in the middle of the island.

Lucas later described the moment a mortar shell struck a dock near where he, Matthews, and Matjasic were taking cover.

Matty did not move. I called to him, but he remained crouched over. Leaving my position, I rushed to him and grabbed him by the arm. He toppled over. I tried frantically to drag him to safety, screaming for Matjasic, who, I learned later, had been badly shocked by the blast. Ray staggered over.

"Help me with him," I gasped.

"Who is it?" he asked.

"Matty," I replied.

Matjasic disappeared. He told me later he did not know what had happened. I learned from others that he passed out.

A third mortar shell hit the water, but some distance away. I ordered a Marine to help me drag Lieutenant Matthews to safety, and ran to hunt a hospital corpsman. I found one and reported:

"Help me, please. My lieutenant was hurt by that last blast."

He looked me over and replied:

"Bud, I've got a hundred men hurt since 9 o'clock this morning. Get you a stretcher and put him aboard a boat."

I was crying. Finally I found an officer who had known Matty. He rounded up a corpsman. Matjasic staggered up, and went back with us. Snipers were covering the dock, and we crawled up to Matty on our stomachs.

The corpsman felt Matty's pulse and heartbeat.

"He's dead," he said slowly.

Matjasic began to cry.

"Let's pray over him, Lucas," he begged, but I was already on my knees. I shall remember that prayer as long as I live. While we prayed, a Marine fell with a sniper's bullet through his head only 10 feet away.

A Marine stepped up to my side.

"A buddy of yours?" he asked. I nodded, unable to speak.

"I lost my only brother this morning," he said.

Lucas went on to describe significant developments in the days-long battle. The printed version of his report ended with the island secured, but his original version provided a few additional details and reflections.

Staff Sergeant George Stutsman, Natchez, Mississippi, brings us two cartons of cigarettes and a carton of matches. We get a five gallon keg of water—a real luxury. It rains briefly, and we stand in the open, soap and shower ourselves off.

Tarawa is completely wrecked. There is not a five foot strip that has not been devastated. Civilian war correspondents with us agree that at no time in history has so small an area been subject to so much fire.

We came ashore not expecting more than 2,500 Japs, the majority of them killed by our advance shelling. We found 6,000, a large part of them still able to fight. Our first wave landed in the face of machine gun fire with appalling casualties. Yet they were able to establish and hold a beachhead. I can count at least 20 of my close friends who died in that landing.

We have begun to bury our dead. Our chaplains are holding mass funeral services.

Our tractors and bulldozers are now busy repairing the damage. In short order, Tarawa will be a major Allied base.

I was the first combat correspondent ashore. I never expected to live to write this story.

Master Technical Sgt. Jim G. Lucas
Tarawa

"It was necessary to shoot all of them to remove that nuisance"
Rivalries within the military services, even backhanded compliments, were forbidden under censorship rules, yet a censor stamped this story "passed" before it was designated "not used." Revealing how a prisoner of war could be employed against the enemy also would have been a concern.

In the battle for Tarawa, even the much-maligned M.P.'s covered themselves with glory. So well did they acquit themselves that all of us have stopped referring to them as the "Gestapo". A feeling of friendship has sprung up that bids fair to continue until we hit our first liberty port.

For the first time in Marine Corps history, the M.P.'s landed with the assault troops. Ordinarily they aren't moved into a contested area until the contest is no longer in doubt.

In this battle they were not sent in as assault troops, but to handle prisoners, guard ammunition and supply dumps and prevent straggling. The M.P.'s that landed with the fourth wave on the north beach under Second Lieutenant W.H. Emery, U.S.M.C., of Madison, Wisconsin, found all hell breaking loose. There were no prisoners, there weren't any dumps set up to guard and the Marines were in danger of losing their tiny toehold on the shore.

The M.P.'s became infantrymen and fought right with the assault troops throughout that day and night. The second batch of M.P.'s, under First Lieutenant Donald D. Pomerleau, U.S.M.C., were stuck on a reef some 300 yards from the beach. They got out just as their boat was hit by 40 mm Jap shells. Under fire constantly, they waded back and forth across that 300 yard stretch of water bringing water and ammunition to the beach where they were needed badly.

When this task was finished, the men went over to the area nearby which was being swept by murderous Jap fire and helped get the trapped stragglers back onto the beach to rejoin their outfits.

Two days later a third contingent of M.P.'s under Second Lieutenant Douglas R. Key, U.S.M.C., of Port Arthur, Texas, landed on the west beach which had been partially secured by the Marines to a depth of some 200 yards. From the sniper fire directed at them it was evident that a number of pillboxes had not been cleaned up yet. The beach was full of mines and booby traps and these had to be cleared up immediately.

The M.P.'s started on the latter task first. It was a job that called for demolition engineers and these M.P.'s knew nothing about such work. Fortunately, their lieutenant had been trained in demolition work. He demonstrated on one mine and then told the men to proceed to clean up the beach under his sergeants, Paul E. Pribble, U.S.M.C., of Parsons, Kansas, and Arthur T. Neal of Hollywood, California.

Afterwards the lieutenant estimated his men had neutralized 150 mines over a 400 yard stretch of beach without sustaining a casualty.

Then they started in on the pillboxes. At the first one, they sneaked around to the rear and set off a charge of dynamite. Eight Japs, their arms upraised, ran out. One of them, afterwards known as "Tojo the Earbanger" (Earbanger is a Leatherneck term for anyone who curries favor) informed the M.P.'s with a smattering of English and eloquent gestures, that there were four more inside the dugout. Another charge of dynamite dislodged them. Three came out with their hands up. A fourth, hiding behind the three, came out firing. It was necessary to shoot all of them to remove that nuisance.

In the next pillbox, the men smoked out 22 Japs. Some, expecting to be shot, came out with handkerchiefs over their face.

"Tojo the Earbanger" went to work on the next eight pillboxes. He went into each one, explaining that dynamite was going to be used on them. Every time he came out followed by surrendering Japs. In some cases he tipped off the M.P.'s that some would come out shooting and when they did they were knocked off.

These M.P.'s, who had come ashore to guard prisoners taken by assault troops and found none, ended up that day capturing no less than 81, according to Lieutenant Key's account.

The captured Japs were given no rest that day. They were set to burying the dead Japs that littered the beach. As night fell, they were crowded into a large gun emplacement. The entrance was covered with barbed wire and machine guns trained on the opening, in case any Jap tried to escape.

With the soul-satisfying feeling of a job well done, the M.P.'s turned into their foxholes for a rest that night—a rest that was disturbed only by occasional sniper fire and a persistent Jap bomber that never once found its target.

Technical Sgt. Samuel Shaffer
Tarawa

"All I could do was yell. Then I hit him with my fist"

The vivid details in this account of a Marine's near death make it all the more harrowing, perhaps too much so for a public already disturbed by reports of heavy losses. That he had been shot by other Marines would violate censorship rules.

Marine Private First Class Charles W. Mitchell, 20, son of Mr. and Mrs. Robert Mitchell, Evansville, Indiana, mistook a Jap for a Marine on Tarawa and was nearly choked to death as a result.

Private First Class Mitchell, who is bound for a rest base on this ship, told his story today.

"It was our first night ashore—the day after the island was first attacked," he said. "We moved 300 or 400 yards in from the beach and set up a security watch that night.

"I had just moved up to the front of our lines to go on watch, changing places with a buddy of mine. I saw somebody crawling toward my foxhole and thought it was my friend in the dark. When he jumped in, I saw it was a Jap.

"He grabbed me around the neck and began choking me. I couldn't get at my rifle which was under me. All I could do was yell. Then I hit him with my fist.

"That knocked him away. Other Marines, hearing the commotion, thought I was having a nightmare. When they realized what had happened, they began firing. Two of the shots got me—one in the right elbow and one in the left wrist. But they killed the Jap."

There was a Jap bombing several hundred yards away that night.

The next day, Private First Class Mitchell's wounds were treated and he was brought aboard here.

Staff Sgt. Richard J. Murphy Jr.,
aboard a transport in the Central Pacific

"He made up his mind to sneak into the first shorebound boat"

This story of courage tinged with insubordination carried a rare written suggestion from the censor who had passed it: "OK for security, but you should consider this from the angle of publicizing personnel who disobey orders." DPR headquarters apparently agreed and held the story.

Left behind when assault forces drove toward their initial landing on Betio Beach, a 19-year-old former Paramarine jumped ship 24 hours later, slipped into an infantry unit ashore, and fought the Japs furiously until all resistance on Tarawa had collapsed yesterday.

Grumbling at first when his commanding officer told him he would have to remain aboard a transport to help with rear echelon work, Private First Class Ralph S. (Blackie) Coleman, of 3 Academy Avenue, Darby, Pennsylvania, nevertheless pitched in and worked like a beaver until word of the bitter fighting seeped back to the ship.

He made up his mind that he would sneak into the first shorebound boat the next day and try to get into the thick of the scrap. He then talked Corporal George J. Heise, 26, of 405 South Third Avenue, Maywood, Illinois, into going along with him.

The morning of the second day they got their chance, and equipped with combat packs and rifles, they stole down a landing net into a boat that was taking ammunition and water to the sorely badgered troops.

Shortly after they reached the beach, the two Marines learned the location of an infantry unit that was sorely pressed, and moved forward until they joined it.

Private First Class Coleman spearheaded a surging drive that saw the outfit take one pillbox after another. During the first morning he burned out two heavy Marine rifles and survived a number of narrow escapes.

With four other Marines and an officer, Private First Class Coleman dropped into a trench to try to wipe out a pillbox that was holding up an artillery piece. At one end of the trench the Japs had dug a rear entrance for their pillbox.

"The lieutenant (I don't know his name) ran to the roof of the pillbox and started shooting through the top," the Marine said later. "But a Jap got him and he dropped, wounded. I ran up there and tried to drag him off, but shooting broke out all around. I struggled with him, but he was too heavy for me to budge. I called my buddies and three of us lifted him down into the trench where he died."

By this time tanks had come forward and Private First Class Coleman and Corporal Heise slipped behind their protective cover, and advanced deeper into the Jap lines. Mortars began getting the tanks' range and they slipped alongside a pillbox they thought was unoccupied.

Private First Class Coleman, looking around to study the terrain, found himself staring directly into the eyes of a Jap in the pillbox.

He fired his rifle at the brown face but missed. He sent two more shots into the pillbox, but the Jap tossed a hand grenade at the Marines. They flattened out and the explosion didn't hurt them.

The Jap raised up to pitch another grenade and Corporal Heise emptied a clip of ammunition into his body.

Then other Japs in the pillbox began hurling hand grenades through its openings. Heise unloaded a couple of his. "We had a regular pitcher's duel," Private First Class Coleman said.

Although more than a half-dozen grenades were thrown by both sides, neither the Marines or Japs were injured. But when the Marines called for reinforcements, the Japs became panicky and started scrambling out their tunnel exit.

"Heise and I just sat about 10 yards away from that tunnel and mowed them down," said Private First Class Coleman.

That evening the two ran out of cigarettes. There were plenty of American cigarettes back at the command post, but the boys were afraid they'd be picked up and sent back to the ship if they showed up around anybody they knew. So they located an abandoned Japanese quartermaster dump, found some Jap cigarettes, and made the most of them.

The next day they continued to campaign with various infantry units they encountered, but the following afternoon when news that the fighting had ended reached them, they were chary of returning to the ship, afraid they might be sorely disciplined for jumping it.

A major heard them talking, Private First Class Coleman said, and set their fears at rest.

"Go on back to the ship, boys," Private First Class Coleman quoted him, "and if anybody gives you any trouble, tell them to see me about it. You two did a real job and heaven knows we needed your help plenty of times."

A former student at Darby Township High School, Private First Class Coleman's parents are Mr. and Mrs. Ralph C. Coleman of Darby. John Heise, the other Marine's father, lives at the home of Corporal Heise's sister, Mrs. H.E. Muir, at Maywood.

Sgt. Pete Zurlinden,
Tarawa

"We're goners but we gotta stay here and keep cool"
Why this story would be marked "not used" is puzzling. Did the DPR editors decide the event described was not that interesting? Or was it seen as casting the Marines as disorganized for failing to order all its men out of harm's way?

Isolated from their company during the final Japanese counterattack in the battle of Tarawa, four Marines quickly counted ammunition and made a firm decision.

Sure they would be killed, they made up their minds to hold ground and kill as many Japs as possible before they "got it." After three hours of the heaviest sort of fighting, they emerged unhurt.

Because of some blazing Jap trucks which silhouetted his men against the fire, the company commander pulled back his lines 25 yards on the night of the counterattack.

Four men failed to receive the order and were left alone in an open shellhole, with an enemy pillbox only eight yards away.

They are Marine Corporal Henry G. Clougherty, of Swissville, Pa.; Marine Private Harry W. Belcher, of Jacksonville, Fla.; Marine Private Daniel J. Kenny, of Detroit, Mich.; and Marine Private First Class Dewey W. Clevenger.

They repelled the first attack, shooting a number of Japs, and the enemy withdrew for a pow-wow. Finally one of them yelled in English, "You'd better give up, you Marines, you can't win."

"We didn't reply," said Corporal Clougherty, "because we didn't want to give our exact position away. I whispered to the boys 'we're goners but we gotta stay here and keep cool. It's no use getting excited.'

"But when it was all over I was a nervous wreck for three days."

Suddenly a Jap rushed the Marines with a sword. He was only one foot away when they got him, and his blood squirted on the men in the hole.

Then a Jap jumped on top of the pillbox and began leaping up and down to attract their attention, while two others attempted to sneak up on them from the sides. The boys killed all three.

Three Jap hand grenades fell into the shellhole, but all of them failed to go off. Then Private Belcher's automatic rifle jammed. "Keep me covered while I fix it," he murmured.

He tore it down in the darkness and completed a swift repair job. It fired two times and the firing pin broke. Once again he took it apart and put it back together.

While he was doing this another grenade fell by his feet. He threw it back at the Japs before it could explode.

The ammunition held out and the four Marines killed at least a dozen Japs before they finally received word from a company runner to withdraw. Corporal Clougherty declared, "I was so certain I was going to die that I made peace with everybody."

But Private Kenny considers himself the luckiest of the lot. One bullet cut the chin strap of his helmet. He said he could feel it "whip through my whiskers."

Technical Sgt. Samuel Shaffer,
Tarawa

"I saw he was a Jap and let him have it"

Written to point out a hero, the following story was nonetheless marked "killed for 134," which may refer to Article 134 of the Uniform Code of Military Justice. It is a catch-all for offenses that, among other issues, bring discredit upon the Armed Forces. Whether the alleged offense was related to this event or a different action by the subject is not clear.

"A pistol is worth a dozen lessons in jiu-jitsu," says Marine First Lieutenant Norman K. Thomas.

Lieutenant Thomas, 30, of Long Beach, Mississippi, should know since he killed two Japs at point-blank range with his .45-caliber automatic on

Tarawa. He was recently praised by his commanding officer for "conspicuous gallantry" in that campaign.

"The only time that Japs dare to do any hand-to-hand fighting is at night," Lieutenant Thomas explained. "You can't beat a pistol at close range."

Lieutenant Thomas, who once taught judo to Marines at Camp Elliott, California, killed the two Japs "at close range" the night before the island was secured.

He had assumed command of his outfit whose casualties were over 50 per cent. One Jap counter-attack had been sustained at twilight. Lieutenant Thomas was the only officer at the command post. Several wounded Marines were lying nearby.

"I saw somebody bending over one of the wounded," Lieutenant Thomas related. "He was stripped to the waist and although he was wearing a Marine helmet I knew he wasn't one of our men. I spun him around, saw he was a Jap and let him have it in the head."

Lieutenant Thomas had to grapple with the second Jap.

"He was bigger than the first one, out-weighed me about 20 pounds," Lieutenant Thomas continued. But you can do more than you think at times like that.

"Just as the first one had been, this one was armed only with a bayonet. I managed to get him down on the ground, then got him with the pistol."

On Tarawa, he didn't get the opportunity to "squeeze off" any shots in the approved pistol-range manner.

Lieutenant Thomas' unit suffered two more counter-attacks, one at midnight and another at dawn. His commanding officer stated that he "made his way up and down his lines, and by his leadership and fearless devotion to duty, turned back the hostile attacks with severe losses to the enemy."

"He didn't pay any attention to Jap bullets," a Marine sergeant who was with him on Tarawa declared. "He walked around as if he owned the place."

The three Jap counter-attacks were organized. In addition, the rest of that night (November 22–23) they kept harassing Marines but failed to penetrate the line. The next morning, with the aid of Navy dive-bombers and gunfire, Jap resistance was broken.

Lieutenant Thomas' unit was relieved at about 8 a.m. The island was secured several hours later.

The outfit was assigned to beach defense, to watch for any attempt by the Japs to reinforce the island. There was none. A few days later, the unit boarded ship for this rest camp.

Up from the ranks, Lieutenant Thomas, who enlisted in June, 1935, was appointed a second lieutenant June 15, 1942, from the rank of sergeant. He became a first lieutenant in January, 1943.

As an enlisted man, Lieutenant Thomas (then Corporal) served three years with the Marines in China from 1937 to 1940. He fought with the Marines on Guadalcanal, although he had no hand-to-hand encounters there such as he had on Tarawa.

Nephew of Miss J. P. Thomas of Long Beach, Lieutenant Thomas has a brother, Major Octave (cq) Thomas, in the Army. Lieutenant Thomas' wife, Mrs. Vera Holmes Thomas, lives at 823 West Mabel Avenue, Monterey Park, California. He has a 10-month-old daughter, Darleen Colette, whom he has never seen.

"My only regret about Tarawa," said Lieutenant Thomas, who calls the Marine Corps "my only profession," "is that we left so many good men there. . . . I hope we'll get a chance to make it up to them."

Staff Sgt. Richard J. Murphy Jr.,
at a Marine Pacific Base

"Caught in the cross fire of one of their own"

Any instance of "friendly fire" might obviously draw the label "not used," as this story did. The close quarters of fighting on Tarawa would have made the battle ripe for being wounded or killed by one's own side, a reality not shared with readers.

Sixty Marines caught in the cross fire of one of their own big tanks in the bloody battle for Tarawa—successfully completed yesterday when the remnants of 4,000 fighting Japanese Marines were annihilated—owe their lives to Private First Class Alva Burkett, 23, of Exeter, California.

The tide of battle surged back and forth over Tarawa's narrow expanse of coral sands so swiftly that it often was impossible to identify our own troops. All of Tarawa was a front line throughout the three days the Japanese bitterly resisted our landing. As a natural result, Private First Class Burkett's platoon found itself pinned in a narrow ravine by machine guns in one of their own tanks which had been ordered to sweep the area in which they were caught.

"Someone had to get word to them to stop, and it might as well be me," Burkett explained. "I ran down the ravine, but was not able to get their attention. There was just one thing to do, and I did it. I jumped out in the open and ran toward the tank, waving my arms and shouting at them to cease firing, they were shooting at their own men."

Miraculously, Private First Class Burkett was not injured, although machine gun fire from the big tank nicked the dirt at his feet. He was forced to charge 25 perilous yards directly in the face of the blazing guns.

Burkett has been commended by his commanding officer for his bravery and is naturally the idol of his platoon.

Master Technical Sgt. Jim G. Lucas,
Tarawa

"Hey, captain, what'll I do with these prisoners?"

Humor was not out of bounds for combat correspondents—indeed, it was welcome within limits—but disrespecting an officer may not have been an acceptable punch line. This piece was marked "not used (taste)."

A Marine artillery officer who was on Tarawa tells this one on himself.

A private marched back from the front with prisoners. Halting near the officer, he called out:

"Hey, captain, what'll I do with these prisoners?"

"Don't call me captain," roared the captain. "Don't you know there are snipers around here just laying for officers? Call me anything—call me Joe, Mac, or stupid, but don't call me captain."

"Okay, stupid, what'll I do with these prisoners?" asked the private.

Staff Sgt. William K. Beech,
a Marine Base in the Pacific

"The best souvenir on this island"

Souvenir hunting apparently occupied many if not most Marines, even while some of the enemy were still a threat. Brief references to picking up mementoes appeared in some stories passed by censors, but accounts focusing on the practice were often rejected. One concern may have been that Marines could have been accused of the unseemly and illegal practice of robbing the dead, especially of their personal effects. Indeed, an October 1944 memo stated plainly that removal of personal items from enemy dead was subject to censorship.

Marine Private First Class William F. Kelliher, 6200 Tracy Avenue, Kansas City, Missouri, came awfully close to getting the best souvenir on this island.

Private First Class Kelliher and a companion came on another Marine trying to open a Japanese safe. They helped out for a while, then gave it up as a bad job. Later returning past the same spot, Kelliher found that the

Marine had succeeded in opening the safe which contained a large quantity of Jap money and one thousand American one-dollar bills.

The unnamed Marine pocketed the grand, but gave Private First Class Kelliher a bunch of Jap ten yen and fifty sen notes.

Bill is sending these home as Christmas cards, with personal Xmas wishes written on the notes.

On another foray Kelliher picked up a Jap suitcase containing a complete hair-cutting outfit, fans, books, a pencil, an opium pipe, and a bugle, all of which he plans to take back with him.

Private First Class Kelliher is a photographer attached to Headquarters Company of the Second Marine Division.

Staff Sgt. Fred Feldkamp
Tarawa

"The island by now is practically stripped clean"

Christmas is still a month off but Marines here have already had a minor version of it.

The Japs on Tarawa obligingly stocked a treasure trove for souvenir hunters.

An abbreviated list includes clothes (shirts, trousers and socks—many of them never worn), beer, rifles, machine guns, pistols, field glasses, flags, postcards, canteens, shoes, watches, money medals, campaign ribbons, toilet articles, dice, cards (manufactured, according to the box, by the "Standard Playing Card Co. of Japan"), hari-kari knives, and a hundred others.

The island by now is practically stripped clean. For awhile, Marines were donning the Jap clothes, but yesterday they were told to take them off for fear that they might be mistaken as the enemy by other Marines.

Some of the souvenir hunters came close to death in their ardor for bringing back a memento of the Battle of Tarawa.

In several instances, Marines entered pillboxes they thought were empty, looking for souvenirs, and discovered live Japs who later were blasted or burned out of their emplacements.

Closest call of all probably came for a sailor from one of the transports.

A group of Marines were out looking for souvenirs when they heard a sound from one of the pillboxes. Approaching it, they yelled for the occupants to come out with their hands up. There was no answer. The call was made several times; still no answer. The Marines were just about to start firing through the pillbox slits when a sailor appeared in the doorway, a bottle in his hand.

"Look," he said, all smiles, "I found some saki!"

Staff Sgt. Richard J. Murphy Jr.
Tarawa

The encounter with the sake-bearing American was recounted in an earlier story written by a public relations officer, Captain Earl J. Wilson. He identified the tipsy man as a Marine, not as a sailor.

"I was there too and I didn't see you"

Criticism of the civilian press was seldom a topic in CC dispatches. DPR headquarters had assured the civilian press that its personnel would not be competing with them, and it would go without saying that the Marine writers would not be criticizing their civilian counterparts in print. How rankled Marine combat correspondent Fred Feldkamp must have been is evidenced by the tone of the following dispatch and the fact that the staff sergeant wrote it the day after Tarawa had been secured and other subjects surely presented themselves. Feldkamp had hoped the piece would be offered to the New Yorker, *but instead it was marked "not used"—twice—and filed. The title above is his.*

The action here which began last Saturday, November 20, has been called by Marine officers "the toughest fight the Marines have ever been in." Covering it for various newspapers, magazines, and news syndicates were eight civilian correspondents, an uncounted number of civilian photographers, ten Marine Corps Combat Correspondents and a group of Marine Corps photographers whose work is distributed to the press in the States by Marine Corps Headquarters in Washington.

Bob Sherrod of Time, John Henry, INS, Bill Hipple, AP, Dick Johnston of the United Press, Frank Filan AP, Keith Wheeler of the Chicago Times, Archie Thomas, Australian morning paper, and the rest of the civilians have done a remarkable job of following the action by staying right up in it during the three days of the main assault. This was no slight feat, for many of the first waves that landed all during last Saturday, the first day, were wiped out completely before their Higgins boats reached the beach.

But it shouldn't be long, I have no doubt, before a series of vivid, eyewitness stories come off the typewriters of correspondents who were no closer to the action here than Melbourne, Australia, or Central City, Colorado.

These stories will all describe the color of the sky when the action began, and in the first paragraphs of all it will be made quite clear that the correspondents in question were standing on the beach, presumably with legs planted firmly some distance apart, arms on hips, and face well up with jaw protruding.

All these stories will be titled "I Was There when Hell Broke Loose" or some variant.

One correspondent who covered the Solomons campaign wrote an I Was There story about a certain Naval action off the islands, describing the scene in great detail, not forgetting the exact color of the sunset over the water, and mentioning prominently the fact that he was standing on the beach, just a few hundred yards away from some of the ships.

I hate to disillusion all the trusting souls who thrive on this type of vicarious journalism, but I must report that at the time of this particular action he was sitting in the office of the Naval censor at a South Pacific base hundreds of miles away.

At a Southwest Pacific base some months ago a civilian correspondent arrived in town, took himself and a few cases of liquor to the best hotel, and contacted a Marine correspondent. "I hear you have a pretty tough obstacle course at your camp," he said after introducing himself. The Marine agreed that they had. "Well, I'd appreciate it if you'd run it and give me the dope about how tough the obstacles are and what they consist of."

The Marine agreed, and shortly a story was being cabled to the States built around the fact that this civilian correspondent, at the relatively ripe old age of forty, got out and ran this course which was one of the toughest yet designed for Marine training.

The Marine correspondent was very glad to help out, and please do not interpret this as a gripe on our part because the civilian didn't break out any of the liquor. I simply feel that it's my duty to report all this to a news-hungry public.

I could go on with other examples, but it might serve to discredit the really fine work which the large majority of the civilian correspondents turn out and the hardships they go through to get their material.

To any enraged civilian correspondents who may be on the point of fuming, all I can say is—If the shoe fits, put it on.

Staff Sgt. Fred Feldkamp,
Tarawa

"To these men . . . this seems the height of luxury"

How did Marines relax after a battle? This story may have been marked "not used" because of its frivolous nature. Yet it illustrates one Marine writer's mindset after the most intense experience imaginable.

With a portion of the Second Marine Division which fought the battle for Tarawa, I arrived a few days ago at a "rest camp" and found:

Navy Seabees building tent "decks" reputedly at the rate of 180 a day.

Showers, washrooms, etc., already constructed, although men (and officers) are still living in tents.

Gay Christmas wrappings everywhere. Every Marine is loaded down with letters and packages; it's over a month since we had any mail.

The Red Cross issuing towels, soap, razors, tooth brushes, etc., to Marines who haven't seen a post exchange in a long time.

Food certainly tastes much better when there's not a Jap corpse alongside or a swaying deck underneath. (The high altitude of this camp, several thousand feet, means that you have to plow through clouds to get to breakfast.)

Nearest town is just a mile away—and there's even a USO which shows movies and has dances! To these men, who still (some of them) are washing Tarawa's sand out of their dungarees, this seems the height of luxury.

Marines enthralled over newspaper clippings describing the slaughter at Tarawa. Most popular is a clipping from The Washington Post containing the eye-witness account by Master Technical Sgt. Jim G. Lucas, Marine Corps Combat Correspondent.

A five-dollar bill feels as crisp as one did two months ago. (We were paid today.)

A folding cot, with a couple of blankets, seems like inner-spring comfort alongside a foxhole or a bunk on a transport.

It's a marvelous sensation to be able to smoke at night without having to worry about "darken ship" or the fact that you'll be making a perfect target for a Jap sniper.

Marines are insatiable music enthusiasts, standing for hours around a jeep in the cold night, listening to programs from the States.

It's difficult to swallow that lump in your throat when you hear, as I did last night, a group of Marines singing, "Hark! The Herald Angels Sing."

Staff Sgt. Richard J. Murphy Jr.
Somewhere in the Central Pacific

"Ski and Jim"

The New York office of the Division of Public Relations rejected this magazine-style portrait of two Marine officers without comment. One practical reason would have been the amount of time that would have passed before it appeared in print, easily several weeks and more likely many months after Tarawa had been in the news. The lack of personal details would have doomed the piece for regular distribution. In addition, the Marine Corps may have hesitated to publicize and even commend men hiding illnesses that could affect their ability to carry out their duties.

This is about two guys with a lot of guts, but not in the way you usually think about those things. Ski is the only name I knew one by while the other we called Jungle Jim. You can put the two incidents I am going to mention about them down to anything you like, but one thing is certain, theirs is the spirit which has always been part and parcel of the Marine Corps pretty well summed up in the last war by the sergeant who yelled to his men about to make an advance, "Come on you bastards, do you want to live forever?"

But, still, this is not essentially of the spectacular "blood and guts" courage that inspires legends and wins medals. No, this is rather the quality of individual fortitude of the kind which has proved the Marine the Jap's superior.

There was nothing unusual about the way I met these two young Leatherneck lieutenants. They were just two ordinary average guys. One had the bunk above me and the other the one below me in the same compartment aboard the transport that took us to Tarawa.

When I finished putting my gear in my bunk I looked up and there was Ski sitting on the edge of his upper bunk with his feet dangling down. He was cleaning his carbine. Ski was tall with the build of an athlete. He came from one of those little coal mining towns in Pennsylvania and was only twenty-three. As a matter of fact Ski had yet to take his first shave.

Ski was second in command of an infantry company. His commanding officer, nicknamed Jungle Jim because of his prowess at Guadalcanal, was a tall slow-speaking Virginian about a year older than Ski, who was very dark and wore a beard.

Both had risen from the ranks, selected particularly because of the leadership they had shown during the long heart-breaking months on Guadalcanal. Although Ski had spent most of his time on the front line there his parents never knew he had ever been anywhere other than in a nice comfortable place with plenty to eat and nothing to really worry about. He "didn't want to worry them."

One of the things that marked Jungle Jim was that he always carried an old fashioned six-shooter on his belt—I think it was a family heirloom—and I was told that he was damned good with it. Someone told me that he had gotten three Japs with it while on patrol and it also had to its credit a three hundred pound wild boar Jim had gotten in New Zealand. He wore the tusks around his neck by his dog tags.

One morning I heard a sharp pop which woke me up. I thought at first a canteen had hit the deck. But when I opened my eyes I found that Jungle Jim had opened his locker and the pistol had fallen out, hit the deck and gone off. The bullet went through the calf of his leg. This put Jungle Jim in the sick bay and Ski in command of the company.

Day and night Ski worried about his men while Jungle Jim lay in the sick bay and worried about missing the coming show. During the days as we approached the Gilbert Islands Jim became increasingly restive and finally—asking for an inch and taking a mile—received permission to get up and walk around the ward. Instead he painfully climbed topside where he limped about the deck to prove he could walk well enough to lead his men ashore. He went through all sorts of facial contortions to hide his pain and tried to keep from hobbling too visibly on his game pin.

Maybe some of his spiritual courage aided him physically, I don't know, but at any rate once up he stayed up and by driving himself improved a good bit.

The evening before D-Day I went to my bunk for a last check on my gear only to find the whole frame rattling and shaking. Ski was having a hard malaria chill. He wouldn't let me get the doctor. He wanted to go in with his men.

He did, and so did Jungle Jim, one limping hard and the other weak and shaking with malaria. Together they led their Marines into the blazing hell of Betio at one of the hottest spots near the pier where Japanese machine gun bullets churned the water first into foam and then to blood.

Somehow I think of both of them as heroes.

Capt. Earl J. Wilson
Undated

"The kind of men who are making the biggest sacrifices"

Occasionally a combat photographer would write a story for distribution, adding a narrative to what he had recorded with his camera. While it is unclear whether any of this story was distributed, editors apparently decided its detailed descriptions of the Tarawa wounded were too stark and marked them with red lines. Those lines are in italics.

A crowd of civilian war-workers had gathered around the pier. Not one of them moved. On the face of each was a still, silent expression, but their eyes were staring at what they saw.

A hospital ship had come directly from the zone of battle, and its passengers were the casualties from the fight for Tarawa. Down the gangplank the men came, in single file. They were walking wounded. Some of them had bandages covering half their faces, others were bandaged about the throat, some had their arms in slings.

I wanted to go aboard the ship and take motion pictures of the men filing down to the shore. The rear gangway was heavy with traffic, so I went to the forward gangplank, where a few men were descending.

I had just got to the top, when I saw four hospital corpsmen carrying a stretcher patient toward me. I brought my camera up to position and shot the scene. After I lowered the viewfinder from my eye, I took a good look at the man. He was a Japanese casualty. I hadn't expected that; he was the first Japanese prisoner I'd seen.

My equipment was at my side, and after gathering it, I started back to the rear of the ship. Soon, Marines lying in stretchers were passing before me. One after another they followed out, each stretcher carried by four corpsmen.

As they were being carried down the gangplank, some of the casualties would raise their heads to see what was taking place. I could see their eyes flash from one side to the other, drinking in all they could see. Some of the men just lay still in the stretcher. They were unable to move at all.

One boy, he couldn't have been more than twenty years old, raised himself on his elbows. I could see in his eyes that he was exhausted. Nevertheless, he wanted to take a long look at the people and the buildings. No longer need he look only at the men lying wounded and dead on the field.

Later, I wanted to photograph the stream of stretchers that passed before me, so I focused the viewfinder of my camera on the gateway. As the stretcher bearers came by with their casualties, they would pass in front of my lens. *On a few occasions I would be peering through the finder watching them pass, when I would notice that a stretcher would come by, apparently empty. The usual form of feet sticking up under the blankets was not there. I would lower the camera from my eye to see if I was photographing an empty stretcher. It wasn't quite that way. There were men in those stretchers, but amputation had taken their legs. I felt pretty sick when I saw that.*

One fellow took my attention immediately. His chest raised and lowered at a fast pace. I could see that he was breathing with effort. His entire left arm, his chest and shoulder, all were enclosed in a plaster cast. When he saw the crowd at the pier, a smile crept over his face.

Later, when I had returned to the shore, I received the greatest shock of all. I had watched one patient as he was being carried down to the dock. Once ashore, the corpsmen placed the stretcher on the ground and waited to place him in one of the many ambulances. A sudden breeze came up and blew the sheet that was covering him off of the stretcher. From the hips down, there was nothing. His part in that battle for Tarawa had caused him to lose both of his legs.

I am sure the impression that came to the crowd of on-lookers that afternoon was extremely significant. I think that war comes to the mind more deeply when something like this is seen, than, perhaps, any words the human can read or hear. These Marines and Navy men who passed before the eyes of all present that day, they are the kind of men who are making the biggest sacrifices in these times . . . for the freedom . . . and for the rights they are fighting to keep.

Private First Class Burt Balaban
Pearl Harbor

The ferocity of the fight for Tarawa, coupled with the relatively small size of the battlefield, was evident in the high number of casualties both sides suffered. Nearly 1,100 Marines were killed along with thirty Navy personnel, most of them corpsmen. More than 2,230 Marines and nearly sixty Navy personnel were reported wounded. In contrast, the Japanese forces embedded on Betio were annihilated. One estimate held that nearly 4,900 men—Japanese troops and contractor workers and conscripted Korean laborers—had awaited the Americans. Only seventeen Japanese and fewer than 150 Koreans survived the onslaught to surrender. With the assistance of heavy equipment the victors quickly turned sections of Betio into American and Japanese graveyards, most of the remains to be identified and relocated in the years immediately after the war. Efforts to find all combatant remains and link them to the men reported missing and assumed killed in action continued into the next century.

In the United States during the week of Thanksgiving in 1943, the day-by-day news reports from Tarawa described a chaotic, bloody fight. It was not until ten days after the battle that officials began releasing details. People were shocked by the accounting of killed and wounded, the grim facts of war driven home by photographs of American dead. The battle served notice to an overconfident civilian population to prepare for a difficult road to victory. Tarawa also highlighted flaws in the military's use of amphibious craft and its overall island strategy, serving as an important inflection in the learning curve. There were still several more islands to conquer.

Master Technical Sgt. Jim G. Lucas's account of the battle—published in newspapers nine days after Marines took the island—was widely admired and won a National Headliners Award. The acclaim for Lucas's story helped prompt the Division of Public Relations to rework the CC's reporting into a book. At 160 pages, *Betio Beachhead: U.S. Marines' Own Story of the Battle for Tarawa* was a concise retelling of the four-day nightmare with the advantage of hindsight and official post-battle reports as well as dozens of photographs. Yet the book did not appear until spring 1945, well after the Marine Corps had sustained several more costly victories in the Pacific that challenged Tarawa for interest and veneration. *Betio Beachhead* was also preceded by more than a year by a book by the *Time* correspondent Robert Sherrod, who was among the civilian correspondents covering the assault. Its lesson learned, the DPR produced a book on Iwo Jima within six months of that battle.

A different medium gave Tarawa its most effective publicity. Battle footage by a Marine combat cameraman, Staff Sergeant Norman Hatch, appeared in newsreels within weeks of the Tarawa assault. It was eventually edited with film from his colleagues into an eighteen-minute documentary, *With the Marines at Tarawa*. Images of Marine dead in the waters off Betio gave officials pause about releasing it to theaters until President Franklin D. Roosevelt's personal approval, swayed by the argument that Americans needed to face the realities of war. The film was well received in March 1944, slightly more than three months after the battle, and it won an Academy Award for documentary short the following year. Both Lucas's story and Hatch's film were proof that the most hazardous public relations campaign imaginable was paying off in terms of promotion.

Close calls were common for DPR personnel on Tarawa, as they were for most every Marine deployed to the atoll. Two public relations personnel remained on the island, buried alongside others in temporary graves. In addition to Second Lieutenant Ernest A. Matthews Jr., a Marine combat photographer, the twenty-four-year-old Staff Sergeant Wesley L. Kroenung Jr. was killed by an explosion near the Betio pier on the first day.

It could easily have been many more. Consider the case of Technical Sergeant Samuel Shaffer. The CC had survived Guadalcanal when his fogged glasses left him unable to fire back at a sniper, with his salvation coming from the rifle of another Marine who could see the enemy. But he was even luckier at Tarawa. Recalling "the worst night of my life," he was in a foxhole at day's end constantly under fire. The next morning two Japanese bodies lay nearby, evidence of how close he had come to being overrun by the enemy. Two nights later, when the island was secured but holdouts remained, Shaffer found himself five feet from a Japanese soldier throwing a grenade from the tank trap in which he had been hiding. Other Marines returned fire, their bullets kicking up the sand around Shaffer's head.

Shaffer recounted those incidents to the combat correspondent Staff Sergeant Richard J. Murphy Jr. A seasoned reporter, Shaffer knew to give his fellow writer a good closing quote: "And I used to think the newspaper business was exciting when I was a civilian."

5 From New Britain to the Marshalls

Celebrating holidays in the Pacific could be bittersweet for Marines. The battle for Tarawa had cast a pall over Thanksgiving week in 1943. A month later, just a day after Christmas, Marines came ashore at Cape Gloucester, a headland on New Britain and one of three landing sites on the island. East of New Guinea and northwest of the Solomons chain, New Britain was critical to the Japanese strategy. No Marines on the island would be celebrating the new year with joy. The First Marine Division had hardly begun what would become an intense four-month jungle campaign. Establishing a base at Cape Gloucester would counter the Japanese fortress of Rabaul on the island's east coast. It had served as a land and air base providing troops for offenses in New Guinea and the Solomon Islands. Taking Rabaul was a primary goal as Army General Douglas MacArthur planned his return to the Philippines. The Japanese had plenty of time to learn to use New Britain's terrain to their advantage. Marines found themselves grappling with swamp and mud, thick forests with dense foliage and exposed tree roots perfect for concealment, heavy foxhole-filling rainfall that could last from hours to weeks, plus an assortment of jungle diseases and insects.

Meanwhile, the US Navy and the Marine Corps prepared for the next island campaign. Their attention had turned in late January 1944 to the central Pacific and three key atolls in the Marshall Islands. Not only would it represent the first assault on territory Japan held before the war, but a successful invasion of the Marshalls would crack what was called the "outer ring" of the enemy's defenses. The Fourth Marine Division was deployed at the Kwajalein atoll, in the heart of the Marshalls, and focused on the islands of Roi, Namur, and Kwajalein. Other elements of the Marine Corps attacked two more atolls, Majuro and Eniwetok. The American forces followed the familiar pattern of bombardment from the air and sea before troops came ashore. Japanese defenders fought from concrete blockhouses, ditches and culverts, downed trees and other brush, and cleverly concealed "spider holes" connected by tunnels. Conquering each atoll took far less time than their Marine comrades required on the larger and more heavily defended New

Britain, ranging from one day for Majuro to a little more than a week for Eniwetok.

All told, the Japanese losses would be enormous compared to American casualties. Staff Sergeant Charles F. Reher, a combat photographer, was aboard a landing boat when he saw the perfect image to illustrate Japan's fate after a naval shell blasted an ammunition dump on Kwajalein Island. "Smoke from the explosion spiraled up into a perfect hand," he said. "It reminded me of the hand of a dying man. It symbolized what was happening to the Japanese empire that day." As Reher reached for his camera, a Japanese shell exploded and showered him with hot fragments. Recounting the moment in a naval hospital, he called the unrecorded image "the greatest picture I ever saw—and I missed it."

The following censored or unused stories were written from the New Britain and Marshall Islands campaigns.

"A survey of the foul odors of war"

At this point in the fight for the Pacific, the Marine combat correspondents rarely offered philosophical commentary on the nature of war. Written amid the New Britain campaign, this realistic if indelicate description of the smells of the battlefield drew a simple "not used."

War to me is a combination of odors, all of them foul and noisome.

Worst of all is that stench of putrefying flesh. It's an ungodly smell that a corpse gives off after lying exposed to the elements for four or five days. It reaches way down to the very innards of a man.

But that odor is gone now. All the dead have been buried in this sector.

All the other foul smells remain with us, however. Each one is to be encountered along the 16-mile stretch of "C-Side Drive" which connects the anchor ends of our perimeter.

There's the everlasting mud and muck. Made up of almost equal parts of earth, water and sodden vegetation, well-mixed by churning wheels and plodding feet, it adds up to an immense hog wallow and a resulting pungent piggy aroma.

Then comes the astringent odor of sweating humanity and perspiration-soaked clothing. Even the almost constant rains fail to eradicate and cleanse the atmosphere. In happier days, it seemed that rains washed the air clean and sweet and left the tang of freshly churned butter arising from the earth.

Here the rain only adds more unpleasant smells. It adds to the mold and mildew. Everywhere is that sickening smell of clothing and equipment, hanging for days without getting dry, only rotting away.

Down at Silimati Point, where the initial assault was made, there's a pile of bags of rice, abandoned by the Japs. The rain and the humidity has caused it to ferment and the fumes are nauseating.

One mustn't forget the hordes of tiny black ants. At first we swore there was a skunk in the vicinity. Learning that skunks are not indigenous to the region, further investigation revealed the ants as the cause. Alive and crawling, no smell. But when crushed—ugh.

Very faint now, but still fresh in memory, is the smell of cordite and burnt powder coming up from the water-filled bomb craters and shell holes up near the front lines. This must be classed, though, as a borderline smell. There are those veterans who sniff these fumes of battle much as a retired firehorse's nose might quiver at the first whiff of smoke.

Thinking myself prejudiced, I've been searching for odors pleasant to the senses. But although the area is covered with dense jungle, not a tropical flower is to be found. It's barren, too, of wild fruit—not even a coconut palm.

The only favorable scent, and a mighty welcome one, comes as do the evil ones from the machinations of man. It is the smell of cooking and baking, wafted into the dark air from the unit's galley.

Technical Sgt. John W. Black
Cape Gloucester, New Britain

"I figure the Lord was with me"

Matters of faith were not off limits to Marine writers, but linking the act of killing the enemy with God's plan may have caused concern. In the case of this story, a censor wrote "suggest no" and "taste."

"I'm a Christian, and I feel that the Lord delivered them into my hands."

Private First Class George O. White, 22, of Route #2, Fayetteville, Ga., was a Sunday school teacher at the First Baptist Church, East Point, Ga., before he joined the Marine Corps "because men were dying and I felt that I must do my part in bringing the war to a quick end."

Today, the third day of battle for his company, Private White plodded along with his buddies behind the tanks leading the attack and matter of factly described how he killed two Japs the day before.

The details, though, came not from the deeply religious youth, but from his buddies, whose respect for the Georgia boy stems back to Guadalcanal days. For Private White, though he never curses, never takes the Lord's name in vain, is a good Marine, and that's the best Marine there is.

A Jap machine gun had pinned down the Marine contingent from a hidden ridge emplacement. White, a scout, skirted around a flank, climbed to the crest, got within 15 feet of the Japs manning the gun, killed two, and scared the others off.

"They never even saw me," said White. "I figure the Lord was with me."

Technical Sgt. Samuel E. Stavisky
Cape Gloucester, New Britain

"He got some measure of revenge"

A censor advised that using the Marine's name in the story below went against policy and suggested the story not be distributed at all because it could result in retaliation against American prisoners of war. Even without the actual name, "story could apply to any prisoner Japs might choose to tie it to," the censor explained in a handwritten note.

When his elder brother was captured defending Bataan with the Army, "Pete," the kid brother, immediately joined the Marines in hopes of obtaining some measure of revenge.

"Pete" fought throughout the Guadalcanal campaign, but never was sure whether or not he had accounted for any of the Jap casualties. Today, "Pete"—whose identity must obviously remain secret—got some measure of revenge for sure.

He killed a Jap for certain—as his buddies will testify—when a Marine patrol fought its way out of a Jap ambush.

Technical Sgt. Samuel E. Stavisky
Cape Gloucester, New Britain

"Leaflets show Australians drowning in a sea of battle"

Censors tended to mark "suggest no" on covering Japanese propaganda, though it was likely that American readers could comprehend the strategy behind such material.

Huge batches of propaganda leaflets designed to chafe the strong Australia-American feeling of comradeship were among the stores and supplies captured here by the invading Marines.

Brightly colored and crudely cartooned, the leaflets, strictly pornographic, hammer away at the theme that while the Australians are fighting and dying in New Guinea, American troops are living a leisurely life in Australia, and wooing the Aussie troops' wives and sweethearts.

Typical of the leaflets is one showing the Australians drowning in a sea of battle, while President Roosevelt, top-hatted and in swimming trunks, swims off with Australia. The text reads: While Aussies shed their precious blood, Ole Man Roosevelt finds his selfish aims going according to schedule.

Technical Sgt. Samuel E. Stavisky
Cape Gloucester, New Britain

"One was driving, one bailing, a third firing at dive bombers"
Marines showed their mettle when they faced setbacks, yet such moments could be kept from readers. Security was the stated reason for rejecting a story, abridged here, describing a series of foul-ups plaguing a Marine amphibian tractor company participating in Army and Marine landings at Arawe and Cape Gloucester on New Britain.

A leak occurred in the tractor's ventilator system shortly after the amphibian was launched from a mothership five miles from the Arawe beach.

"Unable to run the engine, we floated around for a couple of hours watching the show," said Corporal Alfred A. Amirault, 23, of 17 Bartlett Street, North Weymouth, Mass. "We were almost hit by a destroyer in the pre-dawn haze, and later we watched another destroyer engage in a duel with a Jap reconnaissance bomber.

"We then managed to transfer our load of 24 troops to a mine sweeper, and we were towing the Alligator when Jap dive bombers attacked. The ship made an abrupt spurt in maneuvering, and the tractor took a nose dive into the sea. We had managed to get the troops' gear off, but [Corporal Ralph F. Marshall, 19, of 458 Stockton Street, Grand Rapids, Mich.] and I lost everything we had. That is, except my toothbrush."

Amirault, later that day, volunteered and manned a Buffalo armored tractor in leading an infantry drive against Jap positions on the Cape Merkus beachhead.

Corporal George C. Morris, 23, of 32 Williams Avenue, Hyde Park, Mass., together with his tractor teammate, Sergeant John H. Burton, 22, of 508 Calhoun Street, Augusta. Ga., manned Buffalo .50-caliber machine guns and were firing at a dive bomber shot down by the combined fire of several tractor crews at Arawe. "I celebrated New Year's eve on Cape Gloucester," related Norris, "carrying the wounded off the lines."

Another operational accident disabled the amphibian operated by Platoon Sergeant John E. Rintalan, 23, of Walled Lake, Mich.; Corporal Justin A. Bayne, 26, of 2221 La Salle Avenue, Niagara Falls, N.Y.; and Sergeant Nathan H. Godwin, 22, of Dunn, N.C., all Guadalcanal veterans.

Shortly after they were launched from the mothership, the trio observed water leaking into the tractor. Investigation proved that a pontoon plug was missing. The trio transferred their cargo of troops to other amphibians, and attempted to save their own tractor by bailing. They managed to salvage the tractor, although for a few minutes of that hectic voyage the trio had to specialize activities. While one was driving, a second was bailing, and a third was firing a machine gun at Jap dive bombers.

The team of Corporal Samuel J. Alaimo, 23, of 10 St. Marks Place, New York City, and Corporal Michael Hubiak, 29, of 322½ Pleasant Avenue, Herkimer, N.Y., had its own red-hot troubles in the form of an overheated engine. When they got too close to shore during a pre-landing naval bombardment, a Naval vessel rushed up and crashed into them to prevent a possible disaster. The crash was the only effective way to stop the tractor, since a shouted warning could not be heard over the noise of the churning tractor.

In rescuing most of the troops aboard Sergeant Rintalan's amphibian the tractor operated by Corporal William S. Gasteb, 22, of Kirwan Heights, Bridgeville, Pa.; and Corporal Leonard E. Stringfellow, of 4616 Eastern Avenue, Cincinnati, Ohio, became overloaded and unable to proceed.

A salvage boat towed the amphibian to within 50 yards of shore, and the troops disembarked only a few minutes before Jap dive bombers attacked the coral-stuck vehicle. The two lads returned fire.

Technical Sgt. Samuel E. Stavisky
Somewhere in the Southwest Pacific

"I knew then what outfit I was meant to be in"

Word of the Navy censor's disdain for publicizing acts of heroism rooted in disobeying orders may not have reached all combat correspondents. The writers continued to submit such items, perhaps believing that they were textbook examples of compelling storytelling and of Marine fervor for action.

All the world loves a lover, they say—and the Marine Corps loves a fighter.

Many were the tongues that were clucked, many the heads that were wagged, when it was learned that two southern Marines, members of a defense battalion, had "upped and left" their outfit on the night of January 12–13.

But Corporals Bert Dunnam, 23, son of Mrs. Polly D. Dunnam, Route 2, Richton, Miss., and Merdec H. "Drifty" Smith, 29, son of Mr. and Mrs. J.D. Smith, Route 2, Villa Rica, Ga., did not seek to shirk their duty. Rather, they sought to do more and become what they enlisted in the corps to be—real fighters.

To this end, they hiked some seven miles up to the very front lines, convinced the captain of a Marine assault company that they were replacements—and then they really went to work!

A report from the two Marines' battery commanders states the cold facts:

"On the morning of 13 January, 1944, Platoon Sergeants 'X' and 'Y' reported Corporals Merdec H. Smith and Bert Dunnam absent from morning roll call. Upon questioning members of the absented Marines' gun crews, I learned that both Smith and Dunnam had on the previous night meticulously cleaned and oiled their rifles and ammunition and that they made no statements to anyone which might be construed as indicating any intention to absent themselves from their posts of duty.

"At that time there was a story current about two mobile truck drivers who allegedly left their trucks and joined the infantry on the front lines, remained there for several days and then returned to their normal duties. It is my opinion that the act of these two truck drivers appealed to Smith and Dunnam and to them seemed worthy of emulation.

"An inventory showed that they only took arms and ammunition and the clothing they wore."

"Harry E. Kipp, 1st Lieutenant."

Investigation showed that the two Marines had constantly bemoaned their fate—that of staying some distance behind the front lines on the beach and manning the big guns. Both had enlisted more than three years ago in the hope of being among the first in the scrap that they realized was inevitable. But then they were placed in defense battalions . . .

First thing Captain John F. Weber, of 90 Vermont Street, Rochester, N.Y., knew of the situation, two clean Marines approached him and explained that they were replacements from the—Defense Battalion.

Captain Weber's company was at this time standing by to assault Jap-held Hill 60. The company had suffered a number of casualties and it was an easily convinced captain that looked at two fresh "hands" and assigned them to two of his platoons.

Captain Weber said later that he "lost track of both in the wave of destruction left in their wake."

Others in their two platoons were more specific.

Corporal Smith, who had had several years of infantry service in the Army at the Fort Benning, Ga., infantry school before entering the Marine Corps, was immediately pressed into action as member of a patrol going out in front of the lines. His buddy, Corporal Dunnam, was given the same duty the next day.

Captain Weber's company marked time that day (January 13) and continued with its "sounding out" of the enemy with patrols.

Early on the morning of the 14th, as the Marines pressed on and up, Corporal Smith, who was near his platoon leader, said as he pointed to the left and up ahead:

"I didn't know we had any Marines up there."

The platoon leader dryly returned:

"We don't. That's a Jap."

After a momentary swallow, Corporal Smith relates, he fired and had the satisfaction of seeing his first victim topple to the earth.

During the course of the day, Corporal Smith's buddies aver that he downed at least seven more Japs.

Corporal Dunnam's mates were not so specific:

"He was right with us all the while. We all were shooting down Japs," one of them related, "and I'm sure he got his part of 'em."

First patrol actually to reach the top of the hill included Corporal Smith, who was third in line. He disclaims any personal credit insisting that his patrol leader, Private First Class George O. White, of 213 West Washington Street, East Point, Ga., who has since been evacuated from this base with injuries, was the whole show.

After the hill had been taken and the area secured, the Corporals' outfit was relieved and sent back to a rest area.

"Biggest thrill I ever had," Corporal Smith relates, "was when I drove by my own old outfit in a truck coming from the front lines. I knew then what outfit I was meant to be in."

When asked if they ever had any misgivings about their leaving the comparative safety of the defense unit for the front lines, both said that they had not.

"We saw a couple of dead Japs on the way up there," Spokesman Smith said, "and I asked Bert here if he wanted to go back.

"He said 'no' and so we went on."

The two Marines are now staying with their new outfit while arrangements for their odd "request for transfer" goes through.

Old line Marines shake their heads when told of this serious "breach of duty," but it is safe to wager your last dollar that they have their tongues in their cheeks—for if the Marine Corps loves anyone, it's a fighter.

Sgt. Arthur E. Mielke
Cape Gloucester, New Britain

"The incident proves the enemy is still breathing"
Stories cheering American advances were common. Setbacks in the form of effective enemy action seldom saw distribution without some tinge of optimism. Censorship policies ruled out "results of enemy actions . . . which would be of value to the enemy."

If only those "pin point" Marine dive bombers hadn't eliminated the radio station on Mille, we would be hearing—via Tokyo—of the spectacular repulse of an American invasion force by a small Jap detachment on that atoll.

In a harassing raid today, four destroyers shelled Mille while two dive-bombers of the Fourth Marine Air Wing hung over the island for observation purposes. Their work done, they returned to their bases.

The Japs, no doubt, would have claimed a victory, that they broke up an attempted invasion.

The incident, however, does prove that the enemy is still breathing despite 12 weeks of intensive bombing by Marine dive-bombers. Even before the American vessels opened up with their guns, they were greeted with a volley from five Jap coastal defense guns.

The planes overhead had to climb out of the range of heavy anti-aircraft fire. One of the Jap guns was definitely put out of commission before the destroyers withdrew.

It was much more fire than the Marine flyers have ever encountered over Mille. Apparently, the Japs there are holding back for a land invasion and thought today's show was "it".

While the Jap held atolls of Mille, Maloelap, Jaluit and Wotje have been neutralized for any operational purposes, they still kick back at every opportunity. Since the Marine dive-bombers first began their strikes, they have suffered from enemy anti-aircraft fire.

Out of 113 missions, 80 planes have been hit by enemy anti-aircraft fire. Moreover eight Marine planes were knocked down, with a casualty list of six men dead and four wounded.

In one instance, a lifeguard destroyer sent to rescue the crew of a destroyed plane was subjected to severe shelling from Jap coastal guns.

1st Lt. Louis Olszyk
Majuro, Marshall Islands

"He could see that the firing was coming from his own outfit"
Navy headquarters apparently found no humor in this friendly-fire incident, a censor issuing an emphatic "NO" and an additional notation of "killed—Navy"

coming from a different source on this almost whimsical report. The only other censor's marking was the underlined sentence from which the title above is drawn.

Marine Private First Class Chester "Irish" Pawelczak of Toledo, Ohio, single-handed fought off a whole platoon during the battle of Namur. But "Irish" didn't get a medal. All he got was a bawling out from his top sergeant.

"Irish" was digging in on the far corner of the island one night, when a couple of machine guns and about fifteen rifles began to spit hot lead at him. He leaped into his foxhole like a gopher.

"Irish" was catching up on his praying, and was all the way down to the Sixth Commandment, when a flare lit up the battlefield. He could see that the firing was coming from his own outfit. They had mistaken him for a Jap sniper.

He called out, and the echo came back in bullets. He held up a white handkerchief. What happened to his handkerchief, could have happened to him, and it made him shudder. The bullets piled up like a pyramid, and "Irish" lay there all night without moving an eyebrow.

Early the next morning, the firing stopped. "Irish" crept out of his foxhole and sneaked over to his buddies. That was when the top sergeant first saw him. The top sergeant's mouth curled up at the end, as he bellowed:

"Where in the hell you been? Fall in. We're gonna mop up a sniper. If he's still kickin', I'm gonna strangle him with my bare hands for keeping me awake all night. I suppose you were snoring away in some foxhole for the last 12 hours."

The way "Irish" figured, he could have come out with the story, and they might have given him a medal for holding off a whole platoon singlehanded, maybe, and then again it might be the end of a "Jap sniper."

Sgt. Edward F. Ruder
Namur Island, Kwajalein Atoll, Marshall Islands

"Like moving through a nightmare in technicolor"

A disadvantage of the emphasis on security was the loss of first-person reports of Marines and Navy personnel under fire. No specific reason was given for a censor's decision not to release this account of a bombing raid on Roi Island; it would easily fall under the "results of enemy actions" rule. The story shows no effort being made to delete sensitive material that might have rendered it acceptable, which suggests stories about Americans enduring enemy fire were not seen as contributing to the public relations effort. With its focus on Navy personnel, Marine editors may not have objected.

"It was the biggest Fourth of July I've ever seen," said Ensign John P. Smith of Alexandria, Virginia.

"It was Coney Island and the World's Fair rolled into one," said Chief Carpenter's Mate Stephen H. Kreiss of Redwood City, California.

"There aren't any words to describe it," said Chief Ship Fitter Paul N. Barron of 6547 Tyler Avenue, St. Louis, Mo. "It was just plain hell."

In the safety of a rest camp, the three Seabees were swapping yarns of their adventures when a Jap bomber set off an ammunition dump and almost blasted into the Pacific all of tiny Roi Island, with its hundreds of Seabees and Marines working night and day to make it an advance U.S. air base.

"We were unloading 500-lb. bombs from an LST," recalled Ensign Smith, "when the alert sounded. 12 of us jammed into a 5x5 pillbox. We thought it was just another drill when the searchlights went on and some ack-ack was fired. I was outside, about to resume work, when there was a swish and a thud and the first bomb landed. I dove for the doorway, but shrapnel just nicked my legs.

"Then the ammunition dump blew up," chimed in Warrant Officer Frank E. Beadle of 62 1/2 Park Street, Pontiac, Mich. "That's when the first men got hurt. From then on, it was like a scene from Dante's Inferno."

"On the beach, ammunition was piled all around us," continued Ensign Smith. "Two small boats caught fire, and the LST, loaded with bombs and shells, had several small fires on the upper deck set by flying incendiaries. I expected it to go up at any minute.

"The sandbags around our pillbox were beginning to smoke, and the flames were coming closer. We had to decide where to go next. Some men ran into the ocean and swam to the other side of the island. Some carried wounded buddies aboard the LST, which shortly shoved off into the lagoon without even raising her loading ramp.

"We decided to make a run for the trench on the far side of the island. It was like moving through a nightmare in technicolor. Flares and rockets burst and hung overhead. Small arms bullets went off like firecrackers. Smoke, flames, burning brands and sizzling steel whirled by. We came across some wounded." He stopped abruptly.

"Well, we made it," Chief Kreiss took up the tale. "We crawled under a tank set across a Jap trench as a beach defense. About ten minutes later the tank crew came dashing through the smoke, jumped into that oven of a tank, and locked themselves in."

He laughed, remembering it. "Shrapnel bounced off that tank like popcorn in a pan. Those boys wouldn't even open up for their first sergeant the next morning. It took a lieutenant to break them out."

By that time, in the smoking dawn, the Seabees were out of their foxholes and busy rounding up what was left of their gear.

"Our camp was burned to the ground," said Chief Barron, "but we were so glad to see all the boys who survived that we didn't care."

By some miracle, an Army bomber on the airfield was not harmed, nor was the gasoline dump, protected by Jap fortifications, and barely 20 feet from the Seabee bomb shelter.

"If that had caught fire, and the LST with her ammunition had exploded, none of us would be here now," said Ensign Smith. "When we got aboard the transport, they couldn't believe that only 10% of us were casualties. The explosions had knocked men flat on the deck two miles at sea. They thought no one could survive."

"But Seabees, like Marines, are tough," concluded Chief Kreiss. "We dished it out to the Japs when we took that island. Then we them showed we could take it—and keep it!"

Sgt. Bob Cooke
An Advance Pacific Base

"Flame-throwers used on Roi did have many faults"

Marked "confidential—do not release," this story sounded almost like a report on the efficacy of flamethrowers and napalm rather than a newspaper article. Besides describing weapons and tactics, which were banned by censorship rules, the story recorded planning errors, unexpected developments, and on-the-job ingenuity by men in the field—all details of interest to the enemy.

"Flame throwers are among the most controversial of assault weapons," declared Marine Captain Robert C. Culver of (no street address) North East, Maryland, in an exclusive interview today.

The young officer, leader of an assault unit of Marine engineers in the recent capture of Roi and Namur Islands, stated that his men found flame-throwers essential in blasting Jap snipers out of pill-boxes, tunnels, and blockhouses, clearing the way for infantry advance. But engineer assault squads of another landing unit found flame-throwers impractical, preferred bazookas for the same vital job.

Flame-throwers used on Roi did have many faults, admitted Captain Culver. Of an obsolete type now used by neither Japanese nor U.S. Army troops, they were useless when wet, and no special equipment for keeping them dry was issued. Resourceful Marines used gas protective clothing covers to keep the throwers dry on landing craft maneuvering through the choppy lagoon. Only one had to be stripped down and repaired on the beach at Roi.

Spare parts are also hard to get, even back in the States, which makes testing of flame-throwers before use in battle difficult. Captain Culver's men tested two machines on the fantail of their combat-bound transport, and had to replace rubber diaphragms blown out by nitrogen pressure. This they did with typical Marine ingenuity by cutting up inner tubes to fit the space. Neoprene would have been better, the engineer officer declared, but it was a case of anything in a pinch.

In combat, the flame-thrower user is in a highly dangerous position. Carrying the 68-pound weapon, with fuel to last only seven seconds of actual use, the man is practically defenseless without covering rifle fire of his Marine teammates. Captain Culver's men gave personally owned pistols to the flame-thrower boys so they would have some weapon available. These were never used, thanks to the disorganized defenses left on Roi by terrific naval bombardment. But in another engagement, more protection should be given the flame-thrower teams.

The weapons themselves caused only one slight U.S. casualty on Roi. Used on the underground drainage tunnels into which Jap snipers crawled, one flame-thrower backfired into its user's face. This is not surprising, considering that a 7-mile wind is dangerous flame-throwing weather, and there was always a strong breeze in the Marshalls.

Great skill is necessary in using the flame-thrower in battle, Captain Culver warned, especially if the jelly-like Napalm is the fuel. Napalm gives a 40-foot jet, compared to the more diffuse spray of burning Diesel oil, and a steady strong wrist is essential if the flaming jet is to hit exactly the right target. Marines on Roi showed they could handle this tricky fuel, under the guidance of Second Lieutenant Robert Reynolds of Berkeley, California, whose experiments with Napalm accounted for much of the flame-throwers' success on Roi.

Another essential for successful use of flame-throwers is a handy, adequate resupply base, so weapons can be refueled with a minimum of lost time. Roi Island's small size offered no problem here, thanks to the planning of Major L.V. Patterson of Milledgeville, Ga., who personally saw to the testing and refueling of flame-throwers used on Roi.

"Once necessary improvements are made," Captain Culver concluded, "the flame thrower should take its place as one of the most-feared and valuable weapons of the Marine assault engineer."

Sgt. Bob Cooke
An Advance Pacific Base

"He felt himself lifted off the ground in a confusion of flying metal"

A short but lively account of a demolition gone wrong for one Marine may have been rejected by the Navy censor because it highlights a strategic failure and efficacy of enemy fire. The Division of Public Relations may have agreed that an accidental casualty and a fatal booby-trap were nothing to publicize.

Marine Private First Class Lawrence A. Carnevale, 22, of 2 Laurel Place, East Rutherford, New Jersey, has been in airplanes before but the ride he'll always remember is the one he took when a demolition charge sent him flying through the air during the Marshall Islands invasion.

His unit had landed on Namur in one of the first assault waves and had made contact with forward elements of Japanese barricaded behind blockhouses and in dugouts. It was decided to clean them out before setting up night defenses and in the ensuing process of elimination a demolition charge was set off prematurely.

Private First Class Carnevale felt himself lifted off the ground in a confusion of flying metal and scattered earth. He turned a complete somersault through the air and then he went around again before he returned to earth. Mechanically, he crawled around until he found a foxhole.

He was evacuated the next day suffering from first degree burns on his arms, chest and legs. The explosion had also knocked shattered coral into his right eye.

He is now at a naval hospital in this area and will soon be returned to the United States for further treatment.

"That island was full of booby traps," he said today. "We saw a Jap rifle on the ground but didn't bother with it. A Marine came along after us and picked it up. The explosion almost killed him.

"Later, we were walking back to the command post and saw a couple of Marines fooling around some oil cans, but they were hunting for Japanese who might have been hiding there. Suddenly, the whole thing exploded and those boys were killed."

Private First Class Carnevale worked at the Bonis Brothers Fur Machinery Company in New York City until he enlisted in the Marine Corps October 2, 1942. He is the son of Mr. and Mrs. Pasquale Carnevale.

Staff Sgt. Murray Lewis
Somewhere in the Pacific

"We had to admire them, but we shot them, too"

At times Navy censors appeared to steer the Marine writers away from stories in which the resolve of Japanese troops was discussed. Details about

Marines killing the enemy also may have been a reason for this story's rejection.

Marines on an island in the Marshalls found a new way of shooting Japanese during the recent campaign.

Demolition crews blew up pillboxes and the blast would blow the Japanese hiding within 150 feet into the ocean. Dazed by the concussion, they tried to return to shore, but Marines on the beach picked them off one by one.

Other incidents were recalled today by Marine Private William T. Bready, 18, of Memphis, Tennessee, as he recuperated at a naval hospital in this area from a punctured eardrum.

"I was too anxious to pick off another Jap," he said. "I lifted my head and was just aiming at one coming in when they blew up an ammunition dump close by. The concussion almost knocked me to the other end of my foxhole and made me deaf in the left ear."

Private Bready's unit landed on their island the day before the main assault on Roi and Namur. Their job was to protect artillery units which were laying down a barrage and softening up defenses and preparations for the next day's attack. After the beachhead had been secured on the main islands, the group was sent in to help with the fighting there.

"The Japanese on that first island must have been supermen. We couldn't believe our eyes at the beginning when we saw these fellows being able to move after they were blown through the air. One of them charged us and we all pumped bullets into him, but he kept right on coming. When he finally fell, we went over to take a look at him. He had 27 holes in his body.

"One platoon flushed out a bunch of Japs hiding in a blockhouse. They had no weapons, but our boys didn't know it. Suddenly, the whole bunch piled out of the building and attacked our men but all they had to fight with were short sticks with knives tied to the end. We had to admire them, but we shot them, too."

Private Bready is the son of Mr. and Mrs. James M. Bready, of 2364 Autumn Avenue, Memphis. He left Central High School there to enlist in the Marine Corps July 1942.

Staff Sgt. Murray Lewis
Somewhere in the Pacific

"She saved my life, even if she didn't know it"

No reason was given for withholding the story of an unusual encounter between a woman and a Marine on a central Pacific island. Its sheer brutality? A Navy censor made his decision clear by writing "Do Not Release" in large, red letters at the beginning, middle, and end of its two pages.

The strange tale of how a Japanese woman unwittingly saved his life was told here today by Marine Private First Class John M. Bunner, 23, of 1144 Seventh Avenue, Sacramento, California.

To be specific, Bunner isn't certain the woman was Japanese. She might have been a terrified native who crept into the shell hole where the Marine lay wounded, and covered his body with her own.

Bunner and a buddy had been trying to repulse a Japanese counter-attack in the early hours of the morning on one of the islands in the Central Pacific.

"We tried to kill as many as we could with our rifles, but they kept on coming," he said. "Then we ran out of ammunition and we had to fight with our bayonets.

"My buddy got killed and I was alone against four Japs. One bayoneted me in the right leg and another shot me in the hand. I went down and fell into a shell hole.

"About five minutes later, a woman who looked Japanese to me, jumped into the hole and lay on my back. A dead Jap was across my right leg and my buddy was on top of my other leg. I couldn't move and I didn't want to.

"A Jap came by and asked the woman if I was dead. She said I was. He went away, but she stayed there about 30 minutes.

"When she started to get out of the hole, a Jap nearby shot her and she fell back on top of me. Then the same Jap as before came back. She said some word to him beginning with 'k,' which got him mad. He shot her and bayoneted her three times.

"That woman was hard to kill. She got out of the hole after the Jap left, just pulling herself up and over. As soon as she showed herself, all the Japs in the area started shooting at her. She finally died, but she saved my life, even if she didn't know it.

"I would still like to know what went on."

Now in a naval hospital in this area, Bunner has almost completely recovered from his injuries and hopes to return to active duty shortly. He recently received the Purple Heart medal from Lieutenant General Holland M. Smith, commanding general of the 5th Amphibious Corps.

The son of Mrs. Margaret Bunner, of Bellflower, California, the Sacramento Marine joined the service August 16, 1941. He formerly attended Grant Union High School.

Staff Sgt. Murray Lewis
Somewhere in the Pacific

"Carrier pigeons, Japanese rifles, and Mrs. Roosevelt"

Marine combat correspondents often heard humorous accounts—Sergeant Bob Cooke called them "scuttlebutt tales"—once an area had been secured and the pressure was off. A censor accepted some vignettes in one of Cooke's stories but rejected two, both below, without comment. A separate story by Cooke, also below, that referenced First Lady Eleanor Roosevelt, who had visited American troops in New Zealand and Australia in 1943, was rejected about the same time.

Carrier pigeons were reported on nearby Namur Island. With typical Marine humor, the boys tied messages on the birds, reading, "Tojo soon eat dirt," and released them to carry the word to Truk and Tokyo.

Finally, and guaranteed true, is the dilemma of the wounded Marine who had just captured a brand-new Japanese rifle. Amid flying sniper bullets he stood and argued with the four Navy stretcher bearers sent to carry him back to the field station.

The Marine won this point. The bearers carried the precious rifle back to the station on their stretcher. The Marine walked.

Sgt. Bob Cooke
Roi Island, Kwajalein, Marshall Islands

The Marines had been on Roi Island less than 24 hours. All organized enemy resistance had ceased. To two Leathernecks lying in sun-naked luxury on the beach, the easterly wind brought the dull boom of demolitions blasting Jap hideouts, the crackle of small arms from embattled Namur Island across the causeway, the smoke and stench of yesterday's still-burning battlefield.

Suddenly came the strains of the "Marine Hymn," played by a regimental band.

The Marines scrambled to their feet, shaded their eyes to look across the island. Over the former Jap headquarters fluttered a huge American flag. The band was still playing. There was the flash of news photographers taking pictures.

"Good gosh!" said one Marine to the other, "don't tell me Eleanor's here already!"

Sgt. Bob Cooke
Roi Island, Kwajalein, Marshall Islands

"The Minnesota Marine stood up and charged the nest alone"

A censor's red pencil eliminated specific references to "bazooka" in this story, but later the story was marked "no release." The details of strategy and use of a specific weapon may have swayed editors against publicizing the Marine's courageous assault.

The bazooka, famed U.S. rocket gun, is designed primarily for anti-tank defense, or for piercing inches-thick steel plate.

It worked against Jap snipers too for Private First Class Joseph J. Surina, 21-year-old Marine son of Mr. and Mrs. Matt Surina of (no street address) Leonath, Minn.

In the center of bomb-wrecked, bullet-swept Roi Airfield, first pre-war Jap territory to be seized by U.S. Marines, the Minnesota bazooka player was pinned down by deadly cross-fire. With him in the 50-ft. crater left by a 16-inch shell explosion, were two buddies, one with a BAR, the other with a rifle. All Private Surina had was his bazooka.

The snipers were getting the range uncomfortably close, and none of the Marines could spot the enemy. Private Surina decided to run to another shell-hole 100 feet away, draw enemy fire, and have his comrades shoot down the sniper. Lugging his bazooka across his back, he made it safely—and found his buddies right beside him. They had refused to let him act as bait alone.

Suddenly they spotted the snipers—a nest of them around an underground shelter protected by barrels of oil. Private Surina let fly one rocket into the barrels, hoping to explode them, but they were empty. The snipers were plainly visible—so the Minnesota Marine stood up and charged the nest alone, firing his bazooka as he advanced.

He fired seven rounds in half as many minutes, the blasting exhaust from each shell searing his cheek. When he reached the dugout, 14 Japs lay dead around it. The last ones, hit point blank by the deadly tank-destroying gun, had most of their faces and arms blown away.

The dugout they were protecting had survived the war's heaviest naval shelling, and had 3 foot thick concrete walls, reinforced with coral and steel drums filled with sand. In one half were benches, evidently to be used in case of air raid.

The other half was concealed by a steel door which resisted four heavy TNT charges. The Marines finally discovered a back way into the hidden room, tunneled in and found a locker full of baseball equipment.

Sgt. Bob Cooke
Roi Island, Kwajalein, Marshall Islands

"They were just asking to be killed"

This story was not released, but no explanation was offered. The first paragraph was drawn through with red pencil, which suggests downplaying Japanese fervor may have been a factor.

Frenzied Japs, shocked by the most intensive naval bombardment in history, rushed out of their dugouts on this island to jump on top of Marine Corps medium tanks and pounded the steel plates with their bare hands.

This is the most vivid recollection of 24 hours of fighting by United States Marines as they took the South Pacific atoll from the Japanese, fighting that left Private John M. Fagan, 17, of Kansas City, Kansas, with a whole book full of memories.

Fagan was a member of an assault team which followed the lumbering tanks down the island roads. As the fortresses blasted Jap dugouts and pillboxes from point-blank range, Fagan and other riflemen shot the Japanese as they were flushed out of their shelters.

"But these Japs that climbed on top of the tanks were just asking to be killed," he said today. "I could have closed my eyes and hit somebody. Others came out with pointed sticks and tried to rush us.

"Only disappointment I had on the island was being told by our lieutenant not to do any drinking during the night we spent on the island. That broke our hearts because we were bivouaced in a beer cellar and that Japanese beer is good."

Fagan's wife, Mrs. Norma Lee Fagan, and his four-months-old son, Michael, live at 722 South Mill Street, Kansas City. Before joining the Marine Corps February 16, 1943, Fagan worked as a rigger's helper for the Sun Flower Ordnance Works, DeSoto, Kansas.

Staff Sgt. Murray Lewis
Namur Island, Kwajalein Atoll, Marshall Islands

"A modern fairy tale without a dragon or an ogre"

Accounts of relatively easy island landings were rare. Stories that revealed in detail how a former enemy camp was transformed into an American air base were usually withheld for security reasons. This story was marked "No, at this time" when reviewed by a censor in March 1944, suggesting it might be distributed when security was no longer a concern.

For the past seven days I have lived a modern fairy tale in a South Pacific Wonderland complete with an "Alice." There have been no Aladdin lamps or fairy godmothers. In their place have been built bulldozers, tractors, trucks, ships, guns, and men. "Alice" is a six-week-old black and white spotted pig, pet and prospective meal of one of the anti-aircraft batteries.

One week ago tonight 50 Marines came ashore on these islands, in rubber boats, found a handful of friendly Polynesian natives, and some abandoned Japanese barracks. Tonight pup tents stand as thick as cocoanut trees did before they became a part of gun parapets. Bulldozer blades have screeched against coral and crunched sand until a road snakes among remaining palms the entire length of three islands connected by causeways. The road is so heavy with traffic, it threatened to become a major problem during early operations.

The islands bristle with anti-aircraft and seacoast artillery. All guns are manned and ready for action from air or sea. Machine guns alone would make any enemy attempt of a commando raid by land horribly costly.

Days will be few before our airfield will be ready to launch bomber and fighter attacks deeper into Japanese territory.

Most astonishing part of this fairy tale is the complete absence of a dragon, ogre, or any other kind of enemy. If the Japs have known we are here, then they've completely ignored us while this fortress has risen ahead of schedule deep within their perimeter of defense.

If the Japs had any intentions of meeting our Navy, there have been any number of times when they could have found a huge part of it standing by in the lagoon sheltered by this ring of islands.

So fast has been our progress men have gone to sleep deep in a section of underbrush and awakened on the edge of a gun pit or in the middle of a storage area.

First Lieutenant Robert A.W. Brauns, 4403 Underwood Road, Baltimore, Maryland, asked for a tractor to move a load of ammunition "out of the road."

"There's no road running through here," a somewhat amused motor transport dispatcher told him.

"No!" Lt. Brown replied. "Stand aside, brother, here it comes!" (He got the tractor.)

Ships have been unloading on a 24-hour schedule ever since the second day. Marines, working 12-hour shifts at a time, keep the flow of material and equipment from ship to shore moving in a steady stream until it reaches its destination. When the 12 hours off come to the dock crews, it means only that their duties change. There is still work to be done on fortifications, living quarters, mess halls, storage areas.

During the entire week, men and officers have subsisted on cold and simple field rations. Hot coffee is available only when the individual makes it himself. Even then it remains black. Ironically supplementing the skeleton meals, however, is a delicacy seldom tasted by others than millionaires—heart-of-palm—rare because an entire palm tree must be destroyed to obtain it. Here, through necessity, palms are falling by the hundreds. Heart-of-palm is on the "table" of every private. Its flavor is mildly that of cocoanut, color and consistency quite similar to the almond nut. The product from one palm will serve a score of men.

Total casualties to date are two—both drownings. The body of a soldier who slipped into a swift current yesterday while wading between two of the islands was recovered from the lagoon by Private Harold E. Newkirk, Box 21, Eaton, Ohio. The body in a similar case has not been recovered. Both names are withheld pending notification of the next of kin.

Wounds have been limited largely to minor cuts, frequently from opening cocoanuts and field ration cans.

Telephone and radio communications have tied every nook and corner of the islands into one large network. Work never slows because a key man can't be reached immediately—he always can be.

Electric lights glow defiantly throughout the night to speed to final completion this soon-to-be important Allied base.

And still in keeping with all standard fairy tales, this one, too, has a happy ending. We have proved beyond a doubt a practical plan which will likely set the stage for future Pacific operations—seizures of a lightly defended, undeveloped island base to build to order our own garrison at slight cost.

2nd Lt. Mac Roy Rasor
Majuro, Marshall Islands

"Temptation just seemed to reach out and grab him"

In addition to a bold "No," a Navy censor wrote "taste" above this rejected story poking fun at a Marine. A "slopchute," in Marine parlance, is an enlisted man's bar.

A Japanese "slopchute," a bottle of "saki," a live corpse, a sign reading "Alive, Do Not Bury!" . . . it all may sound like a weird dream. That's just the way Marine Private First Class Oscar Hanson of Richmond, Virginia, would like to think of the whole goings-on, as just a weird dream.

Shortly after "Old Glory" was run up the mast on Namur, the outfit set out to uproot the few remaining Jap snipers. Some of the boys uprooted the remains of a Jap "slopchute." Oscar had the luck to be one of them. It turned out to be bad luck, though, when he picked up a half-gallon bottle of "saki."

"Saki," as one of the boys described it, "is an Oriental wine that tastes like 'fu-fu,' molasses, and kerosene mixed in an old sock. But what a way to 'go'!"

Oscar took that first sip. The old long arm of temptation just seemed to reach out and grab him. He had another swig, and another.

When twilight crept over the island, there lay Oscar, clutching a half-gallon bottle, which was as dry as an empty drum. He looked as dead as a herring, and was twice as pickled.

The boys passed by Oscar and paid their last respects. They all agreed that there would never be another Oscar. Then one of his buddies put Oscar and the bottle of "saki" together, added them up, and got a hangover. That's what Oscar had, a powerful hangover.

So that the litter bearers wouldn't cart Oscar away, the boys made a little sign. They tacked it onto the cocoanut tree stump, right where he lay. It was just a simple sign with four words scribbled on it—"Alive, Do Not Bury!"

Sgt. Edward F. Ruder
Namur Island, Kwajalein Atoll, Marshall Islands

"The Jap never was told the name of the song"

Per censorship rules, stories about Japanese prisoners were rejected in whole or in part. Cultural differences between Americans and Japanese were often at the heart of such items written for humor or irony.

A wounded, frightened Japanese prisoner was brought into a Marine field hospital here for medical treatment.

Washed, fed, and given medical attention, the Jap's fright gave way to gratitude, which he expressed with toothy grins and pidgin English. He apparently liked to sing, and during the six days at the hospital, he frequently burst into humming a tune.

One of the corpsmen taught the Jap prisoner a new tune, which the captured soldier took particular pleasure in a humming. The Jap never was told the name of the song, nor the words to it.

The tune? "God Bless America."

Technical Sgt. Samuel E. Stavisky
Cape Gloucester, New Britain

The wounded Japanese soldier was being treated at the first aid station by a Navy doctor when a bulldozer clanked by.

He yelled and scrambled off the table.

"You not scare me," he shouted at an interpreter. "I am ready to be pressed!"

Questioning revealed that Japanese officers had told their men that American Marines liked to run over their prisoners with a steam-roller.

Staff Sgt. Murray Lewis
Somewhere in the Pacific

Not that the Marines ever have to be told, but some obliging Japanese on Eniwetok Atoll were nice enough to tell our boys where to shoot.

According to Marine Private James B. Bauer, 26, of 1210 Bunkerst Street, Kansas City, Kansas, a group of the enemy dashed out of their shelter unarmed, beating their stomachs and pointing to that part of their anatomy.

"That was good enough sign language for us," said Bauer. "We filled their request in the spot indicated.

"Do you suppose they were trying to tell us they had a stomach ache?"

Staff Sgt. Murray Lewis
Somewhere in the Pacific

An air of mystery surrounds a Japanese flyer who landed on the deck of this transport late yesterday. He was immediately interned.

The flyer was a pigeon, one leg banded with the Japanese Navy emblem. Feathers of both wings were inked alternately "K-21" and (this time in Japanese) "61-K."

The mystery involves what the pigeon was doing out here in the middle of the Pacific, 400 miles from the Johnston Islands—hardly the place for a good Japanese Navy pigeon to call home—and more than 1,200 miles from Jap-occupied Marshall atolls. The band carried no message.

Sgt. Charles R. Vandergrift
Aboard a U.S. Troop Transport

"My dear American soldiers, this is my last message"

Recounting an incident in the Marshalls several months earlier, this story was marked "not used" and "killed by Navy." It carried a stamp declaring that publication was not recommended "for reasons of national security," probably under the general prohibition of releasing information about captured documents. Unstated was the likely concern that the story humanized or created sympathy for the enemy.

Marine First Lieutenant Robert C. Replinger has an appointment with Taro Ito in Japan after the war.

Lieutenant Replinger, who lives at 4967 Niagara, San Diego, Cal., doesn't know Taro Ito. He never heard of him until last February when he hit the Parry Island beach with assault troops in the Eniwetok operation.

He scrambled into a shell hole. A dead Jap lay there. In his hand the dead man held a small notebook. The first few leaves were neatly wedged with Nipponese ciphers and red and blue ink. The center pages were marked by the Jap's inserted finger. They were scrawled hastily in English.

"My dear American soldiers," Replinger read, "Please you send to Kita 2 Nishi 13 at Sapporo of Hokkaido in Japan this notebook.

"His name is Taro Ito.
"My name is Chozo Ito.
"He is my father.
"This is my last message. Please Please send him.
"My Dear very Strongly American Soldier!!
"Good bye!!"

1st Lt. Millard Kaufman
Somewhere in the South Pacific

The New Britain and Marshall Islands campaigns continued the lopsided losses Japanese forces suffered against the Americans and their allies. Trying to prevent the seizure of Rabaul cost the Japanese four times as many casualties as the Marines, who lost just over 300 killed and nearly 1,100 wounded. Ironically, the Americans never took Rabaul—they did not have to once its air support was destroyed and its supply routes broken. Rabaul was isolated and left to wither for the rest of the war. The ratio in the Marshalls was stunning. Japanese defenders at the Kwajalein atoll, for example, lost more than 8,100 killed; Americans suffered about 300. Neutering Rabaul and taking relatively light losses during the surprisingly rapid victory in the Marshall atolls allowed the United States to step up its timetable in the Pacific.

As the Marine Corps gained ground, its combat correspondents gained experience. The Pacific war was turning into a beat as familiar as the police station or city hall, except for the constant presence of an enemy bent on killing them. "Being on the lines and diving for a foxhole as fast as anyone gives the correspondent the pole position for his material," Staff Sergeant Benjamin Goldberg wrote for a story aimed at journalists back home in Boston. "Then he has the opportunity to dig up his stories, to scout around and chat. He's just as bearded and dirty and tired as any Marine."

Goldberg later recalled advancing up a trail with other Marines behind a tank near Talasea on New Britain. An enemy mortar shell struck nearby. While a doctor treated a wounded Marine, Goldberg interviewed the casualty and received answers to his questions between grimaces and gasps of pain.

"How bad is it?" the Marine asked.

"The doctor says you're hit in fifteen places, but it's not too bad," Goldberg replied.

"Holy smoke! I'll get the Purple Heart with a flock of palms on it!"

The wounded Marine laughed at his own joke. Then a Japanese machine gun fired on the group and everyone hit the ground. The interview was over.

With the Americans in control of the western portion of New Britain, the combat correspondents and other Marines could enjoy a respite of sorts.

In March 1944, Goldberg was no longer slogging through knee-deep mud all day and sleeping on a hammock in a jungle. He and his colleagues had acquired a tent and built a floor out of logs to lift it a foot above the soggy ground. The tent contained cots for sleeping, a table made from empty chow boxes for a desk, even a light bulb. (Following tradition, they dubbed it the Cape Gloucester Press Club.) Hot meals were on the menu for a change, there were plenty of cigarettes, and each day they could take a dip in the ocean. An outdoor theater hosted a movie once a week. Mail was arriving more often than once a month, and the scuttlebutt had it that a post exchange would be built soon.

Goldberg declared, "We are living luxuriously." Such were the perks that came with victory.

6

Sweeping the Marianas
Saipan, Guam, and Tinian

A boyish look belied Richard J. Murphy Jr.'s experience as a reporter and his status as a Marine combat correspondent. He had been in the first wave of Washington-based journalists recruited by General Robert L. Denig, who ignored Murphy's loss of vision in one eye when he learned the young man had been working for the *Washington Evening Star* after graduating from Georgetown University. Dick Murphy was the right age for Denig's fighting writers, turning twenty-four the summer he joined the Marine Corps. Two years later he was a staff sergeant, a veteran of the battle for Tarawa, and accompanying the Second Marine Division for the assault on the Mariana Islands.

On June 11, 1944, four days after his birthday and four days before the Marines would land at Saipan, Murphy found himself on a transport ship, surrounded by veterans of Guadalcanal, the site of the first American offensive of the war, and fellow survivors of Tarawa, the first strongly defended atoll the Marines had attacked. "Saipan will be still another 'first,'" he wrote in a dispatch. "It will mark the initial engagement of war, European style, in this theater." The comparison would seem apt for stateside readers following the Allied invasion that had commenced the previous week on the shores of Normandy, France.

A booklet provided to Marines aboard the transport noted that Saipan was "almost part of the Japanese homeland," having been under their control for a quarter-century, as had been the island of Tinian, three miles south. Saipan was also home to thousands of civilians, mostly Japanese but some indigenous peoples as well, all living in towns linked by modern infrastructure, paved roads, railways, and telephone and power lines. The pamphlet advised that civilians, even Japanese, were to be treated as soldiers only if they opposed the invading forces. Marines were warned that tales of cruelty could inflame the passions of civilians on other islands.

A Mariana island about 140 miles south of Saipan and Tinian, Guam was also being targeted by the Marines' plan to gain control of the region. A US

Sweeping the Marianas: Saipan, Guam, and Tinian | 123

territory since 1899, Guam would be the first American land reclaimed from the Japanese if the campaign were successful. Most important, the battle for the trio of islands would decide whether the Marianas would become a staging area for aerial attacks on Japan, just 1,250 miles north. Various terrains on the islands were favorable to their defenders—open ground, tropical vegetation, swamp, cane fields, cliffs, mountains, caves—and supplemented by blockhouses and other manmade shelters. The outcome of the campaign was not certain for the United States, but the islands' strategic value was worth committing every resource possible to wrest control from Japan.

A massive Navy armada brought more than 127,000 troops to the Marianas, among them men from the Second, Third, and Fourth Marine Divisions and the Army's 27th Division, plus more than 100,000 sailors and airmen. Waiting for them were 30,000 Japanese troops on Saipan alone. The Americans landed at Saipan on June 15, the beginning of a battle that would last for twenty-four days. On July 21, American forces invaded Guam and, on July 24, Tinian. The following censored or otherwise unreleased stories were reported from island battles in the Marianas.

"I was ready to take a gulp of water and have it over with"

The destination of the vessel that lost a landing craft in a fatal accident was not specified in the following report. The date, three weeks before the assault on Saipan, suggested it may have been part of a convoy. The Navy censor ordering the report not be released was likely concerned it would reveal such movement. In any event, a fatal mishap was not the kind of story the Marine publicity campaign sought to share with the public.

> Survivors of a freak midnight sea accident told today how it feels to be catapulted, half asleep, from a moving vessel into high-pitching waters of the Pacific.
>
> More than 40 Marines and Naval corpsmen were thrown overboard when the small landing craft in which they were sleeping snapped loose from its fastenings on the deck of a larger ship.
>
> At the present writing, five days after the tragedy, there are two known dead and 12 men still listed as missing. Most of the survivors floated or swam from two to five hours in the water before being picked up. Several related encounters with sharks.
>
> The accident occurred shortly after midnight when cables which secured the landing craft gave way under strain caused by the heavy sea. The boat plunged overboard almost instantly.

"I woke up when the cable cracked," related Marine Private First Class Howard H. Hope of 130 East 23rd Street, Jacksonville, Florida, "and my first thought was that it was a torpedo. The next thing I knew I was sailing through the air and a moment later I was underwater.

"It happened so quickly I didn't even have time to drag a deep breath. My lungs were about to burst and I was ready to take a gulp of water and have it over with when suddenly I shot to the surface. I think it was a burst of air pressure from beneath the submerged boat."

Private First Class Hope clung to some floating wooden debris for four hours before he was rescued by a small boat.

Marine Private First Class Richard J. Stuckey of 4508 Penn Street, Kansas City, Missouri, told how he became entangled with ropes within the boat and was pulled far beneath the surface.

"I thought it would never get back up," he said, "but it finally did. I managed to get loose of the boat before it sank and grabbed onto a wooden ammunition box which held me up for two and a half hours, when I was picked up.

"I thought of a lot of crazy things out there I guess. One of them was about the steel cot a sailor had given me to sleep on earlier that night. I remember he told me to be sure and turn it in the first thing in the morning."

Pharmacist's Mate Second Class Thompson E. West of 1619 West 216th Street, Torrance, California, narrowly missed being pulled into the screws of the larger vessel by suction.

"I think the only thing that kept me going was the thought that my mother just couldn't get that second death telegram," he said. "You see my brother, in the Army Air Corps, was killed three weeks ago."

Another corpsman, Pharmacist's Mate Second Class John P. Bagan of 2017 Oaks Avenue, Everett, Washington, who swam without support for an hour and a half, told how the thought of his wife and three children reacted on him in the water.

"Every time I remember them I started swimming so hard that I tired myself out. So I thought of any crazy thing to keep my mind relaxed. One thing I remember was thinking of the last time we had a General's inspection."

Private First Class Harold D. Smith of Box 361, Uvalde, Texas, clung with two other Marines to a life preserver for over four hours. During the last half hour they attracted a shark.

"We were nearly scared to death when we saw that fin," he declared, "but although it bumped into us a couple of times it never did strike."

Another experience with a shark was related by Private First Class Robert O. Hofford of 1427 Mulberry Street, Scranton, Pennsylvania. "One brushed up against me suddenly," he said, "but I screamed and splashed and yelled and I guess I scared him away. Anyhow he didn't bother me again."

Pharmacist's Mate First Class Louis P. Maas of 600 East Raleigh Street, Glendale, California, a former sprint swimmer for Occidental College, Eagle Rock, California, swam unaided for nearly two hours. "I certainly was grateful for that college swimming experience," he told me.

Sgt. Herb Shultz
Somewhere in the Pacific

"Cries of the dying, moans of the wounded"

In fewer than two hundred words, a Marine writer offered a snapshot of one battle's horrors. It may have been too much for a Navy censor, guided by the prohibition of reports of enemy effectiveness, who marked a large red X on the single page of type and wrote "kill" at the bottom.

A murderous sanguine fray was waged by Fourth Division Marines led by Lieutenant Colonel Richard R. Rothwell before dawn this morning against fanatical-crazed Japanese forces, which thwarted an enemy attempt to capture Red Ridge, north of Aslito Airfield.

In the night battle, swollen corpses dotted the slopes of the ridge. Men littered the top of the ridge, lying in horrible grotesque positions as they slumped clutching the dirt in death. Beaten men could be heard crying piteously in terrible fits of sorrow, and now and then one would laugh hysterically.

Corpsmen answering the shrill cries of the dying and moans of the wounded stumbled exhausted upon mutilated bodies of men torn beyond recognition.

After the Japanese force had been annihilated, an ungodly stillness hung over the ridge, and the nauseating stench of the dead clutched at one's throat. No one moved, for he was not certain in his own mind if he were dead or alive.

Dawn was a revelation when it finally broke, and Marines realized then that they still held the vital heights. They had won the battle of Red Ridge.

Sgt. Edward F. Ruder
Saipan

"Japanese prisoners of war dug graves for our men"

A Navy censor and division editors cut or heavily edited nearly half of the following report describing the disposition of American dead on Saipan. The censor's concerns appeared to be detailing the use of prisoner labor and perhaps that women and children were among those being held.

Hundreds of Marines were buried on the sandy beaches of Saipan today, and thus was established a national cemetery in the heart of Japan's island empire.

Tonight, memorial services will be held for them, with Catholic, Protestant and Jewish chaplains participating. *Lieutenant Commander Otto P. Maddox of El Paso, Texas, Fourth Division chaplain, said such services will be held every night from now on.*

Japanese prisoners of war dug graves for our men as they were brought in by crews of their own buddies. So far, there is no accurate check on the number of dead we have suffered, but we know that the communique did not exaggerate when it described casualties as "moderate."

The spot chosen for our first national cemetery on Saipan was under heavy artillery fire only yesterday. I spent three hours there, pinned down by enemy guns and the explosion of our own ammunition trucks. Today, it is clear. Nearby is a gutted Japanese fuel dump, exploded in the first naval bombardment.

Hundreds of prisoners have been taken and today some of them are being used in cleanup details, to dig graves, and to help bring order out of chaos. The vast majority, however, are confined to barbed wire stockades, where family life has already been resumed.

Prisoners of war, particularly those on grave-digging details, show a preference for American cigarettes, which are being handed out in great quantities.

The vast majority of prisoners taken are women and children, of all ages and sizes. Some military personnel also have been observed in the stockades.

2nd Lt. Jim G. Lucas
Saipan

"About midnight, the baby started to cry"
This story was most likely categorized as a report on an atrocity and thus was marked "do not release" under Navy policy. In general, atrocity reports were allowed only if witnessed by the writer; hearsay reports were forbidden.

Through a Japanese interpreter I spoke to a Japanese woman at the captured civilian stockade, and she told a story that might give you an idea of the kind of people we are fighting here in Saipan, and elsewhere in the Pacific.

The story, just as she told it to me follows.

She and her husband and their one year old baby girl, were harboring a Japanese soldier in their home. The Marines were getting close and she and her husband were frightened. The soldier, an old friend of theirs, suggested that they sneak up into the hills to his quarters where they would be safer. They did.

That night, the Marines kept getting closer and closer, and the soldier was not too sure of his safety even in the hills. About midnight, the baby started to cry and couldn't be quieted. The soldier, afraid that the baby's cries would attract any Marines that were in the vicinity, grabbed the baby and strangled it. The father, unarmed could do nothing to prevent the tragedy.

Later, when the soldier fell asleep, the couple took the body of their child and stole out of the house. They returned to their home and then decided to give themselves up to the Marines, figuring that we couldn't be more brutal than the soldier was.

The MP's that run the stockade buried the baby right next to the fence that surrounds the cantonment, and then fed the family.

Later when a permanent place is arranged for these people, the baby will be moved where ever the family wishes.

We would like to end this by saying that the Marines found and killed the soldier, but we don't know what happened to him.

One MP remarked as the interview ended, "One sure thing, if he is on the island, we'll get him sooner or later."

Technical Sgt. Irving Schlossenberg
Saipan

"They were your boys. You never saw them like this"

Below is Second Lieutenant Jim G. Lucas's story from the aid station in Saipan, referenced in the Introduction to this collection. Its antiwar message came from a combat veteran of Tarawa.

If you think war is a glamorous thing, I wish you could have gone with me this afternoon to the row of camouflaged tents back of a wrecked railroad crossing which we call a battalion aid station.

They were bringing our boys there in truckloads. It's not as busy as it once was, but still they were coming in by the dozens. One of the corpsmen told me that incoming patients were only about 50 percent of what they were 24 hours ago, but he still has to see three consecutive hours of sleep.

There was one kid there—he had to be led in—with eyes so glazed that you thought at first he was blind. It didn't take much guessing to decide what was wrong with him; he'd spent five days up on the front lines with Jap mortars bursting around him, and he'd reached the breaking point.

There were seven Marines almost like him in the same ambulance jeep. They didn't walk in; you couldn't even call it a shuffle. One husky fellow stepped on a limb no bigger around than the handle of a garden rake, and it threw him. He just laid there and sobbed until someone picked him up.

You can't always pick your spots in setting up an aid station, and there was a field artillery battery just back of this one. Its first salvo threw those boys into a panic. They'd just come away from that sort of thing. I was watching the boy with the glazed eyes, and if I ever saw stark terror, it registered on his face. There was still no comprehension there; just animal terror. They had to lead him the rest of the way like a frightened child. And when they got him inside, he and another boy clung to each other—because there was nothing else to cling to—and pathetically tried to offer the other encouragement.

And there were others there they were bringing in on stretchers. Some of them went out again because it was too late to do anything for them. One Marine with his stomach shot open insisted on getting out of the jeep under his own power, but he didn't know how far gone he was. A lot of them had their faces covered, to protect them from the sun, and maybe it was better that way.

And there was dust there—dust ankle-deep, dust which made the wounded and the doctors and the corpsmen look like dark faced comedians. And there were flies, and mosquitoes, and all the ingredients it takes to make a hell.

There were doctors, too, fine doctors, the best our country has. Doctors who were bleary-eyed for want of sleep; doctors who operated under a big tree in what was once the back yard of a Jap farm house with guards posted on the road to tell truck drivers to slow down so they wouldn't raise so much dust.

They were doing all that could be done—up there. Later, if the men survived, they'd go aboard hospital ships. But this was the front.

They were your boys. You never saw them like this. When you last saw them, they were cocky and sure, all starched out in their dress uniforms, and proud as peacocks that they were Marines.

Sergeant John T. Campbell of Los Angeles, one of our combat correspondents, told me this story he saw enacted in an aid station. I quote him verbatim:

"I saw a chaplain, he was a priest, I think, administering last rites to a wounded boy. And you won't believe me, lieutenant—I know it sounds silly—but I never saw such an expression as was on that boy's face. It was just like—I know you won't believe me—it was just like that boy was already looking into the kingdom of Heaven."

I believed him, all right. I've seen it, too.

And I wished that the men who make wars could have gone to that aid station and seen the things we saw there. But I knew immediately it wouldn't have done any good. The men who make wars have seen these things, and they call it the supreme goal of human endeavor.

2nd Lt. Jim G. Lucas
Saipan

"I thought I would like to have this"

This brief report on souvenir hunting, titled "looting" by the Marine writer, carried a mocking tone regarding prohibitions against the practice. That alone likely led to its rejection by the Navy censor, but pointing out civilian journalists as souvenir hunters probably would not have been allowed by Division of Public Relations editors, either.

There ought to be a law against it. Americans must be the most souvenir-crazy people in the world. Shortly after the Marines had taken the main section of Garapan you could see them dragging out the souvenirs by the arm load, carrying them off on captured Jap bicycles. And yes, even on ox-cart, actually pulled by oxen.

Marines wearing red, silk Jap handkerchiefs around their heads could be seen working in the fields. Others were trying on the latest thing in geisha girl kimonas.

Even news correspondents weren't immune to the contagion. Pete Stackpole, Life Magazine photographer, was staggering under a load of loot that consisted of a big Jap clock, about a half dozen bottles of brandy and saki, and all sorts of bric-a-brac.

Harold P. Smith, of the Chicago Tribune, proudly displayed a beautifully hand carved scabbard and dagger, and a gleaming, wicked looking hari-kari knife. Staid, dignified Bob Sherrod, of Time Magazine, succumbed to the urge also. He had an insignia of a Japanese tankman, who had been in one of the six tanks knocked out in a counter attack on Garapan. It was the insignia of a Jap imperial Marine. "This is the first souvenir I've ever picked up," Bob claimed, "but I thought I would like to have this."

The writer—well, I picked up a couple of Jap kakhi short shorts. They were light and cool, and although a little big in the waist, could be used pretty well out in this country. Incidentally, as I write this, an order has been issued, absolutely forbidding all souvenir-hunting. Those apprehended will languish in the local bastile or brig, whatever you call it. There will be no exceptions.

Staff Sgt. Gerald D. Gordon
Saipan

"They didn't laugh long"

Judging from a censor's handwritten note, "Flame throwing tanks are out," a Marine writer accompanying such units was wasting his time chronicling their activities.

"When I primed the nozzle with a squirt of fuel, they must have thought the thing was broken, and laughed at me. But they didn't laugh long."

Marine Corporal Jay L. Vincent, 30, husband of Mrs. Velma Vincent, 46 Logan Street, Renton, Wash., flame-gunner on a light tank, then told how he ignited the spray.

"When the flame cleared away, the bare skull of one who had leered at me became visible."

The flame tank has chased the five into a fox-hole. He thinks he got 30 others in an old cellar.

His tank and three others were called up after an infantry group had been fired on from a valley.

Vincent's tank had returned to the tank area when an officer noticed a magnetic mine on the back. After the crew cautiously crawled out, a wire was attached and the mine pulled off. Luckily, it was a dud.

Sgt. Charles R. Vandergrift
Saipan

"A gentlemanly duel at ten paces on a front line roadway"

Embarrassing a Marine in stories would not be allowed by DPR editors. While the Navy censor was on guard for security and other issues, at times he pointed out reports that he thought were unflattering. Writing at the bottom of this short item, a censor advised: "See NO security but doubt Morton would appreciate any such story and also doubt its general good taste from Marine viewpoint." Invoking the issue of "good taste" suggested the story could be seen as offensive to the image of the Corps.

A Marine sergeant major and a Japanese captain fought a gentlemanly duel at ten paces on a front line roadway yesterday.

The sergeant major, Gilbert L. Morton, 31, son of Mr. and Mrs. Thomas Morton, 3220 Iberville Street, New Orleans, La., recounted it thusly:

"I was walking down the roadway. Thirty feet ahead a Jap captain stepped out into the road, raised his pistol, and fired at me. I returned the fire with my carbine. Both shots missed.

"He pulled the trigger a second time. There was a click, but no explosion.

"I thought I had dead meat, sighted in, pulled the trigger. My carbine had jammed.

"The enemy officer smiled, tossed his pistol to the ground. I did the same. We each turned and walked away."

A veteran of the Guadalcanal campaign, Morton, 13 years a Marine, said the two battles were altogether different. This one is probably a lot tougher, he said, although enemy bombing runs have been fewer and shelling by enemy ships nonexistent.

Sgt. Charles R. Vandergrift
Saipan

"The strain of self-control has become terrific"

Most of Staff Sgt. Dick Tenelly's two reports from accompanying Marine units in early July, the third week of fighting on Saipan, were passed by the Navy censor and Marine editors. Penciled out or heavily edited were his references to Marines breaking under pressure and screaming when wounded. So, too, were Tenelly's reflections about the status of the battle and those fighting.

No wilder wilderness can be imagined than Nameless Crag. A long, narrow ridge of porous lava rock, it rises vertically 200 feet from the gentler slope of Mount Tapochau in the center of Saipan Island. Its jagged sides and crest are overgrown with gaunt, shapeless trees and dense underbrush bound together impenetrably with tough, sinuous vines.

There we met an ambush this morning, knocking out three men from a small, *already depleted* Marine unit led by First Lieutenant John C. Chapin, of 457 Lakeshore Road, Grosse Pointe Farms, Mich.

We had a badly wounded Marine some distance along the crest of the ridge. One of a three-man patrol, a sniper's bullet had caught him in the chest, near the heart. Death was certain for him, unless he could be got out quickly. The lieutenant took six or eight men to get him. I followed along.

It was a tortuous path we followed, clambering over horizontal tree trunks, slithering over, under or around huge, sharp-edged boulders, weaving through vines *that clung with true Japanese tenacity*. It seemed impossible to carry a wounded man back over that route. But somehow it was done, with one man going ahead, hacking away vines and trees with a machete.

Then those left started to search for the sniper. One man wandered off too far to one side, alone. A shot sounded. There were several shots as the Marine tumbled, screaming, down the far side of Nameless Crag.

The doomed man's screams were horrible to hear. A week ago our men took their wounds, even death, in silence. But now they have been 16 days almost constantly in attack, seeing their buddies hacked down, bleeding, dying. The strain of self-control has become terrific. The shock of violent pain releases the tension, and now our men scream more often when they're hurt.

Our remaining men fired round after round into the spot from which they thought the sniper had fired. But they never saw their target and couldn't tell whether or not their shots reached home.

Bringing up the rear, I started to move around a jutting rock to join the others. Several bullets splattered the other side of the rock. Seeing my intention, those ahead signaled me to stay put. Machine gun bullets chopped at the leaves above my head.

From somewhere above them, several hand grenades were tossed down upon the forward Marines. *Another of our men began screaming until he was told roughly to shut up.* They fired blindly upward. One man thought he scored a hit, but the lieutenant decided to withdraw.

Our second casualty from this ambush was plainly dead, and his body was, for the time being, beyond recovery. The third casualty was able to limp back along the ridge toward an open spot. *I picked up his rifle and followed.*

Staff Sgt. Dick Tenelly

Saipan

"Nature was a military genius when she carved this island for defense"

Today we stood beside a wrecked enemy gun emplacement high on a ridge northeast of Garapan and looked down upon a panorama of victory for our forces on Saipan. Thusly, 19 days ago, so must have stood the Japanese, looking down upon us as we struggled ashore through *a lethal lashing of enemy* artillery fire.

There is still fighting to be done. More Japanese to be killed. More of our men will be killed or injured, before we occupy the remaining northeastern tip of Saipan. But today's spectacle from the enemy's "Radar Ridge" represented a complete reversal of the situation that obtained even two weeks ago.

Scores of officers and men gathered at this vantage point to watch the scene below. The enemy's complete discomfiture was clear to the naked eye, but for close-up views we took turns at a pair of heavy Japanese field glasses mounted on a tripod.

To the far left, moving up from Garapan, came the Second Marine Division. On their right advanced elements of the 27th Army Division. Directly below us and extending northeastward to our right were the advance units of the Fourth Marine Division. Behind us was our artillery.

Offshore stood *cruisers and destroyers of* our naval task force, adding opportune broadsides to the enemy's confusion. Overhead circled our planes, observing and reporting, diving and strafing the enemy wherever he showed himself.

The center of all attention was the ragged remainder of Saipan's Japanese defense forces, scuttling like frantic ants toward the only remaining high ground left to them. *There was something almost pathetic in their futile continued resistance, but that is of their own choosing, not ours.*

Directly beneath us, a Marine unit besieged a small, palm-treed knoll. An enemy machine gun in an impregnable and unapproachable cave had got six of their men, killed two of their officers. A Marine tank edged around a sharp turn in the road leading toward the cave.

In an open sloping field off to the right, could be seen Japanese riflemen in deep fox holes. Our artillery went over them like a lawn-mower. When the smoke lifted, here and there was one still alive. The live ones were picked off with single shots from 75's.

From here it was clear, if we had not known already, why Saipan is so difficult to take. Nature was a military genius when she carved this island for defense. *We marveled to ourselves how we ever got ashore.*

If the Japanese had been half as clever as they seem to think they are, this would have been a much less glorious Fourth of July for us.

Staff Sgt. Dick Tenelly
Saipan

"The Jap captive was very happy to oblige"

Rules for treatment of prisoners would certainly prohibit enlisting their aid in killing their own men, not to mention deliberately placing them in harm's way. Reporting such incidents in stories would violate censorship rules. A censor simply marked this report "do not release."

Marine Second Lieutenant Moises Diaz, 23, of 715 Gulch Road, Jerome, Ariz., found a helpful Jap soldier today.

"There are two dead Marines in that cave over there," the language officer said to the Jap captive. "Would you be kind enough to get them out?"

The Jap, "very happy to oblige," climbed a steep slope, entered the mouth of the cave and carried down one of the Marines. Puffing from the climb, he still "very gladly" made the return trip for the second Marine.

"Now, do you feel strong enough to climb up again and blow up the cave?" Lieutenant Diaz asked.

The Jap did. He set off a charge which blew the coral rock 50 feet into the air. Lieutenant Diaz didn't bother to explain that the Jap sniper, who had killed the two Marines, was hiding in the depths of the cave.

Sgt. Vic Kalman
Saipan

"Were they mad? Heck, no. They thanked us!"

The Navy censor passing this story pointed out its problematic nature in an unusually long handwritten note: "There's no security involved in this yarn, but I don't think its release would benefit the Corps. Looks to me like the patrol not only put its task off on souvenir hunters but also failed to tell them about Japs in the cave, thus risking their lives. However, do what you please with this." There was no indication the story was distributed.

Souvenir hunters may be a nuisance to some, but they're a boon to one Marine patrol whose job is to rout Jap snipers.

"Yep, souvenir hunters are a big help," said the patrol leader. "Take this morning, for instance. We were ordered to get two Jap snipers in a cave. Well, it was a long walk up the hill. Hot as blazes, too.

"So we waited for some souvenir boys. Told 'em about the Jap rifles and equipment in the cave. Then, we sat down. Sure enough, it wasn't long before there was some shooting and not long again before the souvenir hunters came down the hill with the rifles.

"Were they mad? Heck, no. They thanked us!"

Sgt. Vic Kalman
Saipan

"Some of our boys would like to use them"

Bullets that expand on impact, commonly called dum-dums, were forbidden by international declaration in 1899. A copy of the story below was sent to a judge advocate general. A handwritten note attached to the story indicated that the military legal official told the public relations division the story could not be released and asked that it be held by him, a sign of how sensitive the Navy viewed the matter.

Marines on Saipan Island found large stores of Jap dum dum bullets.

According to veteran Marine Corps officers, use of dum dum bullets is against international law.

Among those who found stores of the bullets was Marine Private William F. Tobin, of 1808 Stanwood Avenue, East Cleveland, Ohio.

Private Tobin declared that he found approximately 50 cases of the outlawed bullets in a cave on the southern part of the island. Many other Marines reported similar finds.

"It is a good thing," said Tobin, "that those bullets won't fit our weapons because I rather think that some of the boys would like to use them on the Japs."

Sgt. Jack Vincent
Saipan

"Still think I'm a Japanese spy, captain?"

Japanese Americans felt pressure to prove their loyalty after the attack on Pearl Harbor, especially when in military service in the Pacific. No reason was given for a censor's decision to write "do not release" on this story, which would challenge those who believed "fifth columnists" were hiding among Americans of Japanese background. Adding to the irony, the potentially Germanic ancestry of the suspicious Marine captain's name did not draw comparison.

For a kid who was once suspected of being a Fifth Columnist, Marine Private Justin W. Warner of 718 Chadbourne Avenue, Millbrae, Calif., is running up quite a record as a Jap killer.

The Fifth Column business came as a result of some highly irregular phone calls young Warner made to his family on the West Coast. His captain reprimanded him severely for subversive activity, and failed to promote him.

The Jap-killing began the day the Fourth Marine Division hit the west coast of Saipan. Private Warner, between dodging mortar shells, again hastened to let people know where he was. An incautious Jap sniper was the first to find out, with a bullet straight between his eyes.

Private Warner's latest exploit was a single-handed advance on what looked suspiciously like a baited Jap trap. In the California Marine's 22nd continuous day of front-line fighting, his company was advancing through a wealthy Saipan farmer's front yard, when he spotted a Jap sitting beside a pile of crated military equipment. It looked like aerial torpedoes, or pontoons, or even gas containers.

The Jap was too unconcerned to be believable. He sat under a tree and sipped saki, fanning himself with a branch. Private Warner reported to his captain and asked what to do with the nonchalant Nip. Captain Adolf Grussendorf of Grand Rapids, Minn., was in no mood to hold up the advance.

"Shoot him!" he told the California kid. And Private Warner did just that, inching his way through the brush. Then, to make sure there was no trick attached, he walked boldly up to the pile of equipment, daring any hidden machine-gunner or sniper to reveal his position. There was no trap. The lone saki drinker had evidently just decided to be comfortable to the last.

After the Marine objective had been taken, Private Warner turned to the captain and asked, with a grin, "Still think I'm a Japanese spy, captain?"

Private Warner is due for promotion any day now, says Captain Grussendorf.

Sgt. Bob Cooke
Saipan

"The first time I ever really hated war"

With its large civilian population, Saipan was the scene of shocking noncombatant deaths. At times Japanese soldiers used women and children as decoys to attack Marines and shot civilians who tried to surrender. Some civilians joined Japanese troops, who preferred suicide over surrender. Occasionally, Marines were forced to shoot civilian shields. With Navy headquarters hesitant to release reports of atrocities, even those witnessed by the writer, a censor marked this story "no" and "do not release."

The few desperate Jap soldiers still fighting on the northern end of this island have begun to use women and children as human shields and grenade bearers in attempts to infiltrate through Marine lines at night.

Three successive nights they have attempted to break through the lines around our command post near Tanapag Village, and at dawn we have gone out to find dead Jap soldiers and by their sides women, children, and even tiny infants dead, wounded, or terror-stricken.

The Marines have become so disgusted with being forced to kill women and children they challenge three and four times attempting to find out if the figures approaching are women before firing. But the Japs come on nevertheless, and the Marines are forced to fire.

Three mornings ago first aid men got a badly wounded Marine who had been driving a truck to the north. He saw two Jap women coming over a hill from a cave. Then a Jap soldier leaped out from behind them and threw a grenade in the truck. That was the beginning.

That night the Japs made a futile 3 a.m. Banzai attack on the command post. After repulsing them at one spot in the dark we heard what sounded to be an injured Jap soldier with women and children. An interpreter instructed him to stay there without moving until morning. An hour later we heard a grenade go off, and at dawn found two of the women were dead, and another minus a leg. All of the six small children were injured in some way.

The soldier was dead. Rather than let them live after him he had thrown a grenade in their midst.

We know the Jap soldiers have terrorized the civilians by telling them we would torture them if we captured them. Just before the Banzai attack a Jap came running down a hill behind us in sheer terror. He ran through our lines before we could shoot him, so one Marine ran after him. Ten feet past my foxhole the Marine shot him. But I was amazed to see a little girl of seven or eight running along behind the Marine, unable to keep up with either of them. She was so scared that when another Marine took her hand and led her to safety in the command post she said not a word. In the midst of this tense vicious night fighting the sight of a little barefooted girl trotting along behind a Marine blazing away with an automatic rifle was a pathetic sight.

In the morning we found the Jap had also been carrying a baby under one arm as he started down the hill. Scared, he dropped the baby and ran faster.

In front of another machine gun we found three dead Jap soldiers with two young women beside them, their pockets filled with grenades for the men.

The next night was worse. About midnight two Japs sneaked through the lines to the first aid station. When the Marines first saw them the Japs acted as if they wanted to surrender. One was carrying a baby. Suddenly the other threw a grenade in the nearest foxhole, injuring two first aid men. The other dropped the baby on the ground and both ran until they were shot twenty yards away. In the morning we found a soldier and a woman.

Fifty yards away another Marine saw three Japs walking directly toward his foxhole, fired, and in the morning found a dead family, of man, woman, and young son.

Last night was the worst. It was early when I heard one machine gunner suddenly challenge four times sharply before firing a long burst. Then a baby began to cry in terror. After a wait to see what the Japs would do, the gunner threw out a flare. We could see soldiers and a woman lying there, but not the baby.

It would have been foolish for any Marine to venture out to find it. So for two hours there in the rain and the dark it cried and whimpered for its dead mother. Around the lines hundreds of Marines listened and swore to themselves at the Japs for bringing this war down to machine gunning babies. In the foxhole next to mine a veteran of Guadalcanal muttered,

"This is the first time I ever really hated war."

We found it there in the morning, still alive, its little head caked with the blood of its mother and still strapped to her back. They were in the midst of six dead Jap soldiers.

An hour later a jeep drove in with five more children, three of them with shrapnel or bullet wounds. The women herding all of them had been killed.

These Marines, veterans of Guadalcanal, Tarawa, and the Marshalls, know the treachery of the Jap. They have lost buddies at those places and here, and they won't hesitate to fire if it endangers other Marines. But they have no stomach for shooting babies. They want to fight men.

Staff Sgt. Frank Acosta Jr.
Saipan

"Japs had told him Americans always torture natives"

A note from a Navy censor indicated this story would be held for review by the secretary of the Navy, saying he would decide what was released concerning atrocities. Whether it was eventually passed or distributed was not indicated.

A native woman on Saipan, surrounded by advancing Americans, threw a naked baby off a 50-foot cliff, pushed an older child over, and leaped to her own death.

That, and other difficulties of saving the Jap-propagandized natives on Saipan, have been revealed here by Marines recuperating from their wounds.

"The Japs filled the natives with lies about how we'd torture them," said Private Stanley Briggs, the son of Mr. and Mrs. Jay Briggs, of Stevensville, (near Missoula) Mont. Private Briggs, who told of the woman killing her two children and herself, continued:

"Just after we'd seen this we came on two Jap soldiers, a man and woman, and five kids. The Jap soldiers were bayoneting the kids, and the man and woman—the parents, I guess—were helping. The oldest kid looked about 10. The smallest was just a baby. We had to shoot the four grown people before we could stop them, and they'd already killed all but one of the kids."

Another Marine, Corporal John W. Gerrard, of 6357 Wayne Ave., Germantown, Penn., told of a group of Saipan natives who didn't believe the Marines were American troops.

"We ran this group out of a cave," he explained. "There was an old man, some married couples, and a bunch of kids—about 15 or so in all, I guess. This old man talked to us through our interpreter.

"He asked us what country we came from. When we told him he seemed puzzled. 'But Americans are all runty and puny,' he said. That was what the

Japs had told him. He said we couldn't be Americans because Americans always torture natives.

"This old man didn't see how we had come to Saipan, either. The Japs had told him and all the Saipan natives that they had captured Pearl Harbor, and controlled all the Pacific."

As soon as the natives found out how well their captured people were being treated, the Marines pointed out, they began to surrender in large groups.

"But even so," stated Corporal Gerrard, "the Japs shot a lot of them as they tried to come into our lines. The bastards didn't even want year-old babies to fall into our hands."

2nd Lt. Milburn McCarty Jr.
At a Base Hospital in the Pacific

"Constantly hearing death scream overhead in bullets and shells"

A report from Tinian on the second day of the Marine assault did not sound as certain of victory as its final line suggested. The early struggle as well as details about strategy may have led a Navy censor to question the story for "policy and taste." Though the story was not used, it provides a clear view of what Marines faced.

Several handfuls of tired, sick Marines invaded this Jap air base island, Saipan's twin in size and importance, yesterday morning. Today they hold, under heavy enemy mortar and machine gun fire, a mile of beach and a half mile inland. And they are advancing steadily.

They are tired from 30 days of the Pacific's bitterest fighting on Saipan, with barely a week to rest, reclothe, re-equip themselves. Many companies of the Fourth Marine Division are still only at half strength. They are sick from six weeks of sleeping on the open ground or the steel deck of a ship, from battling flies and fever, from eating little but canned stew or hash. They are jumping from constantly hearing death scream overhead in bullets and shells, or erupt without warning in booby traps, sniper nests, and land mines. But they keep jumping forward.

The 8,000 Jap defenders of Tinian and its 17,000 civilians had a month's notice and a ringside seat for Saipan, only 2 1/2 miles away, for the kind of show they are getting today. Abandoned by the Imperial Fleet and air forces, they did what they could. They mined all beaches and sea approaches, set trip wires across trails, placed machine gun nests where they could cross-fire all regular exits from the cane fields which cover 80 percent of Tinian's terrain. They hid during the day from air observation, tunneling deeper into the cliffs and caves, saving their artillery until they could use it at point-blank range. Unlike defenders of Saipan, they decided not to fall back from carefully prepared positions to various lines of defense, but to hold each area to the death. This has slowed up the Marine advance and caused some casualties.

They struck at two narrow beaches, barely wide enough for a single company to land at one time, and so steeply rough with coral that amphibian tractors had trouble in making the grade. Mines destroyed some LVT's and jeeps, but Marine engineers soon had the beaches demined and roads established to bring ashore tanks, heavy artillery, supply trucks. The beaches were closest to the Japs' best positions; the airfield in the north end of Tinian, and the sheer central plateau from which their artillery commands the coastal cane fields. The Japs evidently expected us from the south, near Tinian Town, and the Marines' bold stroke at the heart of enemy defenses caught them completely off balance.

Preceded by intensive bombing, strafing, and naval shelling, the invaders still faced heavy opposition from perfectly camouflaged dugout positions which could not be spotted from the air or knocked out by shellfire. Tanks and flame throwers are being sent against these hideouts, ahead of advancing troops this morning. If these latest mechanical devices fail, it will be up to the Marine infantry, as it was on Saipan, to go in and wipe out mortar and machine gun nests by hand weapons.

It's a tough prospect for battle-weary, sleepless Marines to face this morning. But tired as they are, desperate as the enemy is, they have—and will keep—"the situation well in hand."

Sgt. Bob Cooke
Tinian

"I realize we have to kill them, but I just can't get myself to do it"

A Navy censor passed this story of a Marine who could not hate the enemy, apparently overlooking the general rule against "timidity." At division headquarters it was marked "killed." A different marking noted "OK." Whether the story was actually distributed is unclear, but the markings on the single page indicate uncertainty over publicizing Marines who expressed a more humanitarian view of the enemy.

A handsome, mild-mannered Marine who "just couldn't hate anyone enough to kill him" is gaining a name for himself as a scout in the Second Division.

He is Private First Class Wilfred W. Morin Jr., 21, of 52 First Street, Derby, Me.

During the battle for Saipan, he uncovered valuable information about the enemy. Although often at the front lines, he never shot his rifle at either Saipan or Tinian.

"I realize we have to kill them, but I just can't get myself to do it. I don't think I'll ever fire, except in self defense," said Private First Class Morin, who was a student at American University, Washington, D.C., prior to his enlistment.

The Japs, he found, don't share his sentiments.

"One night," he said, "our command post was shelled by mortars. I buried my head, deep in the foxhole, and prayed. Dirt fell on me, but I wasn't injured. In the morning, I found one dud in the hole and five others within a few feet."

Private First Class Morin was on the baseball and debate teams at American University. He was a baseball, basketball and track star at Milo, Me., High School.

Sgt. Vic Kalman
Tinian

"We were subjected to intense mortar fire all the way"

A Marine public relations officer, First Lieutenant Millard Kaufman, wrote a first-person account of a patrol on the opening day of the Guam offensive. It was heavily rewritten by someone else, cut by nearly one-fourth, and played down the description of a shell-shocked Marine and a general sense of disarray. Notably, the revision substituted a third-person narration for Kaufman's voice, probably in response to an edict from DPR headquarters that writers should focus on other Marines, not on themselves. The unedited original version follows.

Ninety minutes after assault troops cleared Blue Beach of organized Jap resistance, a party of 12 Marines landed on the coral from an amph trac. We were to proceed to the Command Post approximately 600 yards inland. That was the extent of our mission. It sounded simple but we had to inch our way through the mud of Guam for three hours to reach our destination. We were subjected to intense mortar fire all the way.

A major, ten enlisted men and I comprised the group. We followed a brackish stream toward the interior. A Jap machine gun cackled crazily on our right. A sniper's rifle bullets whined past us. Most of the terrible noises of war were made by our forces—our planes strafing, our warships shelling, and the steady rumble of Marine infantry firing beyond the first line of hills.

We slogged upstream and cut across a rice paddy. Mortars were beginning to land around us. We took cover in a shell hole, hugging the earth. When the barrage died down an officer approached.

"You'll have to get out of that hole," he said. "Telephone switchboard goes here."

Crashing to the earth every few yards, we got back to the stream. The barrage began again. We threw ourselves close against the slimy bank. Suddenly around a sharp bend a voice yelled, "Corpsman, corpsman."

Our corpsman snaked ahead. I followed with a private first class. Beneath the jagged trunk of a palm were six Marines. Five of them were bleeding and the sixth continued to call for help. One of the wounded was bent double and a whisp of black smoke rose from a hole in his side. The smell of cordite and human entrails was nauseating.

"A piece of shrapnel hit his cartridge belt and ignited a clip," the uninjured man said. "We got to get them out of here," he added. "The Nips got this river bracketed."

The wounded were stiff and silent and their eyes were dull. The corpsman went among them working swiftly, assisted by the private first class. The major asked the uninjured Marine, "How far ahead is the C.P.?"

"It can't be ahead," the man answered. "The front lines are just about fifty yards up."

We left the corpsman there and headed on a diagonal across the rice paddy. Suddenly a burst of shrapnel threw dirt and rocks over us. The noise was deafening. Another mortar landed, sweeping the fronds from a tree twenty yards away. The earth trembled. We crawled toward the stream and I dove over the bank. I landed hard, my face inches from a frog. He sat staring at me. A dead bird lay at my elbow. A private huddled beside me whispered, "Everything on this island is dead or dying except us and that frog."

The major said, "Maybe the guy at the telephone switchboard knows where the C.P. is. We'll go back there." He took off, crouching. I followed, but a man behind me called, "Lieutenant!" I turned and he pointed to a private sitting motionless in the mud.

"He's acting queer," the private said. "Maybe he's hit or maybe it's just shock. . . . He won't move."

Together we walked to the man in the mud. His eyes were glazed and he shook all over. "Are you hit?" I asked. I reached out to touch his shoulder. He drew back shrieking. "I'll kill you," he yelled and he drew his .45 from his holster. His hand trembled as he pointed it at me. I stepped back but I went on talking. Then he put the .45 away and started sobbing. I walked off and he followed.

The major was out of sight now. We headed for the switchboard and the mortars started again. Something struck me sharply on the head. I reached up and felt a dent in my helmet. We lay close to the earth. Two wounded men walked slowly down the middle of the stream toward the beach. They stopped a yard from me. "Get down," I yelled, but they ignored me, just as they ignored the shells bursting around them. One of them said, "I feel faint." Blood was seeping through the bandages on his chest and his arm and his leg. His companion supported him with one arm. His other arm was bandaged. He said, "Let's go on a little farther. It can't be much farther to the beach." They walked on.

When the barrage subsided our corpsman crawled toward me. With an effort he grinned. "I rate the Purple Heart," he said. "I just took some shrapnel in my backside."

I sent a P.F.C. back to the switchboard for information. While he was gone I reached into my breast pocket for a cigarette. The pack was soggy. So was my notebook. Our weapons were crusty with mud. We were soaked with sweat and brown water.

The P.F.C. returned. The switchboard did not know where the C.P. was, he reported. We decided to go upstream again. We overtook a group of military police. I asked their leader where the C.P. was. "We're going there now," he answered. We tagged along, back over the rice paddie to a deep ravine. The major was waiting there for us. I bummed a cigarette from him, took off my pack and wrote this story.

1st Lt. Millard Kaufman
Guam

"The most horrible sight he had seen"

This atrocity report from Guam involving the native peoples called Chamorros was initially passed by the Office of Public Relations of the Navy. Then it was marked "killed," but the authority behind that decision was not noted. The report was stamped "secret."

A Marine patrol today found the bodies of 41 beheaded Chamorros, natives of Guam, victims of a vengeful Japanese massacre.

On each side of a narrow jungle trail, the patrol uncovered the ghastly evidence of Jap sadism, the worst horror these war-calloused Marines had seen.

The murdered Chamorros, all men and boys, were slain in groups. Their hands were tied behind their backs with bandages, rope and toweling, often so tightly that their wrists had bled. They were forced to kneel for the executioner. Twelve of them had knelt in a semi-circle, facing outwards, while the killers went from one to the other, beheading them with swords.

Most of the others were executed in groups of threes and fours.

A mile from this massacre was the mutilated body of another Chamorro. He too had been beheaded and his arms had been cut off. The head, the arms and the upper part of his body had been burned. Then, in an unbelievable example of sadism, the executioner had torn most of the ribs from the Chamorro's half-skeleton.

Marine Private First Class Joseph L. Schwartz, 23-year-old son of Mr. and Mrs. Leon L. Schwartz, of 5326 West 24th Street, Cicero, Ill., was in the patrol that discovered the evidence of the Japanese atrocity. He said it was the most horrible sight he had seen.

"It was something I'll never forget," he said. "All of us on that patrol have seen some pretty nasty things in this war. But this was the worst of them all. It sickened all of us. The Japs know they are licked on Guam. I guess they had to take their revenge on somebody. So they picked these poor people."

The dead natives were clothed in shirts, pants and sandals. Some wore hats.

In some cases, the heads rolled down alongside the bodies. It was evident that the executioners had bungled some of their dreadful work. They had hacked away, again and again, at some of the heads.

The Chamorros had been dead for four or five days. It was difficult because of the bloated condition of the bodies to determine the ages of the victims. But at least three of them were boys, one not more than eleven years old.

Staff Sgt. Francis H. Barr
Guam

"He was much too busy to sit around counting the money"

The discovery of Japanese currency in a cave involved another subject not to be covered by the Marine writers: captured enemy material of value. The Navy noted on the story that it was not to be released for that reason and ordered it killed.

All he has left are a few Jap bank notes, but at one time during the recent struggle for Guam, Marine Private First Class Jack R. Sparks, 19, of De Leon, Texas, was a millionaire.

A gunner with a Marine artillery unit, Private Sparks, a veteran of Tarawa and Saipan, was moving up on the town of Sumay, on Guam, when he happened upon a Jap cache in one of the many caves in the area.

In the depths of the cavern he found eight heavily constructed boxes which held crisp new Japanese currency ranging in denomination from fifty sen to 600 yen notes. A careful estimate of the sens and yens, the latter having an exchange value of 27 1/2 cents in American money, came to a total of about one million dollars. Private Sparks admits, however, that he was much too busy on Guam to sit around counting the money. The figure is that quoted by officers who examined the find.

Enlisting in the Marine Corps September 19, 1942, Sparks' mother followed him into service a month later and is now Sergeant Velma Roch Sparks, WAC Detachment, ASFTC, Camp Crowder, Missouri.

Sgt. Henry A. Weaver III
Somewhere in the Pacific

"We'll give you some work to do"

Interservice rivalries remained a topic not allowed in published stories under Division of Public Relations orders. Still, a Navy censor, apparently not seeing a security issue, passed this story portraying some sailors as lazy tourists on Guam while Marines were still fighting. It was later marked "not used."

While Marines were still fighting on Orote Peninsula, a group of sailors got permission to leave their ship to "see the sights" on the beach.

They made their way to the peninsula bent on collecting souvenirs. Before they had time to get started in what was a collector's paradise, a Marine officer spotted the group of 12 men.

"If you fellows came up here just to look around," said an officer, "we'll give you some work to do."

The men spent the next six hours burying Japanese dead in the wake of the Leatherneck drive for possession of the peninsula.

Staff Sgt. Gordon D. Marston
Guam

"Come along for a visit to the Stump Ward"

A Navy censor saw no security issues in this frank story about amputees at a base hospital in the bloody summer of 1944, but it was marked "not used" at the Division of Public Relations. Keeping in mind that a primary purpose of the combat correspondent initiative was to promote recruitment, such a story would not enhance that goal. The writer, a public relations officer, apparently thought the approach he took would promote the sale of war bonds.

You think the War is over? You think you've bought enough War Bonds?

Then you should have been along this morning when I visited the "Stump Ward" of this large base hospital, where many of the wounded Marines from Guam and Saipan are being treated.

The "Stump Ward" is the ward where they care for the amputation cases. It looks the same as any other big hospital ward—only the patients are different. As you walk down the rows between the beds you notice that every single patient is missing one or more limbs.

It's certainly not a pleasant thing to see, or talk about, but it won't help the War any to close this subject—nor will it help these young men who have suffered most.

One of the first patients I noticed was a thin-faced, red-headed boy, who looked about 17. He was eating ice cream from a paper cup, and was doing it pretty awkwardly because he had only one arm to use. The left one was cut off at about the point where you usually find the vaccination scar.

Next to him was a dark little Italian from New York's East Side. I didn't notice anything wrong with him until we started talking and he matter of factly proffered the information. "Here's where I got it," he said, lifting the sheet to show a left leg which ended at the knee. "I fell asleep in a foxhole late one night, and two days later I wake up on a hospital ship. I didn't know what happened, but someone said a Jap mortar hit right on top of us."

The Italian boy was mainly concerned about a batch of Jap Yen notes he'd found, and then lost in this confusion of being evacuated. "I don't have a single souvenir," he said sadly.

Down towards the middle of the ward a Negro sailor and a Marine were tossing a tennis ball back and forth across the aisle. Both were sitting up in their beds, the Negro with a leg missing and the Marine with one arm gone. The Marine never missed the tennis ball, though he had to catch it with only one hand. He stopped playing [catch] long enough to ask if the Women Marines back home were "good looking." He'd been overseas so long he's never seen a woman in uniform.

At the further end of the ward a Navy barber had set up a chair to cut the men's hair. As the barber finished with one Marine he motioned to two corpsmen, who came forward to carry the Marine back to his bed. This Marine had both legs amputated above the knees.

The "Stump Ward" is only one of more than two dozen wards in this hospital. In all, there are about 5,000 patients here, most of them Marines from the operations in the Marianas.

Surprisingly enough, the men in the "Stump Ward" appeared in a better mood than less seriously injured men in other wards. They were eating ice cream, playing catch, listening to the radio, holding bull sessions—and one was even pecking out letters on a typewriter. You sensed a strong, inner spirit dominating the ward—a spirit which the men called upon to show their gayest front, and to make the best of a situation that couldn't be helped.

As I was leaving, a corpsman told me of another patient who had lost both his legs. This man, a seaman, was injured when a plane crashed on the deck of a carrier where he was working. The crew of the carrier took up a collection for their buddy, and while he was recuperating here he received a letter enclosing a check for $10,000.

"He had me take it down to the War Bond Officer, and put every cent in Bonds," the corpsman said.

2nd Lt. Milburn McCarty Jr.
A base hospital in the Pacific

High stakes equaled high numbers of casualties in the Pacific war. They totaled more than 3,500 American dead and missing plus more than 13,000 wounded during twenty-four days of major conflict on Saipan. Deadly skirmishes would continue for months. Enemy losses were difficult to count because thousands were burned or sealed in caves, but nearly 24,000 were known dead. Fewer than 300 Japanese were taken prisoner. American casualties were fewer on Tinian, just over 300 dead and 1,540 wounded among the Second and Fourth Marine Divisions during the eight days of battle. The Japanese dead who could be counted reached 5,000. Three weeks of major fighting on Guam left about 1,600 dead and more than 5,300 wounded Marines and more than 170 dead and over 660 wounded Army personnel. Nearly 11,000 dead Japanese were recorded. Of the 10,000 remaining on the island, staging small attacks, surrendering or just hiding, about 8,500 were killed or captured over the next year. For decades stragglers would emerge from the island's jungles, the last in 1972.

Among the Marines killed in the Marianas campaign was a combat correspondent. Staff Sergeant Solomon L. Blechman, a native of New York City, had worked on high school and college papers, as a college stringer for other papers, and then briefly for the *Mamaroneck Daily Times* before joining up. A combat veteran from the Bougainville campaign, he had ruminated in a story that the steamy, sniper-ridden island was no paradise for a CC. Less than a year later Blechman volunteered to accompany combat units on Guam as they established a beachhead. To gather firsthand material for his stories, he exposed himself to fire from machine guns, mortars, and small arms. A mortar round exploding on the beach wounded Blechman, and he died on July 21 aboard a hospital ship, just twenty-three. He was buried at sea and later awarded a Bronze Star.

And what of the boyish Marine combat correspondent Richard J. Murphy Jr.? He had been in the initial landing at Saipan, but he would not file a single story on the hard-fought yet successful advance across the Marianas. For days Murphy was unaccounted for, not unlike when he was reported missing and feared wounded or killed during the chaotic battle for Tarawa before turning up unharmed. Three months after the landings on Saipan, his parents received a telegram that he was missing in action. One family story passed down over the years had it that the amphibious craft carrying Murphy became stuck on a coral reef. He was last seen helping a wounded man escape the damaged craft when a shell struck it and exploded. The Division of Public Relations sent Murphy's parents his final dispatches, typed aboard a Navy transport on the journey to Saipan. A year passed before his personal belongings arrived at their home. The fate of his remains was an open question for the family.

Nearly eight decades later the answer came in a phone call. A researcher who specialized in matching unidentified remains to missing service members had concluded that Murphy's remains were likely those in a US cemetery in Manila. He had linked Murphy's Marine Corps dental records with those of the remains labeled X-15 in Section L, Row 9. DNA testing comparing the remains with two of Murphy's living relatives confirmed the identity. In 2018, Murphy's remains were buried next to his mother's grave in Silver Spring, Maryland.

Four Marines with the Division of Public Relations on Cape Gloucester, New Britain, January 19, 1944. Left to right: combat correspondents Technical Sgt. Albert F. Monteverde, Technical Sgt. Samuel E. Stavisky, and Staff Sgt. Jeremiah A. O'Leary; and combat photographer Robert R. Brenner.

Bodies float amid the wreckage of amphibious tractors and lie beyond a seawall along a Tarawa lagoon, November 1943. A public relations officer and a combat photographer were killed during the assault.

Technical Sgt. Earle W. Johnson, a combat correspondent, uses a ration box as a desk for his typewriter as he reports on the battle for Bougainville, December 1943.

A Marine public relations officer, 1st Lt. Jonathan C. Rice, examines a Japanese flag held by combat correspondent Sgt. Milburn McCarthy. The souvenir was taken during the assault on Bougainville, December 1943. Their "city room" had been a sniper's foxhole.

Combat correspondents Staff Sgt. Jeremiah A. O'Leary and Technical Sgt. Samuel E. Stavisky examine Japanese dead on Cape Gloucester, January 2, 1944.

Technical Sgt. Earle W. Johnson, left, receives congratulations from a fellow combat correspondent, Staff Sgt. Solomon Blechman, upon his promotion to second lieutenant. Guadalcanal, March 20, 1944.

Combat correspondents Staff Sgt. Hy Hurwitz and Sgt. Herb Shultz write their stories on a Saipan beach, June 1944.

Working in the Saipan Press Club are two public relations officers, Capt. W.F. McCahill and, at the typewriter, Lt. Jim G. Lucas. At lower right is combat artist John Fabian. June 1944.

2nd Lt. Pete Zurlinden, a combat correspondent promoted to public relations officer, writes about the Marines' advance on the city of Garapan, Saipan, June 1944.

Combat correspondent Staff Sgt. Jack Pepper interviews Private First Class James H. Moos, 20, of Oklahoma City, Saipan, July 12, 1944. Pepper had been a reporter for the *Oklahoma City Times*.

Sgt. Cyril J. O'Brien types a story on Guam during the early days of the Marianas campaign, summer 1944.

Combat correspondents Technical Sgt. Joseph L. Alli and Technical Sgt. Benjamin Goldberg write their stories from a dugout on Peleliu, September 1944.

Combat correspondent Sgt. Joseph D. Donahue sits on the wing of a wrecked Japanese Zero while studying his notes, Peleliu, September 1944.

Black Marines – Cpl. Willis T. Anthony, Pfc. Emmitt Shackelford, Pfc. Eugene Purdy, and Pfc. Horace Boykin (on bicycle) – take a time out from supplying ammunition to the front lines, Saipan, June 1944.

Two unidentified Black Marines turn from drivers into riflemen after enemy blasts destroy their vehicle, Iwo Jima, February 1945.

Reporting from the dark volcanic sands of Iwo Jima are combat correspondents Staff Sgt. Bob Cooke and Sgt. Dan Levin and public relations officer Capt. John W. Thomason, February 1945.

Combat correspondent Technical Sgt. Keyes Beech balances a typewriter on his lap while reporting from the summit of Iwo Jima's Mount Suribachi, February 23, 1945.

Combat correspondent Sgt. Walter Wood works from a makeshift desk on Okinawa, May 1945.

7 Payback at Peleliu

A tough but quick campaign awaited Marines heading to the island of Peleliu, part of the Palau island group, in September 1944. Or so the campaign's planners thought. The initial prize would be the Japanese air base at the island's southern tip. Controlling the skies over the Palaus was judged necessary to protect American forces as they advanced to liberate the Philippines. There was every reason to expect that an intense preinvasion shelling from ships and bombing from the air would leave Peleliu's Japanese forces reeling. Planners believed ground troops would quickly establish numerous beachheads and that the rush of men and machines across the island would be unstoppable.

"Is it really impossible to blast a tiny island—a mere speck in the big blue, two miles wide and five miles long—right off the map, completely out of the Southwest Pacific?" One of the Marine combat correspondents covering the battle, Sergeant William Boniface, posed that question in a heavily edited dispatch. The answer came when Peleliu reappeared through a curtain of smoke, in Boniface's eyes looking more like an "eruptive volcano" than a coconut-rimmed atoll. A new question came to his mind. "Could humans—even Japs—be alive on that burning inferno, a glimpse of hell?" Again, a disquieting reality provided the answer, this time delivered by Japanese mortar fire. By the end of the operation's second day, with a main roadway taken without opposition, Boniface felt confident enough to tell readers that "the most difficult part of the invasion of Peleliu was behind us."

Boniface was not alone in being optimistic—as well as tragically wrong. The Peleliu campaign would turn out to be tough but hardly quick. Another Marine combat correspondent, Technical Sergeant Benjamin Goldberg, soon described Peleliu as "three days and two nights of sleepless horror." Many such days and nights followed. The battle lasted more than two months, ending in late November with a hard-fought American victory. Historians later pointed to a pair of critical errors in its planning. Marine commanders had misread the terrain and did not realize their men would face an uphill battle toward an extensive network of caves and tunnels, built by its defenders to exploit Peleliu's coral base. The mountainous area housing those emplacements, which were all but unaffected by the preinvasion bombardment, earned the brutally understated nickname Bloody Nose Ridge.

A worse error, perhaps, was the Marine commanders' not anticipating a new resolve by the Japanese military to fight to the death as a strategy rather than an outcome. Replacing a suicidal attack in the face of defeat—the feared banzai charge—was cool determination. As Gordon D. Gayle, a Marine major at Peleliu who retired as a brigadier general, later wrote in a concise examination of the battle, "Japanese soldiers would dig in and hunker down, to make their final defenses as costly as possible to the attacking Americans." After the Marines suffered unexpected losses at Peleliu, the Japanese would continue to apply those tactics at Iwo Jima and Okinawa, a suicidal but effective payback that set the stage for defending their mainland.

"A tongue of flame shot out like a hundred flame throwers"

A Marine public relations officer, Captain Earl J. Wilson, flew in an observation plane over Peleliu as Corsairs dropped flaming gas, more than 32,000 gallons over eight days, on the island's defenders along Bloody Nose Ridge. For security reasons a Navy censor cut operational details of those Wilson called the "Death Dealers" of the Second Marine Air Wing. Below is a section deleted from Wilson's thirteen-page, magazine-style feature, which division headquarters recommended trimming and converting to a regular story.

Napalm gas is the hottest thing this side of hell. When they drop it from a plane they call it a fire bomb. On Tinian Army Thunderbolts splashed the stuff on the cane fields there burning off great patches of the vegetation and some miscellaneous Nips along with it. That was the first time it had been used in the Pacific. But it had never been used for pin-point bombing, that is not until the "Death Dealers" drew the assignment on Peleliu.

Standard QM gas thickened with Napalm jell is loaded into an ordinary belly tank, each tank holding one hundred sixty five gallons of the fiery liquid and weighing around 1200 pounds. When it hits the deck the tank bursts and the gas shoots into crannies and crevices. Its psychological effect is terrific and it does the Nips strictly no good.

On "Bloody Nose" the Nips were still holding out, Bushido stuff, and our boys couldn't get their flame throwers up close enough to the caves to give them a squirt. So the Corsairs were to become flying flame throwers in an attempt to reach the hidden Nips.

But there were a couple of catches to the deal. First off there was the problem again of hitting a little area surrounded by our troops—that is hard enough with ordinary bombs. With belly tanks the only way you can release them is to pull a lever, pray, and let the slipstream pull them free. An error of only three seconds would put the fire on our own lines.

And if you can't get rid of the bomb the orders were, "get off the island and hit the silk. Don't try to land with that stuff."

The target was tricky, a ridge about two hundred yards long and the cliff on one side of that ridge. Object, swing the bomb so that the flame hits on top of the ridge and the rest of it whips around on the cliff.

Nothing to it, easy as wearing a bow tie on liberty. The top of the ridge was around ten feet wide and the "safe" area wasn't more than fifty yards across.

The best place to watch the show was from a Grasshopper plane hanging around about two hundred feet up. From there you could see the first ship cut in doing better than two hundred and fifty knots. He made a sharp banking curve and headed for the target. It looked like the ship would scrape its belly on the sharp-edged ridge when the belly-tank cut loose and went footballing end over end through the air. The bomb hit on top of the ridge, skittered for half a second and burst. A tongue of flame shot out like a hundred flame throwers in action and slid down over the face of the cliff while hundreds of balls of flame shot out from the impact.

Again and again the gull-winged Corsairs slid in until the entire ridge was a sea of flame while a coil of thick greasy smoke towered up a thousand feet into the air like some hovering genii.

All over Peleliu men stopped at their work to watch "Bloody Nose" become a volcano. A bible student said, "and fire came down out of Heaven, and devoured them." Men on the lines could feel the searing heat of the soaring frames.

Captain Earl J. Wilson
Peleliu

"A contest to see who would get the most Japs"

A Navy censor passed this report of two Marines in a contest to see who could score more kills, but someone else along the copy chain rejected it because of "doubtful facts."

Private First Class Benjamin E. Lewis, 19, of Linden, Ala., and Robert Lee Honeycutt, 19, of Albemarle, N.C., make a pretty good combat team. They fight together in the same infantry squad.

During the recent invasion of Peleliu by the First Marine Division, they hit the beach together and started the advance inland with their unit. The Alabama Marine scored the first round in their contest to see who would get the most Japs during the campaign. Retreating from heavy machine gun fire, a Jap dashed from a foxhole to seek sanctuary in an enemy pillbox. Lewis killed him. Turning to Honeycutt he said: "We're goin' to be too busy to mark these down—no cheatin' now."

A flame thrower operator advanced on the pillbox and flushed out five Japs, with a singing burst from his weapon as they streamed out the pillbox entrance. Honeycutt got three and Lewis cut down the other two. The score was even!

During the advance inland, several days later, the unit to which the 'teen age Marines were attached halted their advance to set up night defenses. The extreme left flank of the line bordered on a deep cave that had been cleaned out during the afternoon. Lewis and Honeycutt drew guard duty on this flank of the defense during the night.

Shortly after midnight Lewis noticed five forms outlined against the entrance of the cave. He challenged them. The reply came in the form of a bullet that flattened itself in the coral behind him. The bullet was followed by a charge toward his position—Japs had somehow occupied a hideout in the cave!

As the enemy lunged toward him only a few feet away Lewis leveled his Browning automatic rifle. The trigger jammed. Yelling to Honeycutt, "Tojo's here," Lewis flung his rifle in the face of the leading Jap who was almost upon him. As the Jap staggered back into the bodies of the oncoming group, Honeycutt opened fire and Lewis grabbed for another gun to join the firing. The entire event was over in less time than it takes to relate it.

Drawled Honeycutt, "You all was taught in boot camp that them rifles is to shoot and not to throw around—score eight to three."

Three of the dead Japs were within arm's length of the Marines' foxhole.

Mumbled Lewis, "I think I knocked off the Jap I threw the rifle at—he didn't get up again—score seven to four; I'll catch up with him tomorrow night."

Some game!

Sergeant Walter F. Conway
Peleliu

"You're going to be surprised when you try to land at Palau"

The infamous propaganda broadcaster Tokyo Rose was well known to the American public as well as to the Marines. While a censor passed a report about the accuracy of her typical warnings of doom facing Marines at Peleliu, apparently others in the Navy had second thoughts and ordered the story killed. Japanese gloating over a tough campaign was likely seen as poor subject matter for readers back home.

Tokyo Rose delights in giving the First Marine Division needle-jabs on her propaganda broadcast, and for more than a year has predicted utter annihilation of these veteran Marines.

But today, with fighting still raging fiercely in devastation on the nearly impregnable ridges, the boys readily admit she was more accurate on her latest prediction—that we would have a surprise in store for us when we "try to land at Palau."

In New Guinea, over a year ago, we heard her promise destruction by air raids, for "the butchers of Guadalcanal." Then she told us that "Japanese Imperial Marines are waiting for you at Cape Gloucester."

The latter operation, smoothly-executed, failed to quiet Tokyo Rose. Before we sailed for this island she said, "You First Division Marines had it easy at Cape Gloucester, but you're going to be surprised when you try to land at Palau."

When this island is secured, First Division Marines are anxious to hear her next prediction.

Technical Sgt. Benjamin Goldberg
Peleliu

"They thought he was equipped with an outboard motor"

Mocking the death of a lone enemy soldier pursued by four planes apparently struck the wrong note with both a Marine public relations officer, who deemed the story in "bad taste," and Navy command, which prohibited its release. Those listed in the opening paragraph, including the Tarzan film stars Johnny Weissmuller and Buster Crabbe, were well known champion swimmers.

There is doubt that a Weissmuller, a Crabbe, a Kiefer, a Medica, or a Spence brother would be chesty enough even in their heyday to think that they could match their swimming prowess with that of the flying ability of a Corsair.

Yet, one Jap who was trapped in a small craft in Ngatpang Bay in the northeast corner of Babelthuap Island, of this group, made the mistake of trying to outdistance four of them today.

The aquatic Jap was discovered in the bay about 150 yards from shore this morning by a quartet of Marine fighter pilots, of the Second Marine

Aircraft Wing, returning from a bombing and strafing mission of Japanese positions on Babelthuap.

First Lieutenant Billy H. Cantrell, of 1219 N. Sherman Ave., Springfield, Mo., and Phillip E. Heinley, of 532 South Spruce St., Wichita, Ka., were the first to notice the Jap in the water. They made a pass at him, saw him leap out of the craft into the water before they could cut it in half with machine gun fire.

The Jap stayed submerged until he was certain that the Corsairs had passed over him. Then he cut water for shore.

Fifty-yards closer to shore Major Jack E. Conger, of 6009 N. Waterbury, Des Moines, Ia., the division leader, who has 10 Jap planes in the air and four on the ground to his credit, and Second Lieutenant Winton E. Balzer, of 376 Chestnut St., Gardner, Mass., joined in the chase.

The airmen circled over the Jap for a few minutes at several hundred feet and recalled that he was swimming so fast that they thought he was equipped with an outboard motor.

A second run was made on the fish like Jap who remained under water, fetching all the time, until the planes passed over again.

It was during the third run on the Jap when he was within 50 yards of shore that his luck ran out on him.

Major Conger, and Lieutenants Heinley and Balzer dropped out of the circle and started the final run on the Jap. Lieutenant Cantrell lingered a little while longer in the circle than the other three. The Jap ended his fetching after the trio passed over and, just as he came up to catch his breath Lieutenant Cantrell was well down on him.

The Jap had just stuck his head out of the water when the Corsair and the hot lead caught up with him.

Technical Sgt. Bill Goodrich
Peleliu

"If we got sick, we were shot"

The Navy went back and forth on whether to pass or reject a story about a Korean laborer recalling mistreatment by Japanese forces on Peleliu. While it carried two separate "passed" stamps by censors, the story also was marked "killed by Navy" and "no" at the top and bore a rejection stamp from the Navy's Office of Public Information, citing national security. This excerpt includes two sections and several phrases struck from an approved version.

Chamorros kissed the robes of priests on Saipan, and freed Europeans greeted conquering Yanks with smiles and flags, but this was different—this meeting of joyous Koreans and their "Honorable Teacher," Marine Second Lieutenant William A. Linton, Jr., of Chicago, Ill.

For some of the prisoners knew Lieutenant Linton when he was a boy and many went through his father's mission school in Korea.

The Marine was born in Korea 21 years ago and spent the first 17 years of his life there. He saw the United States for the first time in 1940, and his first football game in 1942, when he was a student at the University of Tennessee.

Lieutenant Linton was accustomed to hearing tales *of Japanese oppression*, but even he wasn't prepared for the story *of starvation and torture* which spun from the lips of his childhood friends in Peleliu's stockade today.

Palpek, a powerful little man with the complexion of a Cherokee, foreman of 100 Korean workers in the Palaus, was spokesman.

"We used to work in the gold mines back home," he said. "The Japs offered us good jobs in the Palaus and promised to send our families to us. That was years ago.

"They were fine to us until they got us aboard ship. Then they threw us into the hold and chained us there. We were in darkness, living on bread and water, for several weeks. If we complained, we were beaten."

The Korean workers were paid five yen—$1.15 a month. They were permitted one cup of water and one meal a day. The meal consisted of bread and a Japanese vegetable. Once a week they were given rice.

"There were no medical facilities for us," Palpek said. *"If we got sick, we were shot. We managed to stay alive by foraging for food. One day we ate a dog, but it was a Jap's pet and five of our men were tortured to death. It was a long time ago, but nights I can still hear their cries of pain."*

The Koreans weren't allowed to write or receive letters. None knew what had become of their families and they bombarded Lieutenant Linton with questions about home.

They were overjoyed to learn that the Marines had landed, but surrendering was a problem. They were killed by the Japs when they tried to give up and were shot by Marines who mistook them for the enemy. One Korean, in a cave with a Jap, strangled the soldier and then spent three days attempting to surrender. He finally made it, but had bullets in the leg and side.

"But more than 50 percent of them were saved," Lieutenant Linton said.

Sgt. Vic Kalman
Peleliu

"They were running with a case of bottles between them"

Writing about Marines risking life and limb for alcohol was an activity a Navy censor determined did not violate guidelines; that the men had left their unit without permission apparently was overlooked. For its part, the Division of Public Relations decided not to publicize the escapade.

For two Marines just humoring a thirst, Sergeant Martin M. Ruddy, 22, of 455 Post Avenue, Rochester, N.Y., and Private First Class Edward H. Hansberry, 21, of 10 South New Jersey Avenue, Atlantic City, N.J., got into a lot of trouble.

During the drive northward along either side of Bloody Nose Ridge, advance scouts reported that there was a Jap warehouse about 200 yards ahead of the Marine line. Furthermore, unless the scouts' noses were wrong, there was beer and sake (rice wine) in that same warehouse.

Ruddy looked at Hansberry. Hansberry looked at Ruddy. They slipped out of the little group and headed north. They next appeared on the road, headed south for the Marine lines and safety, running with a case of bottles between them. Rifle and machine gun bullets were spraying the dust all around.

A Jap stepped out in front of them from a foxhole beside the road. They stopped, carefully set down the case, and eyed the Jap. He drew a grenade but they shot him before he could throw it.

The Leathernecks picked up the case and started to run.

Three more Japs came out of their holes and opened fire. Again the Marines set down the case of bottles, turned and started shooting. The Japs fell and the lads picked up the case and nursed it back to the lines.

They reassured themselves that neither was injured. Then, being generous fellows and badly outnumbered, they split their loot—10 bottles of beer, two of sake—with their comrades: one swallow per man.

"Well," said Ruddy, smacking his lips rather mournfully, "I guess it was worth it."

Staff Sgt. Ward Walker
Peleliu

"He was badly wounded, then the ants came . . ."

A Navy censor passed this tale, but the medical and surgery division of the Navy waved off publication. Was the medical aspect of the story accurate? Other than the notation "Killed by medical & surgery," no specific reason was offered, not even taste.

Red ants and a strong constitution undoubtedly saved the life of one Marine at Peleliu. Red ants, for the coagulating power to stop the flow of blood, and a healthy body to maintain its ebbing strength.

The marine, a perfect specimen of human endurance, because of calisthenics, is Corporal Leonard R. Schultz, 22, of 8205 Molina Street, Detroit, Mich. He never followed morning and afternoon exercises in civilian life, but when he came to the Pacific he decided to stay fit. He used dumbbells fashioned from jeep axles.

But at Peleliu came the final test. He had come through the Guadalcanal and New Britain campaigns without any trouble. On D plus 1, in his final campaign, he was struck in the groin about 12:30 a.m. by shrapnel. Badly wounded, he lay for seven hours, with only a battle dressing between his legs. But there were red ants . . .

Blood flowed freely through the dressing from four painful wounds. Then the ants came—a continuous stream of them—over the bandage and under it. They crawled into the wounds and over themselves—like a swarm of bees. And they stopped the flow of blood.

Half-consciously, the wounded man started to brush them off. But in his subconscious mind he knew that they were helping him. His half-raised hand slid back to his side. The ants were there to stay.

Evacuated by hospital ship, Corporal Schultz is now in a Pacific Naval hospital, recuperating from his wounds. He has been awarded the Purple Heart medal.

"It's odd," he said, "I thought I was going out that night, but these little ants were my companions. I believe they were my saviors. I guess the morphine kept me from dying of pain.

"It had been an awful night before 12 o'clock. The Japs counter-attacked about 10:30 p.m., but we threw them back. I was with a bazooka outfit, working with a machine gun section. When the shell got me I was lying on my back in a Jap tank trap. I could see straight above me in case any of the enemy got close enough to peer over the side. The doctors tell me if I'd been on my stomach I would have been killed.

"I was knocked out when the shell fragments hit me. Five other guys had just been killed on either side of me. When I came to I just gave up hope. And then the ants came . . ."

Sgt. James F. Moser Jr.
Somewhere in the South Pacific

"Japanese caves were outfitted almost luxuriously"

A Marine public relations officer wrote this short item on the use of captured Japanese materiel, later marked "do not release," as well as two separate but related stories that added names for a hometown angle. A Navy censor may have found the stories too detailed and thus of potential use to the enemy—a sign that even officers could err by revealing too much information.

Almost the entire flight line of a Marine aviation squadron here is being operated by captured Japanese equipment found near the rubble-strewn air field and taken from steel-doored caves in "Bloody Nose" ridge.

Japanese generators and motors operate Japanese lathes and milling cutters for precision instruments which were hauled to the flight line in Japanese trucks. Metalsmiths, carpenters and mechanics work with electrical tools operated by Japanese-generated power. Japanese tents cover the equipment. And some of the Marines are wearing clean Japanese clothing, sleeping on Japanese cots and eating out of Japanese mess gear.

Assault troops of the First Marine Division who stormed the ridge found the Japanese caves to be outfitted almost luxuriously with electric wiring, showers and a basic plumbing in addition to the compartments for various types of equipment. Word of the equipment filtered back to where aviation Marines were setting up gear in preparation for the arrival of Marine garrison planes and forage-wise mechanics headed for the caves with trucks and a swinging crane.

The captured materiel has been in use for several days now and it is expected that much of it will be kept in operation even after regulation equipment has been unloaded from supply ships.

Capt. James A. Kelly
Peleliu

"All of the heroes of a fighter squadron are not in the air"

While passed by a Navy censor, this story about noncombat deaths was not used by DPR headquarters. No reason was noted. The story lacked names for hometown interest, and it was a tacit acknowledgment that wartime deaths could occur in mundane ways, qualities that would not promote recruiting.

All of the heroes of a Marine fighter squadron are not in the air.

Two of its ground crew members, whose names cannot be divulged, were struck dead by lightning tonight amidst a severe rainstorm as they loaded bombs on the Corsairs for a raid on Jap pockets of resistance in "Bloody Nose Ridge" in the morning.

Both aviation Marines were working on the same plane which was not affected by the streaking bolts of light.

Two other Leathernecks of the same outfit who were loading a plane a short distance away from the deceased men were shaken up considerably.

After a night's rest in the squadron dispensary they returned to duty to do the job they began before the lightning struck.

A fire was also started by the lightning behind the plane ready tent of the same unit. Before it could cause any serious damage several members of the outfit extinguished the fire with carbon dioxide cylinders.

Technical Sgt. W.F. Goodrich
Peleliu

American forces won the battle for Peleliu, but the Japanese tactic of "bleeding" their opponent was successful, too. More than 1,250 Marines and Navy corpsmen and doctors were killed, and nearly 5,300 others were wounded. Army replacements, brought in during the final weeks, suffered more than 270 dead and over 1,000 wounded. Japan lost 10,900 troops, with only a relative handful of them taken alive. While Japanese forces could not sustain forever a ten-to-one deficit of troops killed in battle, the question became whether the United States would continue to accept even lopsided losses. The modern-day debate that atomic weapons were necessary to force Japan's surrender relies in part on Japan's fierce defenses of Peleliu, Iwo Jima, and Okinawa. Further evidence of Japanese resolve appeared after the war: In April 1947, more than two dozen Japanese troops who had been hiding on Peleliu agreed to surrender after weeks of negotiations, finally convinced the war had ended.

Another debate coloring Peleliu's standing in history gained attention in the ensuing decades: Was taking Peleliu essential in the effort to defeat Japan? The arguments against the invasion, voiced during its planning, were amplified by its costs. Other events in the world war overshadowed the Marine fight at Peleliu and drew the public's attention from it, both then and later. The Allied push across western Europe, which began on the Normandy beaches on June 6 of that year, dominated the war news. In October, the midpoint of the fight on Peleliu, Army General Douglas MacArthur kept his promise to return to the Philippines, signaling a critical phase of the liberation of the Pacific. In the decades that followed, Marine Corps actions at Guadalcanal, Tarawa, Saipan, and Iwo Jima grew to dominate the history of the Pacific front. In some quarters the fight for Peleliu was branded a "forgotten battle."

Never by the men who were there, of course, and certainly not by the Marine combat correspondents. Among them was Technical Sergeant Donald A. Hallman Sr. He was one of the oldest of the fighter-writers, thirty-five in 1942 when he quit the *New York Daily News* to join up. He insisted that his Marine Corps byline carry the suffix denoting fatherhood because his fifteen-year-old namesake was a Marine, too, who had transferred from radio school to combat duty. The senior Hallman wrote for the Marines while under fire at Cape Gloucester, then volunteered to go to Guam. Afterward, with only two weeks of rest he shipped off to Peleliu. His widely published account of the Marines' initial assault described a "night of hell" punctuated by artillery fire, Japanese fighters creeping into foxholes, and hand-to-hand combat. Several days later, on Bloody Nose Ridge, a Japanese shell tore off his left leg below the knee. Hallman used his belt as a tourniquet and waited three hours to be evacuated. Still recovering in a West Coast hospital the following spring, he learned that Private First Class Donald A. Hallman Jr., then seventeen, had been killed in action on the first day of the battle for Iwo Jima.

8

Invisible Heroes
Black Marines and Sailors in the Pacific

An explosion shattered any semblance of Christmas time aboard the American naval transport ship. That day, in late 1943, troops and supplies were being unloaded at a Bougainville dock when a Japanese dive bomber evaded the transport's antiaircraft fire and dropped its payload. The blast killed six sailors and wounded twenty other military personnel, leaving the stern gun twisted like a pretzel. Although it was the ship's worst hit since the Guadalcanal invasion, the attack could have been far more deadly. Other bombs had missed as its guns brought down three other Japanese planes.

One of the wounded sailors, Cook Second Class Leroy A. Chisholm of Charleston, South Carolina, who suffered a flash burn, described the attack to Technical Sergeant Maurice E. Moran, a Marine combat correspondent. "I was too scared to be scared," the twenty-three-year-old admitted with a laugh, "but I did remember to hang on to a live shell so it wouldn't explode and raise more hell." A fellow cook, twenty-year-old Hillavery Thompkins of Knoxville, Tennessee, sustained fragmentation wounds in the face and neck while handling ammunition in the magazine below deck when the blast's concussion knocked him down. Both men, who had left their mess duties for battle stations, were in line to receive a Purple Heart.

A buddy, Steward's Mate Freddie Singleton, a twenty-seven-year-old from Beaufort, South Carolina, described a close call. "I was loading when that bomb hit and I had a live one in my arms," he said. "The hit was six feet away from me and I never got touched—man, howdy!" He asked Moran, "Don't they give Purple Hearts for 'almosts'?"

The wisecrack was just the sort of conclusion needed for a solid if routine dispatch about danger and duty in the Pacific war. Moran added a note at the end of his story to raise a point with editors at the Division of Public Relations. "These men are all Negroes," the CC wrote. "Not identified as such in body of story because Negro publications resent such identification. Suggest they be so identified if distribution is made to white southern dailies which segregate Negro news." For reasons not disclosed—a significant time lag may have been a factor—the story was marked "suggest no release." In general, the effect of enemy fire was not to be reported per censorship rules. Was the race of the heroic sailors another reason their story was not shared with American readers?

The DPR had already decided how it would cover African Americans, whether Navy personnel or Marines, in the stories sent to newspapers and other media. The October 30, 1943, edition of the DPR bulletin—Moran may not have seen it yet—advised its writers:

> Whenever a man named in your copy is a Negro, be sure to identify him as a Negro. This is especially necessary for copy distributed in the Southern Procurement Division, inasmuch as Southern newspapers for whites do not publish Negro news or carry it on a separate page. Consequently, stories concerning Negro service personnel are sent by the SPD to the Negro press. The SPD reports receiving some stories about Negroes that have not made their identification clear.

Essentially, the policy called for segregating stories based on the Marines' race. In time a handwritten note and, later, an inked rubber stamp appeared at the top of the first page of such stories: "For Negro Press." Whether additional DPR dispatches featuring Black Marines were distributed to other news media, even outside the South, is not always discernible from files at the National Archives. Such decisions were probably left to the individual Marine Corps personnel in charge of the regional procurement divisions; they were expected to know what various media sought from the DPR. Handling stories about African Americans serving their country was not referenced again in the bulletin, suggesting that publicizing Black Marines drew no special attention beyond keeping their news separate from that of other Marines.

Racial segregation for DPR dispatches was not surprising given the Marine Corps' fraught history with African Americans. The Marine Corps was founded in 1798, but Black Americans were excluded from its ranks even as late as World War I. In April 1941, with Europe at war again and the United States preparing for a role in the new conflict, the commandant of the Marine Corps, Major General Thomas Holcomb, held fast to the policy that Black men were unwelcome. "If it were a question of having a Marine Corps of 5,000 whites or 250,000 Negroes," he said, "I would rather have the whites." Holcomb did not change his racist views even months after Pearl Harbor, when the United States needed troops for wars in both Europe and the Pacific, accusing Black volunteers of "trying to break into a club that doesn't want them." However, for years Black leaders had lobbied President Franklin Roosevelt for better treatment in the military services. In spring 1942, Roosevelt's navy secretary, Frank Knox, told the Navy, Marines, and Coast Guard to begin accepting African Americans for general service. It was the same spring that Holcomb allowed General Robert L. Denig to seek recruits from newsrooms for his new public relations initiative.

Joining the Marines did not give African Americans an equal place in the Corps or quell racist attitudes toward them. All the American military services segregated their white and Black personnel throughout World War II. (Not until President Harry Truman issued an executive order in 1948 did the military begin the long process of racial desegregation.) Care was taken not to place Black officers in charge of white men, though white officers could command Black men. For the Marine Corps, including Black Americans but segregating them meant establishing a separate training facility. Instead of enduring the Marine rite of passage of boot camp at Parris Island or facilities near San Diego, Black recruits were trained at Montford Point, a western section of Camp Lejeune in North Carolina. Nor were Black Marines given an equal opportunity to directly fight as riflemen in assault forces, which would have helped prove their value and patriotism to any doubters.

Instead, many Black Marines were trained for one of two defense battalions or in depot and ammunition companies, which delivered supplies in support of amphibious forces in battle. Some were trained as cooks and for other steward duties to cater to officers. The defense battalions were needed in case of aerial attack or other efforts by the Japanese to retake bases, though that proved to be relatively rare. The depot and ammunition companies, on the other hand, were on the beaches and in the jungles during island assaults from Saipan to Okinawa and suffered most of the casualties among Black Marines. The Navy expanded its Black personnel, too, continuing its practice of using Black sailors as cooks and stewards but adding them to the ranks of construction battalions, better known as Seabees, and called on them to load and unload supplies under fire. Any assignment in a theater of war put men at risk no matter their race.

As US military forces advanced across the Pacific, African Americans in the Marine Corps and the Navy began appearing in stories from Marine combat correspondents. Sometimes the CCs referenced them in demeaning jokes; such stories do not appear to have been distributed. More often, CC dispatches lauded the African Americans for aiding Marines in combat by bringing them ammunition, water, and food or for carrying the wounded to safety on stretchers. Yet these stories, too, would be declared "For Negro

Press." Many American readers—particularly those in the segregated South—would likely not learn about Black Marines despite the very information system the Marine Corps created to record and celebrate the exploits of its men. The relatively few dispatches that were written about these invisible heroes were dwarfed by the thousands of other stories coming out of the DPR.

Online searches of digitized newspapers indicate that the two most widely used Black-centric stories by CCs were published in 1944. Sergeant John R. Hurley's story about Black Marines under fire on an undisclosed island in the southwestern Pacific was released on March 1. It appeared in at least six Black publications in six different states that month, but mainstream papers that can be searched digitally did not carry it. Some did publish Sergeant Charles R. Vandergrift's story about Black Marines' outstanding service on Saipan, which appeared in five mainstream papers in August, including the *Atlanta Journal* and the *Dayton Daily News* (Ohio), in addition to three Black publications.

The original version of the Vandergrift story, held at NARA, documents a rare effort to gain wider publication for a story about Black Marines. Typed at the top of the first of five pages was a note from the CC himself: "Requested 6/30/44 by Gen. Denig for OWI," which references the DPR commander and the Office of War Information, President Roosevelt's wartime government propaganda agency. Noted in pencil, likely by DPR editors, were distribution points including Associated Press, United Press, and International News Service, a common directive for major DPR releases. Unusual, however, was another designation: "For White Press." The addition suggests that, unlike the typical stories about Black Marines and Navy Seabees, this one was aimed at readers beyond "Negro Press." (The original version of Hurley's story is not in his file, making a comparison to Vandergrift's impossible.) In his history of American media and the Pacific war, the historian Steven Casey has noted that the Roosevelt administration promoted more news coverage of Black Americans in the war, at least in the Black press, as the presidential election of 1944 approached and Black leaders urged a larger role for African Americans in the fight.

Other DPR dispatches about Black Marines and Navy Seabees appeared to reach mainly Black-oriented publications, judging from the few found through digital searches. For example, a 1944 story written by Sergeant Vic Kalman reported that Black Marines had braved four days and nights of gunfire on Peleliu to save Marines of the First Division. Notably, a Navy censor deleted a passing reference to racial segregation in the American

South. A digital search showed that Kalman's story had appeared in four newspapers, all of them part of the African American press. Similarly, a story from Peleliu by Technical Sergeant Donald A. Hallman Sr. showcasing how two hundred Black Seabees had stepped forward to answer a call for volunteers for stretcher-bearer duties appeared in five African American newspapers but no mainstream press. By the time Marines were fighting on Okinawa, in the spring of 1945, little had changed. Sergeant Harold E. Foreman's story about Black stretcher bearers only appeared in one paper, an African American publication, according to a digital search.

Worth noting is a DPR-produced feature profile of a Black Marine from Chicago. Private First Class Vincent T. Cullers helped guard stretcher bearers during the fighting on Peleliu. He had studied at the Chicago Art Institute for a year before enlisting and spent his free time capturing images of Marines in watercolors. Kalman's profile of Cullers in the fall of 1944 appeared in one African American publication, in Alabama, but not in the *Chicago Tribune*, one of his hometown's major dailies. After the war Cullers had a significant career in advertising, founding the first African American–owned advertising agency and credited as having "revolutionized ethnic-targeted advertising." Culler's success in the postwar American advertising industry was highlighted in his 2003 obituary in the *Chicago Tribune*, nearly sixty years after the newspaper had overlooked his unique wartime profile.

With Black Marines and Seabees deployed to the Marianas, Peleliu, and the ensuing campaigns, the DPR began distributing the stories cited above and a relative handful of others focusing on them. Some of those dispatches have been included in this collection because they apparently were not distributed as widely as stories about white Marines per the division's racist policy, an ugly nod to their public relations mission. Examples of stories about Black Marines and Seabees that went unpublished are also included.

"Negro Marines aid in manning key base in Southwest Pacific"

Sergeant John R. Hurley's story described the general duties of Black Marines on a Pacific island. By listing forty-four men from twenty-four states and providing their hometown addresses, the story would have allowed newspaper editors to highlight the local connection. As noted earlier, a digital search shows that only a half-dozen Black papers carried the story, excerpted here, and no mainstream publications. The title is from a copy of the story as released.

Negro Marines are undergoing almost constant air attacks as they help man this island, a key supply base for American forces fighting the Japanese.

The Negroes, trained at Camp Lejeune, New River, North Carolina, received their baptism of fire at Guadalcanal, where ships they were aboard were raided by Jap planes.

From Guadalcanal, they moved forward into more active combat zones. Japanese bombers made regular nightly runs over the areas but the Negro Marines grew accustomed to the air raids.

Coming from all parts of the eastern and southern United States and the first Negroes to be recruited by the Marines, they are a part of America's fighting forces in the Southwest Pacific area.

Trained as infantrymen with some later specializing in antiaircraft artillery, other special weapons and tanks, they are nearly all volunteers. Retaining marked good humor and spirits under the trying conditions imposed by remoteness and tropics, they continue to work hard at their assigned duties, taking the good with the bad.

The former cooks and clerks, mechanics and drivers, carpenters and farmers are from Alabama, Mississippi, New York, Michigan, Florida, Tennessee, Ohio, Pennsylvania, Georgia, Alabama, Illinois, Arkansas, Virginia, and California. They average about 20 years of age.

There is friendly competition in boxing, volleyball, softball and in musical and singing contests when duties are completed. They have set up their own rings and courts.

Pocket-size grammars help the Negro Marines eliminate the language problem in their trade with natives. They vent their souvenir craze by dickering with the natives, later sending home grass skirts, seashells, war clubs and canes, and other curios. The natives take money first, then cigarettes, tobacco, pipes, soap, junk jewelry, etc. The visionary brought along ample supplies of the latter from dime stores.

At night, when air raid sirens are not blowing, can be heard the moan of spirituals such as "Join the Band," "Bread of Heaven" and "Father Prepare Me," mingled with livelier modern tunes.

Sgt. John R. Hurley
Somewhere in the Southwest Pacific

"They worked around the clock and did a swell job"

Sergeant Charles R. Vandergrift, writing on orders from the DPR's commanding general, produced four and a half pages on a unit of Black Marines on Saipan that drew praise from their commanding officers. The following excerpt focuses on the actions of the six Black Marines named in the story.

"Praise the Lord and pass the ammunition" became an actuality here when a Negro Marine unit including two student ministers moved in with the assault troops to ensure an ever-ready supply of artillery shells for front line orders.

Other members of the unit also sought solace from above as they stacked the "big stuff" in neat rows and dived into over-regulation foxholes when the Japs pattern-fired the beach with mortar and artillery shells.

"I ain't got time to think about nothing but the Lord," said 19-year-old Private Edward H. Seals, son of Mrs. Emma Calhoun, 1728 Germantown Street, Dayton, Ohio. He explained that this was prompted by the crash of a Nip plane—bested in a dog-fight with Naval aircraft—150 feet from him the night of D-day. "I prayed night and day after that."

They set what Second Lieutenant Howard E. Tucker, son of Mrs. J.E. Deardorff, 1236 Fifth, East, Salt Lake City, Utah, a platoon leader, believes to be a record of 5,600 tons of ammunition in 33 hours.

"I'm very pleased with the way they worked," said Captain Louis P. Shine, son of Mrs. Frances Shine (no street address), Osage, W.Va., unit commanding officer.

"One was killed, four were wounded, but they worked around the clock and did a swell job. Several officers congratulated us on the way we had the ammunition they wanted ready when they wanted it."

Besides the two prospective pastors, the unit contained a former professional boxer, a dance band leader, several defense plant workers, a former electric washing machine salesman, and others with a wide variety of pre-Saipan occupations.

Neither Private First Class Fred Washington or Private First Class Augustus Witcher are actually ordained pastors, but both hope to be after the war.

Washington, son of Mr. and Mrs. James Washington, Magnolia, Ark. (no street address), conducts regular Sunday night services, reporting an average attendance of 60 to 70. Witcher leads the singing for the Sunday service and holds a prayer meeting in song service each Wednesday evening.

"I held first services here on D-plus-10," said Washington, "using the story of Daniel, because I thought it fit in best, both from a morale standpoint and because it showed that protection is simultaneous with danger."

Washington lived at 3317 Stanford Avenue, Los Angeles, Cal., and worked as a welder for the California Ship Yard before entering the service October 10, 1943. For several months he was an assistant pastor at the Zion Hill Baptist Church, 1319 East 22nd Street, Los Angeles, conducting services at least once each month. He was studying prior to entering the Baptist Seminary Theological school at the time of his induction.

"Everybody was happy—it seemed kinda like a big football game," said Witcher of his D-day landing. "When we were near a shore a Jap mortar shell landed in a nearby 'alligator.' The singing and joking stopped."

"We dug foxholes and then started unloading ammunition. When explosions got too close, we'd dive into the holes until it slackened up. My foxhole was only about two feet deep to start with, but it was double that depth before the first night was over."

Witcher, 20, son of Mrs. Olive Witcher, 910 Anderson Street, Charlottesville, Va., hopes to enter Virginia University, Richmond, after the war to study for the pastorate. For three years before entering the Marine Corps, September 26, 1943, he worked with Rev. E. Lord Jamerson, pastor of the Mount Zion Baptist Church, Ridge and Main Streets, Charlottesville, leading the junior choir and heading the Young People's Training Union. During the week he sold electric washing machines.

Here's a sample of the experiences others had:

Private First Class John M. Jenkins, 20, son of Mrs. Berlina Jenkins, 1218 C Street, S.E., Washington, D.C., knocked out a Jap machine gun with a hand grenade. "They moved us up to the front to help halt a counter-attack," he said. "This gun opened on me from close range. Must have been 20 shells as I jumped into a ditch. I could see three Japs moving about the gun. After pulling the pin on a grenade, I got to thinking they'd have time to throw it back, so I held it two of the 6-second delay period and let 'er go. It landed right on the gun. Guess I got 'em all."

Back in 1942, at New Orleans, Afro-American Leo Mann knocked out Lew Jenkins, former welterweight champion. Mann, 21, son of Mrs. Daisy Mann, 1308 Heiner Street, Houston, Texas, is now a sergeant. He directed one of the unloading groups. "I jumped into my foxhole when the mortar shells began moving in, for about the 10th time. One thudded down right beside me. I covered my head. When I looked up, I was lying outside the foxhole. Guess I was blown out." Sergeant Mann, who fought variously as a light, welter and middle weight, won 24 of his 27 professional bouts.

Patrons of The Barn, unique Cincinnati alley night spot—including myself—recall a colored boy who nightly tried to tear a sturdy piano apart. Here he manned a .30 caliber machine gun during a brief Jap Charan-Kanoa counterattack. "Don't know for sure whether I hit any Nips or not, but I shot up a lot of ammunition," said Pfc. Robert Payne, 20, son of Mrs. James Brown, 418 Cutter Street, Cincinnati, Ohio.

Sgt. Charles R. Vandergrift
Saipan

"There was a time we wouldn't ride in the same street car"

Sergeant Vic Kalman's story of courage and sacrifice by Black Marines on Peleliu was passed for distribution to "Negro Press," but not with a reference to racial prejudice. The deleted sections are in italics. The references to "antics" and "comic relief" could be taken as condescending. Rather than pejorative, they may have been an approving nod to the aplomb often ascribed in CC dispatches to Marines under fire.

This is the story of Negro Marines who ducked enemy fire and machine-gun fire for four days and four nights to save the lives of First Division troops.

Their antics brought comic relief to the frontline Marines—men who fought at Guadalcanal, Cape Gloucester and Peleliu's "Bloody Nose Ridge."

But more, their feats brought awe and caused more than one Southern Marine to remark, "To think there was a time we wouldn't ride in the same street car with them."

The story began the second day of the campaign, when Second Lieutenant James C. Walker, 23, of St. Louis, Mo., confronted the Seventh Marine Ammunition Company, a Negro contingent attached to the 16th Field Depot.

"Casualties are heavy," he announced, "and we need volunteers for stretcher bearers. Do you think you men can fill the job?"

The question needed no verbal answer. It was hardly uttered when four of the men started up a path for "Bloody Nose Ridge." Among the quartet was Private First Class Majorie McLeod, 22, of 117 West 121 Street, New York City, former bus boy at the Hotel Taft.

They hadn't quite reached the ridge when a shot rang out. Three of the men ran for cover, but Private First Class McLeod kept walking.

"Careful, there, Junior," he shouted, "or someday you'll hit somebody."

After that, the Jap sniper was "Junior" to the entire company.

"I'll bet 'Junior' used up 200 rounds and he never touched one of us," said Private Phillip Miller, 19, of 2215 12th Place, N.W., Washington, D.C., former athletic instructor of the Police Boys' Club.

"He once hit a branch over my head—the closest he came in all the times we walked up that path," added Private Leslie R. Valrie, 21, of 436 East Ohio Avenue, Deland, Fla., who formerly drove a school bus in Deland.

For 96 hours, with only a few hours sleep each night, the men hauled ammunition, water and food to the front lines and carried wounded back to the hospital. Often, they had to dash through machine-gun fire to reach the wounded Marines.

"We knew they were losing blood, so we practically had to run all the way back to the hospital," said Private Robert J. McCloud, 20, of 2 Star Street, Raleigh, N.C., who left a defense job with the Norfolk Navy Yard to join the Marines.

They trudged almost a mile with the wounded, arriving at the hospital in time to save dozens of lives. They were handicapped by crushing heat the first two days, a driving rain the third, and mud up to their knees the fourth day.

The stretcher-bearers weren't armed, but armed guards accompanied them—one in front and one in the rear. The third day of the siege, a stretcher was borne by Private First Class Joe N. McKnight, 19, of 289 Front Street, Georgetown, S.C.; Private First Class Leonard F. Mayo Jr., 19, of 215 Woodland Avenue, Morton, Pa.; Private Raymond Breaux, 26, of 1932 Clouet Street, New Orleans, La.; and Private First Class George W. Henderson, 22, of Henderson, Texas.

"A Jap opened up on us and our front guard was injured. Then the man in the rear got it. How that sniper missed us, I don't know. Maybe we just prayed harder," Mayo said.

They made three trips to the hospital that morning—came back for the two guards—without a pause.

A few days later, when "Bloody Nose" had been secured, the stretcher-bearers heard that "Junior" was dead. Private James Grey, 18, of 230 Drew Hill Avenue, Baltimore, Md., couldn't believe it. Cautiously, he walked up the familiar path. Nothing happened. He walked halfway back. Still no shots. He shook his head slowly.

"It's just not going to be the same without 'Junior,'" he said.

Sgt. Vic Kalman
Peleliu

"Not a single man has shirked even the toughest and most dangerous job"

A Navy censor and Marine editors passed Technical Sergeant Donald A. Hallman Sr.'s story from Peleliu, nearly six pages long, praising Black Seabees in general for courage under fire and saving lives. Nine men were cited by name. Yet the story, excerpted here, was marked "for release to Negro Press."

Two hundred Negro Seabees, grimy and weary from two days of unloading ships under enemy fire, were lined up on the beach here.

"I want volunteers for stretcher bearing on the ridge tonight," a white officer was telling them.

And 200 Negro Seabees stepped out as one.

The incident is typical of the record chalked up by a Seabee stevedore battalion which landed immediately behind assault waves of Marines here and have been working night and day since. They unload ships, wrestle ammunition and heavy supplies to the beach dumps, carry ammunition to the front lines, and bring back wounded. On occasion they have filled in as frontline troops, and for more than a week they have been going forward to drag in wounded Marines.

"They are the hardest workers, and the most willing, I have ever seen, no, even excepting my own Pioneers (Engineers)," declared Marine First Lieutenant William S. Selfridge Jr., 23, of 21 Poplar Avenue, Pittman, N.J., a veteran of Pacific fighting.

"There has not been a single man to shirk even the toughest and most dangerous job. Every man volunteers for everything," commented one of the battalion's white officers, Navy Lieutenant (j.g.) T.F. Gaffey, of 39 Fullers Lane, Milton, Mass.

Seaman, First Class, Edward Scott, 20, of 313 Dickenson Street, Fremont, Ohio, was on the line four times as a stretcher bearer. The second night he was in a foxhole with a Marine officer when four Japanese started moving in. When the Marine fired, one Jap fell and played dead for a time; then he attempted to flank the position while the other three came on. Seaman Scott got two of them, the Marine officer accounted for the others.

Seaman, First Class, James Key Nichols, 20, of 5047 South Parkway, Chicago, has a souvenir of one trip across the exposed airport. He was carrying one end of a stretcher when a Japanese machine gun killed the Seabee on the front end. Nichols' canteen was pierced by two bullets. He delivered the wounded Marine by himself two hours later.

Machinist Mate, Third Class, Emory L. Jennings, 586 Post Office Street, Altus, Okla., heard there was a wounded man on the edge of the airport. Despite continuous sniper fire, he went and got him.

Technical Sgt. Donald A. Hallman Sr.
Peleliu

"Whenever we get tired of eating rations, we have broiled fish"
This story was written with the note that it was for "Negro Press." It was rejected with scrawled notations of "No" and "Kill," probably for the same reason that similar stories about the unauthorized use of explosives were not accepted for distribution. Parity, it would seem, crossed racial lines when it came to publicizing questionable behavior.

When one sees him with a grenade, it doesn't mean that Marine Private Phillip Miller, 19, of 2215 12th Place, N.W., Washington, D.C. is hunting for Japs.

He's probably going fishing!

"The first time I threw a grenade in the water, the concussion killed two fish. The second got five," he said. "Now, whenever we get tired of eating rations, we have broiled fish."

Private Miller, formerly an athletic instructor at the Police Boys' Club in Washington, is attached to the Seventh Ammunition Company, a Negro outfit which has seen action with the First Marine Division.

Sgt. Vic Kalman
Peleliu

"Where you all fin' some souvenirs around heah?"

On occasion Black Marines appeared in comical stories or jokes and at times were quoted in dialect that, in retrospect, appears designed to demean them. However, the use of dialect in CC dispatches was not unusual, typically appearing only when referring to Marines from the American South or Brooklyn, New York. The first of these stories was part of a collection of supposedly humorous tales that a Marine editor rejected as "old jokes." Whether any of these stories were distributed is unclear.

A choice tidbit of this campaign concerns two Negro engineers who arrived a week after the Marines launched the invasion.

"Where you all fin' some souvenirs around heah?" they inquired of a Marine MP directing traffic.

The MP waved vaguely over his shoulder. "Over that way, back in the swamps a couple of miles, you ought to find plenty. There's a lot of Japs in through there."

"Marine, we ain't looking for no live Japs," one of the newcomers spoke up. "We wants to know where you Marines is fighting. We knows they ain't nothing dere but dead Japs."

Technical Sgt. John W. Black
Cape Gloucester, New Britain

The only change in the edited version of the following story was replacing "colored" with "Negro." The tired joke passed a Navy censor, though whether the story was distributed is unclear.

Two colored Marines of the veteran Fourth Division were huddled in a foxhole on Iwo Jima during a heavy Jap shelling.

When one shell hit dangerously close and sent a spray of sand over them, one asked:

"Was that friend or foe?"

"Foe," the other replied.

"Foe?" restated the first.

"Yes," said the second ending the discussion, "it was meant 'foe' us."

Sgt. Jack Vincent
Iwo Jima

Meanwhile, "colored" was unchanged in this anecdote, part of a collection killed by the Navy.

Then there was the story of the colored Marine that went up and down the beach. Caught out after dark and challenged by a sentry on a night automobiles comprised the password, the Marine replied, "Boss, I'm no Jap—I'm a Buick!"

Sgt. Jack Vincent
Iwo Jima

It was the first night of the Marines' assault on Peleliu. A Jap leaped into a foxhole occupied by a husky Negro Seabee. The Seabee dodged the bayonet and grabbed the Jap at the throat.

When asked to explain his kill next morning the huge Negro reported:

"Ah just squeezed and squeezed until ah was shaking hands with mahself."

Technical Sgt. Benjamin Goldberg
Peleliu

"Among the more conscientious sniper hunters are Negro Marines"

While its relationship to Black Marines was tangential, the following unused story—rejected for lacking names and covering souvenir hunting, a problematic topic—was notable. The Black Marines, taking on a dangerous duty voluntarily, were described in positive terms as compared to their comrades, whom readers would assume were white.

Whenever there's a lull in the battle, Marines go out on S 'n' S expeditions—hunting Souvenirs and Snipers.

The more adventurous, of course, specialized in snipers. They'll hoist their rifles on their shoulders and penetrate brush and swamps and deserted buildings for the pesky Jap riflemen who never do any serious damage, but who can be terribly bothersome, especially at night.

Among the more conscientious sniper hunters are a group of Negro Marines stationed behind the front lines. Every afternoon, when their work slackens, they make their voluntary patrols.

Souvenir hunters are more numerous. They're out for anything Japanese, as long as it can be easily identified as such by proud folks back home.

Troops in the rear lines, who get leftovers, generally accept the more commonplace tokens such as Japanese paper money, clothing, or bayonets.

Those in the front lines are more fastidious, though. They specialize in officers' swords, rifles, and one fellow has blandly announced that he is holding out for a complete Jap light machine gun, with accessories.

Sgt. Stanford Opotowsky
Saipan

"Marine, is my husband there?"

The tone of this story of a Marine's wife could be interpreted as sympathetic, even poignant. With the addition of her race, it could be seen as a sly jab or ridicule, since race was not pertinent to the situation. There was no indication the story was distributed.

I had returned from overseas the previous day and was waiting in the Ferry Building in San Francisco, while a buddy was obtaining accommodations for our cross-country train ride. A colored woman, shabbily dressed, stoop-shouldered and about 35 years old, approached me and said, "Marine, could you tell me where the Marines are in San Francisco?"

"There are some at Treasure Island," I replied. I had spent my first night back in the States there.

"Is my husband there?" she asked, handing me a soiled envelope. In the upper left hand corner was the name of the Marine sender, his unit and "c/o FPO, San Francisco, Calif."

"Is this letter from your husband?" I asked.

She nodded, "Uh, huh."

"He's not in San Francisco, he's overseas. FPO means Fleet Post Office, and his mail is sent to his outfit from there. The Fleet Post Office is in San Francisco."

She was silent for 10 seconds.

"I came here to surprise him," she said in a dull voice.

I said nothing.

"I came from home. I live in North Carolina."

She pushed the letter into her coat pocket and walked away.

Technical Sgt. Benjamin Goldberg
San Francisco

"Just plain tired of being the men behind the guns"

Navy and Marine officials usually did not want to publicize the actions of men who left their posts, even if it was to go into battle. This item was passed by the Navy censor and sent to DPR headquarters, where it was marked "not used." That one of the men was identified by race might reflect the writer's effort to point to a Black Marine's patriotism—or to follow orders to identify them as such in copy.

Incognito is the way they want to remain but two Marines, one a Negro, were just plain tired of being the "men behind the men behind the guns" and did something about it.

Several days before his outfit was to leave the Pacific coast, one was transferred unwillingly to base duty. He stowed away aboard ship when it left a west coast port bound for combat. After a week out, the stowaway was found, reprimanded for his act but allowed to rejoin his old outfit.

The Negro Marine, a dock worker at a rear Pacific base, decided he had loaded enough ships and wanted to go where the cargo he loaded was going. Several days after the ship left port the stowaway was discovered. He will be in a beach supply unit when Fifth Division Marines invade Iwo Jima.

Both stowaways will be "men behind the guns" now in the Marines' greatest Pacific campaign and they are elated over it.

Sgt. Chester H. Smith
Aboard a transport en route to Iwo Jima

"They have been pinned down while carrying wounded Marines"

This story of two Black Marines was cut to two sentences and passed "For Negro Press." Besides wordy sections of sentences, lost in editing were details describing their actions, the dangers they faced, their backgrounds, and the names of their families. Such personal information, key to the hometown quality of the stories, was common in reports on white Marines.

Stretcher bearers are called upon to perform some of the most dangerous missions in combat and once again Negro Marines are distinguishing themselves with bravery on Okinawa Shima.

Two of these men, Corporal Willie Crenshaw of Bessemer, Ala., and Private First Class Warren N. McGrew Jr. of Waco, Texas, have been working day and night evacuating the wounded of the First Marine Regiment.

Numerous times here on Okinawa Shima they have been pinned down for long periods of time by sniper fire, machine gun fire and enemy mortar shells while carrying wounded Marines back from the front lines to rear areas where their wounds can be treated.

There is little chance to fire back at the enemy while carrying a stretcher and the wounded cannot be set down in an exposed area. So when snipers open up, Crenshaw and McGrew just make a run with the wounded man to the nearest place of cover.

These two men have alone been called upon to carry ammunition up to the front lines and to go out on patrols searching for snipers. Crenshaw already has one Jap sniper to his credit.

Corporal Crenshaw, whose wife and three children reside at 500 South 20th St., Bessemer, attended Dunbar High School and then worked as a funeral director at Blevins and Son Funeral Home in Bessemer prior to entering the Marine Corps on April 3, 1943. He also saw action with the First Marine Division during the Peleliu fight.

Private First Class McGrew, who is the son of Mr. and Mrs. Warren N. McGrew of 700 Johnson Street East, Waco, attended the A.J. Moore High School and then worked as a bell hop at various hotels in Waco prior to entering the Marine Corps on November 3, 1943. He is now in combat for the first time.

Sgt. Harold E. Foreman
Okinawa

"I have to be with the boys in action"

This profile of Marine Private First Class Vincent T. Cullers, the future advertising executive, was a typical DPR-produced feature story showing the Everyman nature of wartime service—except that the subject was a Black Marine, which resulted in the label "Negro Press."

"Who did that?" she demanded, pointing to a chalk caricature of Teacher.

New teachers in Chicago, like anywhere else, have difficulty in ferreting out such culprits. But this time something—perhaps it was the softness in her eyes—prompted little Vinny Cullers, a spindly Negro lad with black wavy hair, to confess.

"Vinny," the teacher said, her voice more kindly than he had ever heard, "I want you to work hard. You've real talent. I want you to be a great artist."

That was 10 years ago.

Today, Vincent T. Cullers, a handsome, powerfully built Marine private first class, may be seen at the front lines, his carbine in his hands, his water colors and brushes slung over his shoulder in a captured Japanese case.

Cullers guards the Negro stretcher-bearers who have saved so many First Marine Division lives during the current campaign on Peleliu. He has been fired at often, once was pinned down for 20 minutes by a Jap machine gunner.

Invisible Heroes: Black Marines and Sailors in the Pacific | 177

His keen eyes take in the scenery. Then he returns to his foxhole with the 11th Depot Company and goes to work on a make-shift easel.

"I have to be with the boys in action, to get the feeling," he said, eagerly. "I haven't yet been able to put down that feeling on paper. I need a lot more experience. But someday . . ." and his husky voice trailed off into his dreams.

Cullers' work is not the best of the war, but his commanding officer thought enough of it to relieve him of many general duties so that he could continue painting. Few artists have had to work under similar conditions—in foxholes, often rain-filled, on an easel he made from the top of an ammunition box. He ran out of materials weeks ago. His paints are poor and he has to sketch on any scraps of paper he may find.

His portraits are excellent. He did several for Chicagoans before he joined the Marines in July, 1943. One of his best is a self-portrait which he painted aboard ship while the Marines were enroute to the Palaus.

Vinny attended Du Sable High School in Chicago, where he started on the football team. Although honored as an athlete, his greatest thrill came when he won a scholarship to the Chicago Art Institute, where he studied until the war interrupted his career.

His mother, Mrs. Letty Cullers, lives at 4855 South Dearborn Street, Chicago. A brother, Samuel, 26, is a pilot-technician for Douglas Aircraft.

Sgt. Vic Kalman
Peleliu

"We tried to dodge them mortar shells, but they just kep' on coming"
This story of a Navy Seabee did not mention its subject was a Black man. The writer, however, suggested in a note that it be sent to "Negro Press" because "This CB is a Negro." A Marine editor wrote "Negro Press" in large letters at the top for clarity. Notably, the writer's use of dialect was changed to more formal usage in the edited version, suggesting there was no clear policy on the matter.

Wherever there are Marines there are Seabees. And at Peleliu, attached to the First Marine Division, these construction men of the Navy did more than their "share."

One of the Seabees was Seaman First Class Winton E. Cooper, U.S.N.R., of 8 William Street, Montclair, N.J. Attached to a Specialist Battalion, Cooper worked at everything from unloading ships to carrying wounded from the front lines. He would carry ammunition on his shoulder up to the front, and return as a stretcher bearer with wounded. These men were credited with saving the lives of many Marines.

Wounded by concussion on September 19, Cooper is now in a Pacific Naval hospital, recuperating from his "near miss." He has been awarded the Purple Heart medal.

"It shore wuz a rough fight," he said, "and us Seabees took a walloping too. But it did me good to see them Japs take a worser one!

"The furst thing I did, after bein' pinned down on the beach for a half-hour or so," he said, "was to take ammunition to the Marines, who'd landed furst and gone on ahead. On the way back, I helped bring out wounded. This kep' up a long time.

"We tried to dodge them mortar shells—but they just kep' on coming. I was carrying an '.03', but I don't kno' whether I killed a Jap or no. I don't know how many ships we unloaded later, but they jus' seemed to cover the water. There wus a lot of little boats and alligators knocked out, too.

"I don't know how close that shell came that got me, 'cause I didn't know nothing about it 'til I woke up on the ship. I was soon on my way back here then."

Cooper is the son of Mr. and Mrs. William E. Cooper, and is married to Willie Gee Cooper, all of the William Street address. He enlisted in the Seabees September 8, 1943, and following basic and advanced training at Williamsburg, Va., was sent overseas December 16, 1943. He first saw action at Emirau.

Sgt. James F. Moser Jr.
Somewhere in the South Pacific

"His unit loaded much of the cargo for the Tarawa raid"

Filed a year after the Marine assault on Tarawa, this story was still marked for distribution to "Negro Press," but at half its length after editing aimed at more concise wording.

Marine Private First Class Joseph Elliott of Norfolk, Virginia, a winch operator with 15 months overseas duty, hasn't seen any actual combat with the enemy but he figures his "behind the line" work has played a big part in helping Nippon soldiers join honorable ancestors.

His unit loaded much of the cargo for the Tarawa raid in November of 1943. He recalled that oftimes they worked around the clock, helping to load and unload ships with the supplies that made the Gilbert Island occupation possible. During this time Jap bombers came over on three separate occasions in an effort to wreck as much of the supplies as possible.

Cpl. Collie J. Nicholson
Somewhere in the Pacific

"He helped to wipe out a cave of Imperial Engineers"

Black Marines in combat was news, given the Corps' efforts to keep them out of the front lines. Nonetheless, a story featuring a Black Marine was again directed to African American media.

Marine Private First Class James H. Barnes, of 1432 "S" Street, N.W., Washington, D.C., who landed with Marine assault troops on D-day plus one on Guam Island, was one of the few colored Marines to get a front line crack at the enemy in the Marianas.

Going ashore with a .30 caliber machine gun crew the day after the first wave hit the beach, Barnes remained in the thick of the fight until the island was secured. In addition to doing duties with the machine gunners, he went on several combat and reconnaissance patrols. It was during one of these patrols that he helped to wipe out a cave of Imperial Engineers.

As far as he was able to observe, according to PFC Barnes, the enemy troops contacted by his unit fought desperately until those in command had been seriously wounded or killed, then they became disorganized and seemingly unable to cope with the situation.

Cpl. Collie J. Nicholson
Somewhere in the Pacific

"Someone heard a faint cry for help"

Marines risking their lives to save a sailor would be a natural subject for a story. The race of the men relegated this dispatch to "Negro Press."

In keeping with the highest tradition of the Corps, two Negro Marines here, a corporal and a PFC, were credited recently with saving a man's life when they pulled a struggling sailor out of the ocean some distance from the shore. The sailor had been washed out by waves while attempting to cross from one island to another during low tide.

The Marines were Corporal William H. Orr Jr. and Private First Class Manuel Jones. They were traveling by LCM between the islands when someone heard a faint cry for help and saw a man struggling in the water off to their left. Immediately the two Leathernecks, both excellent swimmers, removed their shoes and went to the rescue.

Orr is the son of Mr. and Mrs. William H. Orr Sr., of 5614 South LaSalle Street, Chicago, Illinois. Jones is the son of Mr. and Mrs. Charlie G. Jones, of 39th Valley Street, Vauxhall, New Jersey.

Sgt. Collie J. Nicholson
Somewhere in the Pacific

These last three stories came from a Black Marine whose desire to cover the war appeared to be as frustrated as the yearnings of many other Black Marines to join the fight. Collie J. Nicholson had grown up in Winnfield, Louisiana, the son of an illiterate Army veteran of World War I turned sawmill worker. Segregation was a fact of life, and straying outside the racial boundaries came at a cost. Reading opened the world to Nicholson and showed the many possibilities beyond the sawmill. At sixteen he was writing a sports column for a weekly Black newspaper, the *Shreveport Sun*. He was in his freshman year at what would soon become Grambling College, playing baseball and working between classes, when the Japanese attacked Pearl Harbor. He finished his second year before joining the Marine Corps in September 1943, at twenty-two. The racial segregation of troops was hardly a new environment for him. When Nicholson was placed with the 51st Defense Battalion, his newspaper experience landed him in the base public relations office. He pushed to accompany the 51st when it went to the Pacific, hoping he would become a CC.

Nicholson did write for the Division of Public Relations, but evidence indicates he was never granted the coveted title of Marine combat correspondent. None of the edited stories in Nicholson's file at the National Archives, stretching from 1944 to 1945 as he rose from private first class to sergeant, carries the title under his byline. When he included the title in a story, it was crossed out before being distributed. Nor was Nicholson's name on a list of hundreds of combat correspondents and public relations officers in a 1947 collection of wartime dispatches. Decades later, his obituary in the *New York Times*, a 2006 article that focused on his long association with Grambling State University, initially as a student and later as its sports information director for thirty years, noted that he was the first Black war reporter for the Marines. The distinction between war reporter and combat correspondent may be a fine one to civilians, but the formal title was a sign of achievement and a source of pride among Marine writers. It was an honor not always granted its white writers. If other Black Marines wrote for the DPR, they too may have been denied the formal designation.

One reason Nicholson was at a disadvantage in competing for space with CCs was his assignment to cover the men and activities of the 51st Defense Battalion. He spent much of his time in the Pacific in American-controlled areas of the Gilbert, Ellice, and Marshall Islands. He often covered musical performances and sporting events, such as island baseball and basketball championships and boxing matches. His features about individual Black Marines focused on unusual off-duty activities, such as creating and selling greeting cards, running a for-profit laundry, or drawing and painting. He reported more about what a subject did back home than his duties in the Pacific, which may have been mundane or restricted from coverage in the media because of security concerns. Some of his stories were written by request of the *Shreveport Sun* and other Black publications.

Nicholson was not assigned to accompany the 51st Battalion during any island assault, a standard duty for CCs that could yield front-page bylines. When Black Marines were under fire on Saipan, Guam, Peleliu, and elsewhere, the Marine combat correspondents on the scene decided whether to write about them. Another source of competition for Nicholson was the Black combat correspondents who worked for the Associated Negro Press and major Black newspapers such as the *Chicago Defender* and the *Pittsburgh Courier*. Perhaps the greatest impediment to his becoming a bona fide Marine combat correspondent was the relatively narrow readership for his stories. Nearly all of Nicholson's dispatches in his National Archives file were marked "for Negro Press," per DPR policy. A search of digitized newspapers showed Nicholson's byline appearing exclusively in African American publications. Of the ten Nicholson stories found in a search of the years 1944 and 1945, most were about sports. Apparently the DPR considered his stories to be an expenditure of time and effort in service of a small number of readers and a pool of potential recruits to which the Marine Corps was ambivalent. His contributions to the war effort, like those of other Black Marines, went unseen by a large majority of American readers.

Nicholson was among the Black Marines of World War II who lived long enough to see the prejudices they endured exposed, their patriotism and faith in American ideals vindicated, and their membership in "the greatest generation" celebrated. He remained proud of his service and held no grudges for opportunities denied him. "Being in the Marine Corps was the greatest thing that ever happened to me," Nicholson said, according to his biographer, Michael Hurd. "Everything I am or have accomplished, I owe to the Corps." In 2002, six decades after his service, the Marine Corps Combat Correspondents Association honored Nicholson at its national convention, one hero who was invisible no more.

9 Thirty-Six Days on Iwo Jima

Marines under heavy fire found a reason to cheer during the difficult opening days of the assault on the volcanic island called Iwo Jima. At midday on February 23, 1945, a large American flag tied to a section of water pipe rose on the peak of Mount Suribachi, signaling the completion of a key early objective. Sergeant William H. Genaust, a Marine combat cameraman working with the Division of Public Relations, recorded the moment with a Bell & Howell movie camera containing color film. Standing next to him was a civilian, Joe Rosenthal, an Associated Press photographer, who captured the flag raising with a single frame of black-and-white film in a Graflex 4x5 Speed Graphic camera. His photograph of the five Marines and Navy corpsman raising the flag produced the iconic image of Marine Corps resolve, if not World War II itself, and appeared in newspapers across the nation. Genaust's color footage contributed to the public acclaim for the Marines in its own way, appearing in newsreels and serving as the climax of the twenty-minute battle film *To the Shores of Iwo Jima*. In those years before national television, millions of Americans saw Genaust's footage at movie theaters. Navy Secretary James Forrestal said those relatively few seconds of film "rallied the American public as no other sequence in war photography."

If Genaust's mother had had her way, her son would have been with her and his wife, Adelaide, in Minneapolis, Minnesota, instead of standing on Mount Suribachi. The previous October, Jessie Genaust had asked President Franklin Roosevelt to order her son Billy, thirty-eight, sent home as soon as he recovered from a bullet wound to the leg he had sustained on Saipan. "I feel he has done his part in this war and I really need him," the widow wrote in a letter to the president. "You would make me the happiest mother in the world." A Marine captain politely denied her plea. Genaust had his own plans, and they would not have surprised his fellow Marines. He had been wounded on Saipan while helping wipe out a nest of eight to ten snipers. Back on his feet, Genaust passed up an opportunity to go home and instead volunteered to go to Iwo Jima.

The flag raising was far from the climax of the fight for Iwo Jima, a five-week battle that proved to be the bloodiest in Marine Corps history. A high death toll on both sides had been assured: 110,000 American troops were deployed to take the island, which was defended by an estimated 21,000 Japanese, who'd had close to a year to fortify the island with defenses linked by tunnels. Not unlike the defense of Peleliu, the Japanese soldiers and sailors defending Iwo Jima did not expect to survive the battle—and the great majority did not. Marines and Navy corpsmen counted for more than 24,000 casualties, over 6,100 killed. Army and Navy losses pushed the US dead on the island to nearly 7,000. Capturing an air base that had bedeviled its bombers attacking the Japanese mainland, America secured a shorter, unimpeded route to Tokyo.

Fighting on Iwo Jima made a commensurate impact on the ranks of those working for the Marine Division of Public Relations. Four Marine writers died covering the campaign, the most in any single conflict of the war. These stories, censored or otherwise unused, came out of their efforts.

"Unexpectedly tough Jap opposition resulted in considerable confusion"

The Navy killed this second-day story reporting confusion among assault troops. The writer apparently thought heralding the Marine captain's ability to bring order and effectiveness amid the chaos outweighed admitting there were problems.

> One of the toughest jobs on this very tough beachhead was handled by Captain William C. Law, of Hartsville, S.C., intelligence officer for the second battalion, 14th Marines, Fourth Marine Division.
>
> The unexpectedly tough Jap opposition on this island resulted in considerable confusion amongst assaulting troops. Points that were supposed to be taken were not taken; key officers were casualties and communications were erratic, indeed.
>
> Originally it was Captain Law's job to locate on the ground positions selected on the map for the firing batteries of his battalion. He landed under heavy fire on the heels of the assault infantry on D-Day, only to find the Japs still in these positions.
>
> Ultimately the batteries were brought in on the beach and it was up to the captain to determine infantry positions and acquire the various types of information required for operation of artillery. This he did both by personal reconnaissance and radio. On D-night, his battalion began to fire the steady series of missions which have so greatly contributed to the Marines' slow but sure conquest of this Jap bastion, only 760 miles from Tokyo.

Captain Law is a graduate of Clemson College and has seen action at Roi-Namur, Saipan and Tinian, as well as Iwo Jima. His wife, Mrs. Louise Williams Law, and his parents, Mr. and Mrs. H.L. Law, reside at 1404 Home avenue, Hartsville.

Staff Sgt. J. B. T. Campbell Jr.
Iwo Jima

"Their dead and wounded demonstrated their bravery under fire"

Rare was the dispatch to be rejected with the words "killed by the Commandant." That the top Marine had weighed in showed that this report, coming after three weeks of fighting resulting in heavy casualties, was not to be shared with the public. A brief dispatch written earlier by a different CC, Sergeant Bob Cooke, related that Hill 382 was now called "Meat-Grinder Hill" and wrote, "It ate up men as fast as they could be fed to it." It too was withheld from distribution.

Sixteen more casualties and this would have been a "lost battalion," lost to the last man.

Probably this unit, a valiant, hard-fighting, hard-luck battalion of the 24th Regiment of the veteran Fourth Division, paid a greater price in dead and wounded in 22 days of battle on Iwo Jima than any other group in the history of Pacific warfare.

Hard-fighting—it took the worst the Japs could administer and was still fighting the gallant fight until its sector of Iwo was secured; hard-luck—it drew the toughest area, the high ground leading up to Bloody Hill 382. Is it necessary to add that it took it?

The battalion, commanded by Lieutenant Colonel A.A. Vandegrift Jr. until he was cut down, landed with 814 men. It had 798 casualties, among them more than 135 dead. If it had suffered 16 more casualties, it would have lost 100 percent of its original strength. Somewhere along the line, it picked up 226 replacements so that its strength today is around 350 men.

Even with the replacements, the thinness of its ranks is testimony that this fight to take this island 650 miles from the Japanese mainland was the worst in the 169-year history of the Marine Corps. Nor need there be any other citation to these infantry troops of the 24th Marines. Their dead and wounded, by their very numbers, demonstrated their bravery under fire.

Other battalions in the 24th Marines lost nearly as many men. The regiment's total casualties during 22 days of fighting comprised 2,326 enlisted men and 80 officers. Its losses in the officers' and noncommissioned officers' ranks were so severe that, at times, corporals and privates first class were leading squads and platoons.

One of its battalions lost 661 men and 23 officers in killed, missing and wounded; another 763 men and 26 officers; Col. Vandegrift's battalion 798 men, including 21 officers. Nowhere was the fight easy.

The 24th Regiment, commanded by Colonel Walter I. Jordan, of Virginia Beach, Va., suffered the most severe casualties as it captured the high ground leading up to Hill 382. Here, the Japs from pillboxes, caves, gun emplacements and rocks and crevices had troops of the 24th under savage shell, rocket and mortar fire as well as machine gun and small arms fire. Those Marines who came through said that the shell, rocket and mortar fire was the worst part. They saw their buddies not just shot and killed or wounded. They saw them mangled.

The advance of the 24th was made foot-by-foot, yard-by-yard across a no man's land of indescribably tough terrain. For days the regiment was pinned down, almost unable to move and never able to move without drawing shell or mortar fire. The Japs from the high ground beyond nearly always had them under perfect observation. That was the trouble, nearly always the trouble on this island.

The 24th, at this writing, had suffered heavier than any regiment in the Fourth Division, and the Fourth, the veterans of the Marshalls and Marianas campaign, had fared worse than any other division. It had taken the most of Saipan and Tinian to make the B-29 raids on Tokyo possible; now it had to pay another price to give American planes a necessary base within fighter range of Nippon.

Sgt. Jack Vincent
Iwo Jima

"The boy lost his mind"

Marines who left the battlefield suffering from shock over losing their buddies would not be a story to publicize, a fact a seasoned public relations officer would have known. Yet Jim Lucas wrote an item anyway.

This is one of the saddest stories to come out of the bitter battle for Iwo Jima.

A young Marine was taken from his regular place in a tank crew and left behind to assist in repairing a disabled vehicle. While he was safe on the beach, his tank hit a mine and four of the five crewmen lost their lives.

When he heard what had happened, the boy lost his mind and had to be evacuated from the island.

2nd Lt. Jim G. Lucas
Iwo Jima

"Honey I know you will write as soon as you can"

Marine Sergeant Dan Levin aspired to write about more than Joe Blow's contribution to the war effort. Several of the CC's stories from Iwo Jima, including this creative portrait of worry and loss, were marked "not used" at division headquarters. Did they suspect fiction over fact or had they no use for an artful approach to reality?

The sulphur shells were bursting in Hell's Acres, just North of the awful airport, and East of the Brimstone Pit.

(A letter lay abandoned in the bottom of a rocky foxhole.)

All morning corpsmen had been walking through Hell's Acres, finding the dead.

("Dearest darling, How are you today OK I hope. The baby is fine and hope you are the same. Honey I didn't get any mail as yet this week. I hope I get some soon. Honey I don't know what is wrong but I guess it is cause you are on the move. Honey I know you will write as soon as you can. Honey I didn't get any mail since the 26th of Jan, I hope I get some soon...")

The remnants of the company of the Fourth Marine Division were awaiting the word to move up again. They watched the corpsmen carry away the dead and crouched low when the sulphur shells hit fifty feet away.

("Honey I love you dear and hope you are still in love with me as I miss you very much and I do love you very much too. Honey please write to me as soon as you can Honey. Please Honey I don't know what is wrong...")

The fighting in Hell's Acres had been terrible yesterday, and in the morning, and now there was only the desolation of acrid earth, and ripped rocks, and torn barren trees, and the gleaming weird green-yellow mound of sulphur which marked the Brimstone Pit.

("Honey the baby is getting along in school he likes it very much he gets a star on all his work... Please write soon Honey... Honey he said to me today that he wished his daddy was home to help him with his homework too. Well Honey...")

The last page of the letter is lost.

The morning's and yesterday's dead had been covered with ponchos and carried down the crags from Hell's Acres for burial. The living now moved up, toward where the sulphur shells fell and the mortar howled and the sniper's rifle snarled. Toward the Brimstone Pit and the last terrible mile to the sea.

Sgt. Dan Levin
Iwo Jima

"At least one Jap agrees with the Marines"

A story about a Japanese soldier's complaints about the draft being similar to Americans' drew a rejection from Navy headquarters even after a censor had passed it. A different story by the same CC, also below, suggesting Marines and the enemy likewise groused about life in the service, drew a simple "no" at DPR headquarters.

As this operation continues it appears that everybody including the enemy has something in common.

Marines who landed 15 days ago have already formed their opinion of Iwo Jima, its horrible terrain, lack of water, flies and all the rest of the natural discomforts.

Strangely enough at least one Jap has been found who agrees with the Marines. A prisoner of war captured during the Fifth Marine Division's assault on Suribachi Yama proved to be a very talkative fellow, telling captors that he felt he had been given a bad assignment being in the garrison of Iwo. This was his opinion even before the Marines' landing.

The Jap prisoner, whose age was 39, explained that he was married and had two children, apologizing for the size of his family, explaining that he should have a larger family at his age.

His main complaint, miserable Iwo notwithstanding, was the draft situation. He claimed that there was something very unfair about the draft.

While Marines grinned a bit to themselves he said that there were a lot of younger men running around in Tokyo, and he "saw no reason why he, with two children and a wife should have been drafted and sent to Iwo. At least they could have let him stay with the Japan army on the home island of Honshu."

Sgt. Henry A. Weaver III
Iwo Jima

Ration biscuits have always been the source of common complaint. And Marines have always applied very tired gags to the hard tack and "stomach grenades," as some call them.

So men of the Fifth Marine Division were not surprised to find, upon smashing through enemy positions, that the Japs who had stolen rations at night had eaten most all of the "C" and "K" rations as evidenced by the empty cans and cardboard containers.

But Marines smiled when they saw scattered about the caves and countryside, the familiar cellophane envelopes still holding their rock-ribbed biscuits.

Sgt. Henry A. Weaver III
Iwo Jima

"Don't ask me why I left the galley"

Heroics aside, Navy headquarters still vetoed the distribution of stories about deserters. In this case, reporting that the Marine's commanding officer complimented the man who had left his post instead of punishing him likely reinforced the nonpublication policy.

Marine Private First Class Utah C. Henson, 24, of Sneth, Mo., was AWOL from his galley post for almost three weeks on Iwo Jima, but he received a high compliment, rather than punishment, from his commanding officer. He says he was scared all the time on Iwo, but his actions were otherwise.

Henson, a cook with the 9th Regiment of the Third Marine Division, deserted his chow preparing duties, and voluntarily served as a stretcher-bearer and ammunition carrier.

Dodging enemy and mortar fire, Henson hauled supplies to the front lines and returned with casualties. Leader of a stretcher team, Henson was forced to take cover on every trip but did not lose a patient.

A farmer in civilian life, Henson had never been near an injured person until Iwo Jima, but in the absence of corpsmen and doctors, he frequently rendered first aid and there are Marines here who say his treatments are greatly responsible for their survival.

"It was my first combat experience," Henson explained. "Frankly, I was scared the whole time I was up there. Don't ask me why I left the galley; or what kept me going. I guess when a man sees another fellow bleeding, he just can't help but try to do something for him."

Shell fragments struck Henson twice: One piece pricked him on the arm and the other landed in a dungaree pocket and burned a hole.

"I did not know it was there," he said, "until I felt my leg stinging. I thought a bug was biting me."

Henson, whose wife, Sleen, and daughters, Eunice, two years, and Blythe, nine months, live on Route No. 3, Kennett, Mo., has been with the Third Marine Division for eight months.

He went through boot camp at San Diego and trained later at Camp Elliott and Camp Pendleton in California.

Sgt. Red O'Donnell
Iwo Jima

"I'll not even take off my helmet to scratch my head"

A Navy censor passed this story in which a Marine private praised the value of his helmet after an encounter with a sniper. But the story ended up being killed for an unfortunate reason.

"I'll never again gripe about my helmet being too heavy on my head," a Third Marine Division Browning automatic rifleman declared emphatically, when he returned recently from the front lines.

The Leatherneck, Private First Class Richard Barella, son of Mr. and Mrs. Clorindo Barella, of Route 1, New Hartford, Conn., was thoroughly convinced of the importance of wearing a helmet in combat during the battle for this Japanese Gibraltar of the Pacific.

A sniper's bullet penetrated his steel head-piece and creased the inner-lining.

The 21-year-old Marine, a former employe of the Torrington Manufacturing Company, Torrington, Conn., was having a duel with an enemy sniper when a second sniper found the range.

"My ears rang for a while," Private First Class Barella said, "but I only suffered a burned neck.

"From now on, I'll not even take off my helmet to scratch my head when I'm on the front."

Staff Sgt. Francis H. Barr
Iwo Jima

DPR headquarters editors dropped the story above in April when they discovered that the once-lucky Marine had been killed in action only hours after his close call. A similar dispatch, below, that reflected Marines tempting fate was not used, either.

It was less than a week before he was killed by mortar fire while leading his company of the 21st Marines in an attack that Captain Edward V. Stephenson of Madison, N.C., gave this to reply to a sergeant who warned him to get in a foxhole:

"Hell, I'd just as soon get killed now as later."

The former druggist, whose parents live in Seaboard, N.C., met his death while in the forefront of a drive that took his company to the furtherest point reached by any Marine unit up to that time when he met his death.

Sgt. Dick Dashiell
Iwo Jima

"The cost of one artillery unit firing one day to win Iwo Jima"

DPR headquarters wrote an emphatic "no!" when cutting out the final paragraph in this story about an artillery unit. Unstated was whether the concern was over the idea of putting a dollar amount on the unit's performance or the accuracy of the writer's conclusion.

Marine field pieces have had a field day here.

Hard-hitting artillery, always a prime ingredient in the Marine formula of amphibious assault in the Pacific, has played its most pretentious role to date in the epic battle against Iwo's virtually impregnable defenses.

In action—and firing record amounts of ammunition—has been the largest concentration of Leatherneck field guns yet seen in the Pacific war, if not the entire 169-year history of the Corps.

One artillery unit alone—the veteran 12th Regiment of Major General Graves B. Erskine's Third Marine Division—expended more than 21,000 rounds during one day's firing. Total weight of steel hurled at the enemy in preparation for and during two attacks that day was estimated at 310 tons.

Approximate cost of firing one round—including ammunition, projectile and depreciation—is about $50.00. Or about $1,050,000 spent that day, by one regiment, to win Iwo Jima.

Sgt. Bill Ross
Iwo Jima

"A strategy being used extensively in this operation for the first time"

CCs eager to tell readers of success during the long battle at times shared too much information about tactics and technology. Surprisingly, they even reported on Japanese missteps that could have been corrected on Iwo Jima or in future battles. Such stories, examples of which follow, were not passed by the Navy censor and were marked "do not release." The last item was written five weeks before atomic bombs ended the war.

Like a cat crouched at a mouse hole, First Lieutenant Philip N. Austen, of Spokane, Wash., sound ranging officer for the 14th Marines of the Fourth Marine Division, waits in the night for a Jap gun to show its head—and then pounces.

Lieutenant Austen locates the positions of Japanese guns by the noise they make in firing. This is called "sound ranging" and is being used extensively in this operation for the first time in any Marine Corps engagement of this war. The reason is that the Japanese control all the high ground on this fortress island and are firing upon Marines from concealed positions. It has been extremely difficult for either forward observers or aerial observers to find these emplacements.

Through the use of certain secret devices, Lieutenant Austen and his team compute the position of Jap guns and even mortars. They then adjust Marine artillery upon the Jap position, picking up the sound of the exploding Marine shells in the same way they recorded the sound of the Jap gun—or guns.

Then the sound rangers get a battalion of artillery loaded and trained upon the Jap emplacement. The gunners have their lanyards in their hands, waiting for the word, "fire." Lieutenant Austen listens at his earphones for the Jap weapon to roar again. Sometimes the wait is a long one. Sometimes nothing happens at all. But nearly a score of times the Jap gunners have taken that one more shot that brings a full battalion of Marine artillery crashing into their emplacements. For with the first decibel of sound coming from the Jap position, long before the Jap shell has landed—Lieutenant Austen has commanded "fire" and the American shells are on their way.

Staff Sgt. J. B. T. Campbell Jr.
Iwo Jima

The Japanese mined one Iwo Jima beach so heavily that Marine engineers worked for two hours before assault troops could land.

Sixty anti-tank mines and 25 "yard stick" mines, with 50 to 100 pound serial bombs attached, were removed from the volcanic ash.

A mine disposal group led by Marine Second Lieutenant William G. Piper, of 213 Yale Avenue, Swarthmore, Pa., cleared the entire minefield without suffering a casualty.

"We probed the whole area with bayonets to locate the mines," he said. "It was a tedious job as some of the mines were wired to booby traps."

Anti-tank mines were placed six feet apart and in rows of three deep. "Yardstick mines," or anti-personnel mines, were scattered along the shoulder of the beach road at irregular intervals.

"After the men spotted the mines," the lieutenant said, "they prayed and dug in! It is a particularly intense moment as the mine is lifted from the sand."

Staff Sergeant Robert E. Bardto of Butler, Pa., and Private First Class George W. Minnich of Oaks, Pa., kept on digging though enemy shells fell dangerously close.

Sgt. Edward F. Ruder
Iwo Jima

When the Japanese trapped at the northern end of Iwo Jima sent up one of the heaviest rocket and buzz bomb barrages of the battle for this island fortress two nights ago, Marines were puzzled that none of the "Monsters" exploded.

Today, they learned the reason. Not one of the otherwise death-dealing missiles was armed. The Japs simply fired them into our lines without their war heads, often with wooden plugs in the fuse openings. The rockets fell harmlessly at the southern end of the island. The nearest approach to a casualty came when a hot 100-pound motor fell in a foxhole between two sleeping Marines.

Marine First Lieutenant William Bellano, Scranton, Pa., said there were other instances in which the Japanese simply sent rocket motors buzzing over our lines. Apparently, it was their idea of a war of nerves.

No one was able to figure the reason. It may be that the Japs hoped to brain someone with a direct hit, but it was, at best, costly sniping. Each bomb is worth several thousand dollars.

2nd Lt. Jim G. Lucas
Iwo Jima

Call it curiosity or sheer bewilderment—or a typical example of perverse enemy psychology, say Leatherneck pilots.

But the Japs "just can't keep a blackout," according to crews of Fourth Marine Air Wing Mitchells returning from nightly anti-shipping strikes to Empire waters aimed at extending our aerial blockade of nearby Bonins strongpoints to strategic coastal ports.

Technical Sgt. John T. Kirby
Iwo Jima

"Almost no use killing those damn gooks just for postcards!"

A Navy censor passed this story despite its criticism of fresh Marine troops and the subject of souvenir hunting, but DPR headquarters declined to use the story. The presence of a racial slur drew no comment or change.

Old hands of the Fourth Marine Division hit the deadliest defenses here in their fourth beach-head under enemy fire. They saw their buddies blown sky-high by vicious Jap mortar and artillery fire from both flanks, by "rice-kettle" mine fields, by giant rocket barrages. They want no souvenirs of this nightmare volcanic island.

But the boot replacements with them, making their first landing on enemy soil in this bloodiest battle of the Pacific, want a flag or a saber to send home. Two of these "old salts" returned from their first day and night at the front thoroughly disgusted.

"We got two Japs apiece," they said. "Got them with grenades ready to throw in their hands. But hell, they were only Superior Privates. Nothing on them but a bunch of postcards. Almost no use killing those damn gooks just for postcards!"

Sgt. Bob Cooke
Iwo Jima

"That one didn't have our number on it"

Dark humor likely was not welcome after more than five weeks of fighting and a record number of casualties, which could have prompted editors at DPR headquarters not to use this brief item.

It isn't malarkey about shells that have numbers on them.

That was the opinion of Marine Private First Class John N. Neal of Bulger, Pa., who said a mortar shell landed smack in an Iwo Jima shell hole, where he and five other leathernecks had taken cover, but not one of them was scratched.

"That one didn't have our number on it," one Marine said.

A minute later another Jap shell landed outside the hole. Four of the six Marines were wounded.

"That one did!" was the next remark.

Sgt. Edward F. Ruder
Iwo Jima

"Orders are orders"

Put aside as "not used" was this story about a Marine who followed orders but did not exercise much common sense or initiative. The final sentence, noting his position was under fire, may have been included to assure readers that the Marine was not merely avoiding combat.

Come shot or shell, never let it be said a U.S. Marine can't follow orders no matter what the obstacles . . .

Minutes after his assault company of the Fifth Marine Division's 26th Regiment landed D-Day on this shell-spattered beach, Private First Class Charles E. Hughes Jr., 19, son of Mr. and Mrs. C.E. Hughes Sr. of Box 52, Diamond, Ohio, was ordered by his sergeant to remain there and guard two reserve flame-throwers until relieved.

Twenty-six days later and still following orders, Hughes was still guarding the flame-throwers on the beach, a bee-hive of construction activity now. His sergeant, the only man knowing Hughes was on the beach, was killed two weeks after landing.

"Finally on the twenty-sixth day I decided something was wrong so I went up to our first battalion command post some three miles up the island and asked what to do," Hughes said. "A jeep was sent after the flame-throwers and I was put to work as a litter-bearer. Had I gone off and those flame-throwers carted away by someone else, it might have left our company in a bad way if they needed them so I stuck to my orders."

Although Hughes didn't see action as a rifleman, he spent days on the wreckage-strewn beach, plastered day and night for two weeks by Jap fire and one of the island's most dangerous spots.

Sgt. Chester A. Smith
Iwo Jima

"I want to be accepted as an American, because that's what I am"

Nisei, generally considered American-born children of Japanese immigrants, tried to coax enemy troops to surrender rather than be killed or commit suicide. This story about the effort on Iwo Jima proved problematic for the Marine Division of Public Relations for several reasons. First, the Japanese Americans depicted in the story were Army personnel. Second, stories about strategy and the use of translators were generally out of bounds. Moreover, the soldier quoted anonymously told the Marine combat correspondent that Marines often mistook Nisei for the enemy and fired at them, which an editor opined in a typed note "should come out in any case." In the end, a Navy censor passed the story, but DPR headquarters decided not to use it, most likely because public relations officers were not keen on promoting the Army. In the lightly edited original text, references to "Nips" were changed to "Japs"; the original language appears below.

Helping the Third Marine Division to flush Nips out of their caves during the battle of Iwo Jima was a group of Nisei whose job was to talk to the Japs in their own language in an effort to get them to surrender. Much of their work involved the hazard of walking through the tunnels with flashlights playing on their faces.

First, the Nisei—U.S. Army personnel who are American-born sons of Japanese—spoke over a loudspeaker rigged up to a sound truck parked in front of a cave or tunnel.

They asked the Japs to consider their plight: There was no possibility of the Nips winning the fight; there was no truth to the propaganda that the Marines would torture them if they surrendered; there was no way to escape death save by laying down arms.

"Come out stripped to the skin," the Nisei told them. "Keep your hands raised. Walk out slowly. We will give you food, water, cigarettes and, if you need it, medical attention."

Sometimes, the Japs—usually those who were without ammunition or water, or both—walked out as instructed. More often, they defiantly tossed a grenade out of the opening or simply remained in their caves without response. Then Marine demolitions men went to work.

One group told the Nisei to "come and get us." They were got, by dynamite. Another bunch replied: "Wait 15 minutes." At the end of that time they blew up their cave—occupying the innards of a whole hillside—and, of course, themselves.

If the Nisei were unsure the Nips heard them, or if they thought the enemy needed a little more personal persuasion, they then undertook one of the more dangerous jobs of the whole campaign. They cautiously entered the cave, talking to the Nips all the time.

As they walked through the black emptiness, the Nisei threw flashlight beams upon their faces to show the Nips that they were "blood brothers" despite the difference in nationalities. A Nisei's face, thus lighted, gave the Japs a perfect target there in the cave, either for a rifle, bayonet or sword. But at Iwo Jima, none of the Nisei was attacked.

One of the Nisei, a technician fourth grade nicknamed "Kelly" from Los Angeles, explained it this way:

"I guess they didn't kill us for a couple of reasons. One was that they could see that we were of Japanese descent. The other was they figured we certainly weren't going to try to trick them with flashlights shining on us and making such beautiful targets."

"Kelly," a chubby, smiling bundle of energy, was typical of the danger-shrugging Nisei at Iwo.

"I've been shot at more by Marines than by the enemy," he grinned. "Sometimes the boys don't take time to look at my uniform after they see my face, and they let go. Just the other day, a Marine threw a grenade at me when I came out of a cave. It bounced off my back and down a little hill before it exploded without hitting anybody.

"I've been shot at three or four times by Marines, but I'm still here."

Usually, the Leathernecks shot at "Kelly" when he forgot himself and sauntered away from his escort of a white-faced American soldier or two.

During the Guam operation "Kelly" became lost at the front and wandered around for hours thinking that any second might be his last. Naturally he was in mortal danger from both sides. The Nips might have killed him because he wore a Marine uniform, and the Marines might have plugged him because of his Nipponese face.

"Kelly," who has no living relatives, took the perilous job because he thought it would help him get adjusted in peace-time.

"After the war," he said solemnly, "I want to go back to the United States and be accepted as an American, because that's what I am. I think if people know I had a job like this with the Army it will help me in my business, or whatever I want to do."

Sgt. Dick Dashiell
Iwo Jima

"Marines kill the Japs, Marines should bury them"

Marked "not used," this report on a Marine who buried the enemy dead highlighted an unpleasant duty few would envy or seek out.

His is not the most pleasant task on this island, and he will probably never get a medal for the risks he has taken for the past 23 days, but Marine Gunnery Sergeant Ben G. Avram, 35, of Philadelphia, Pa., has the growing respect of other members of his regiment in the Fifth Marine Division.

A battle "handyman" since the early assault waves struck Iwo, Avram, a Marine veteran of 14 years, has done the dirty work. He helped clear a path for food and supplies to his men, he carried out the wounded, he helped maintain security about command posts, helped lead sniper patrols and demolitions parties blasting enemy caves. And of late has resigned himself to the call, "Hey, Gunny" if and whenever there is something unpleasant to be done.

The most distasteful task he has assumed has been the vital job of burying the enemy dead. From the first hours of the Fifth Marine Division's assault on Suribachi, and during the later fighting at the north of Iwo, he has gone down into the enemy lines under constant fire to bury the Jap dead. Aside from the displeasure attached to the duty, he has been a neat target for snipers and has taken "pot luck" along with other front line Marines as far as mortar or artillery fire is concerned.

More than one piece of equipment he called to his aid has been either shot up or knocked out of the fighting. Avram has had many a narrow escape with both booby-trapped enemy dead and lurking snipers. But as far as the latter are concerned he "doesn't even count them anymore."

With a rather philosophical outlook towards his job he says, "Marines kill the Japs, Marines should bury them."

It may sound strange but he now resents the interference of other units in his "work." His ambition being to see at least one thousand Japs in his scattered little cemeteries which follow the advance of the Marine lines.

Sgt. Henry A. Weaver III
Iwo Jima

"White sheets fell limp over what was once his legs"

A report from a hospital ward for Marines maimed by enemy fire would have added to the grim news from the Pacific—and the details hardly attractive for recruiting.

Many Iwo Jima Marines worry that they will be sent home.

They are the men who were blinded or maimed on the battlefield. At night they lie awake in their hospital beds and wonder if they have the "right" to expect love from those they left behind.

We visited a Marine sergeant. He was propped up against the back of his bed. The white sheets fell limp over what was once his legs. Near his pillow were several rumpled sheets of stationery. We talked to him and he confided that he was trying to write his girl and tell her he had found someone else. They had been waiting for three years to get married.

"It's a damnable lie," he said. "But it wouldn't be fair to her any other way."

The man had not lost his faith, but his conscience had been working overtime. We set him thinking about artificial limbs, and he promised he would hold the letter until he had given them a try.

A Marine youngster not more than 18 years old was brought into the ward. He had taken a Japanese hand grenade in his face. He told us he was not worrying about himself.

"I was never very handsome, anyway," he said, "but my mother would never be able to take it."

He explained that his mother had told him she would never forgive herself for signing his enlistment papers if anything had happened to him.

But perhaps the strangest case was that of a Marine private who was not seriously wounded. He had been shot through the leg and had been told he was going to be evacuated to the United States to convalesce.

"It isn't right that I should be sent back now," he said. "It was my first time in battle and I got wounded so fast I never had a chance to do any good. Back home the folks were expecting me to get a few Japs myself."

Sgt. Edward F. Ruder
Iwo Jima

"One of the more touching things were baby shoes"

This undated story about the disposition of personal effects of Marines killed on Iwo Jima probably was submitted shortly after the battle ended. Penciled on its first page were "not used" and "bad taste." It may have been judged too soon to share such a morbid and matter-of-fact process with the public—and with Marines themselves—as the war in the Pacific seemed far from over.

Home and hobbies.

Those were the chief sources of effects left in seabags by those who were killed in action or who died of wounds on Iwo Jima, to judge by bags returned to the quartermaster section of the Third Marine Division's 21st regiment.

Among the objects more commonly found were pictures of family and friends. Most of these were snapshots, although occasionally an expensive photograph turned up.

"We found a surprising number of nightclub pictures," said Private Robert Renardson of 538 Summer Street, Mount Holyoke, Mass., who was in charge of sorting and inventorying the gear, clothing and equipment. "Most of these were taken, evidently, in San Diego or Los Angeles before the Marine shipped out. There usually were a buddy and girl friends in the picture."

Grass skirts, one of the easiest-to-find souvenirs in the Pacific, were also much in evidence. So, too, were various Japanese pictures taken from the bodies of Jap soldiers as well as Japanese rifles, sabres, pistols, field glasses and wrist-watches, plus Purple Heart medals received for wounds suffered in previous campaigns.

One of the more touching things one saw in the seabags were baby shoes. There were also marriage licenses. Birth certificates of sons and daughters were plentiful, as were letters written on everything from fine linen to scraps of wastepaper, and in every type of penmanship from aristocratic scrolls and flourishes to penciled, misspelled scrawls.

One thing that surprised Renardson were the number of watches which the Marines left in their seabags at base camp. Other valuables included pen-and-pencil sets, metal—and sometimes jeweled metal bands—wrist bands, and cash. One Marine left $380 in bills in his bag. Good wallets were also common. A number of wallets found on the bodies of Marines contained bullet holes.

Prayer books, miraculous metals, sacred hearts and prayer beads were much in evidence.

A large number of Marines had stored several days' rations of beer in hopes of celebrating the end of the campaign. Others tucked in lobster, cherries, shrimp, turkey, chicken—all, of course, canned.

More than 2,000 bars of soap were found in more than 500 seabags. These were turned over to the American Red Cross. Several sets of fancy Marine blue dress clothes turned up.

And it seemed that every Leatherneck possesses an address book crammed with names of girl friends, old and new, buddies, former schoolmates, and aunts, uncles and cousins.

The valuable effects, such as money, valuable papers and keepsakes, were sent to the Commandant of the Marine Corps in Washington, D.C., for determination regarding the legal representative or heirs at law, and final disposition.

Items of a non-valuable nature, such as pictures, souvenirs which were passed by censors, sweaters, civilian caps, address books and clothing of officers (who pay for their clothes themselves instead of having them issued to them as do the enlisted men) were shipped to the Marine Corps' Personal Effects Distribution Center in Farragut, Idaho. From there they were sent to next of kin.

Handling the effects of those killed in action and those dead of wounds was a section of two officers and 23 men. One officer was in charge of the entire section and the other acted as censor. Four of the unlisted men were sorters, four were recorders, four wrappers, four runners, one typist, one who compiled the shipping list, one crater, one typist in charge of form and routing and three general helpers.

They inventoried, wrapped, packaged, censored and shipped the contents of more than 500 seabags inside of a month under the supervision of Second Lieutenant Frederick T. Field of 95 Cedar Avenue, Newark, N.J.

Personal effects not left in rear areas by those killed in action were forwarded to the section via battalions by men of burial and graves registration details. Effects of those who died of wounds were forwarded by hospitals or hospital ships.

Staff Sgt. Dick Dashiell
Iwo Jima

An estimated one in three Marines killed in World War II died on Iwo Jima, but the Marine Corps was slow to share such statistics with the public. When it did, the breadth of the casualties was another shock wave for a war-weary United States. President Roosevelt himself turned to the government's public relations machine to emphasize the Marines' sacrifice and ordered Joe Rosenthal's flag raising photo to become the logo of the latest war bond drive. Later, the Marines' performance on Iwo Jima was memorably described by Navy Admiral Chester Nimitz when he said, "Uncommon valor was a common virtue." Heavy losses obscured the fact that the Marine Corps and the Navy had learned from their past mistakes in the Pacific. The historian Joseph H. Alexander noted that, while hardly free from error, the Iwo Jima campaign was a high point for planning and sustaining via logistical support such a massive amphibious assault. Cooperation between the Navy and Marine Corps was superior, too, according to Alexander, and contributions from the other military services were important.

The battle also raised the bar for the public relations effort that was central to the mission of Marine combat correspondents and cameramen. Stories, photographs, and motion picture film from Iwo Jima were picked up in Guam and flown to Chicago and then New York, where the film was processed, and the stories were sent on by train to Washington. Along the way a story by combat correspondent Sergeant Keyes Beech was dropped off in Philadelphia, processed, and transmitted by national wire services. The opening carried the hometown elements that gave the CCs' reporting its distinction:

> Out of countless tales of heroism there came today the story of a Marine lieutenant and two enlisted men who fought their way through pillboxes, bunkers, blockhouses and machine-gun nests to cross to the western shore of this island only 90 minutes after they landed on the east.
>
> When he hit the beach at H-Hour, Feb. 19, 2nd Lt. Frank J. Wright, 25, of Pittsburgh, Pa., had a platoon of 60 men.
>
> By the time he had crossed the island an hour and a half later two of the 60 remained with him and instead of being a platoon leader Lt. Wright was a company commander.
>
> Four of his company's officers, including the company commander, were killed or wounded as they attempted to follow him across.

Beech provided a stirring account of the three men as they "blazed a death strewn trail" for 800 yards, including their names and hometowns. In Pittsburgh, the story was headlined "Pittsburgher and 60 Men Start Across Iwo, 3 Make It." Newspapers across the country carried the story even without a local angle. The passage of ten days from the landings at Iwo Jima to publication on March 1 had not lessened its news value.

The DPR city room worked into the night to process sixty more stories within a few hours. Subsequent batches of copy from Iwo Jima arrived within seven days of being airmailed from the field, which the receiving officials regarded as "excellent time." The copy from the initial fighting arrived far ahead of the "en route" stories that had been written aboard transports as troops moved into the area, rendering them out of date and unusable. The Marine Corps' own record of how its troops fought their most famous battle of the war benefited from a publicity staff that by then had two and a half years of practical experience.

Just as the battle cost the Marines dearly, the men working for the Division of Public Relations mourned losses of their own. Ahead of the Iwo Jima landing, combat correspondent Sergeant James J. McElroy, who had worked for newspapers in Rhode Island and Massachusetts, was aboard a B-25 bomber that went down on February 12 during a bombing mission to the Bonin Islands. A little more than a week later, combat correspondent Staff Sergeant William T. Vessey, an Oregon native who had worked for newspapers in Oregon City and Portland, became the first of the CCs to land on Iwo Jima. He was wounded during the battle for Mount Suribachi and died on February 20. (Several of his final stories, written aboard a transport, went unused because of the time lag.) On the second day of the battle, mortar fire wounded combat correspondent Sergeant John M. Barberio; he died the next day aboard a Navy ship. He had spent his newspaper career in his New Jersey hometown at the *Red Bank Daily Standard*. While not designated a combat correspondent, Corporal William J. Middlebrooks, who had worked for the *Pensacola News-Journal*, was reporting from Iwo Jima for the DPR when he died of wounds on February 24.

As many as four combat photographers or cameramen were reported killed. One of them was Sergeant William H. Genaust, the Saipan veteran whose mother had begged President Roosevelt to send him home. Nine days after he filmed the flag raising on Mount Suribachi, Genaust was reported missing in action. A witness later said Genaust had entered a cave with other Marines and was shot and killed by enemy troops hiding inside. The cave was sealed off with explosives, burying Genaust's body as well as any Japanese. Despite efforts over the decades that followed, his remains were never recovered. Yet his color film of the Marine Corps' proudest moment endured, appearing in television documentaries and then on the internet in the new century. Genaust himself never saw the footage.

10 Okinawa and Imperial Japan's Last Stand

Sitting at his typewriter, Sergeant Harold E. Foreman searched for a word to describe the feelings of the frontline Marines on Okinawa, the final island conquest before invading the Japanese mainland. Four days earlier, the combat correspondent had landed with them and then marched alongside as they made their way across the central region's hilly and terraced countryside. The Marines discovered hundreds of pillboxes, caves, and other emplacements but hardly any Japanese troops. The few enemy snipers they encountered were killed or taken prisoner. The handful of casualties sustained by Foreman's unit came not from enemy action but heat exhaustion, sprained ankles, and bad feet. In those four days they took control of territory they thought would require fifteen.

Foreman settled on a word seldom found in Marine combat correspondent reports from the front lines in the Pacific. "We are a bewildered lot of Marines," he wrote in a dispatch dated April 5, 1945. "We have been searching for the little yellow man who wasn't there." Foreman ended his story with an optimistic tone: "Just what will happen during the remainder of our stay here remains to be seen, but I wonder what General William Tecumseh Sherman would have thought of this invasion." All too soon, however, the Union general's famous if apocryphal observation, "war is hell," would be borne out in Okinawa.

Those first quiet days were soon betrayed by the now-familiar Japanese military strategy of attrition, in which troops were sacrificed to inflict huge enemy losses and alarm the American public. After the fast start, Operation Iceberg, the codename for the Okinawa campaign, slowed to a glacial pace. The Japanese had turned the southern portion of the island into a fortress to protect ports and an airfield. They heavily fortified hundreds of caves in ridges and hills along three lines of defense, then lay in wait to train artillery and deploy troops against the Americans. A Marine corporal, Warren G. Evertz of St. Louis, later told a Marine writer that the toughest part of the campaign for Okinawa took place at one particular area known as the Shuri Line. "We fought the elements as well as the Nips," Evertz said. "For three days we received no food, water or ammunition because the rain made the lines of supply impassable. On the fourth day we were dropped supplies by parachute." His description left out the misery of watching Japanese bullets and shells kill his comrades.

Gaining control of Okinawa took Marine, Army, and Navy forces eighty-two days, from April to June 1945, and shed more American blood than any other Pacific campaign. More than 12,500 troops died in combat, nearly 3,000 of them Marines. On the sea, the Navy's Fifth Fleet suffered through wave after wave of kamikaze pilots, who sank thirty-four ships and other craft and damaged hundreds more. Japanese forces numbered some 110,000; about 7,000 surrendered, more than 100,000 were confirmed killed, and still more died in sealed caves. The noncombatant population suffered as never before in the Pacific; as many as 100,000 died in June alone.

At the time, Marines on Okinawa had no reason to believe they were fighting the last major battle of the Pacific war. In fact, the will of Japanese troops to face certain annihilation had already prompted America's military planners to consider how ships, planes, and boots on the ground could be used to invade and conquer the Japanese mainland. In Japan, a defensive plan to repel the Americans included civilians as young as fifteen and as old as sixty, male and female. Unimagined death and destruction on both sides were the outcomes in all such scenarios. Meanwhile, only a relatively few American officials knew another option was possible, one based more on nuclear physics than military tactics, which might save countless lives of Marines, soldiers, and sailors. But first Okinawa must be vanquished.

"Convincing civilians to surrender is bringing headaches"
Navy command killed this story, excerpted here, even though it cast a positive light on Marines giving aid to Okinawan civilians. Interactions with them as well as Japanese troops were often withheld from public release per Navy censorship regulations.

> Bombers and long-range artillery that have paved the way for American ground forces on Okinawa have driven many civilians out of their homes and into caves left by Japanese soldiers. When interpreters catch up with the tiny Okinawans they find Jap propaganda has left its mark about how treacherous Americans are supposed to be.
>
> Once the language men get the natives out of hiding they find them friendly enough, but it's convincing them to surrender that is bringing the headaches.

Marines are risking their lives every day trying to rescue civilians. On April 3, Private First Class Joseph L. Wingate, 19, of 182 Byron Avenue, Lawrence, Mass., was killed when he approached a cave believed occupied by civilians, only to find a Jap rifleman concealed in the dark. Wingate's buddies in the 29th Marines, Sixth Marine Division, led by Private First Class Ray E. Morse, of 1511 Eighth Avenue, Beaver Falls, Pa., and Private First Class R.A. Smith, of 199 Sherman Street, Albany, N.Y., got even with grenades and a flame thrower.

A five-man patrol heard a low moaning as they passed one cave yesterday afternoon. They found two old women and an old man hovering around two dead babies. Lieutenant Glen Slaughter, 25, of 1416 Spring Way, Berkeley, Calif., interpreted their story.

Shellfire the day before had killed one of their babies, and the old people figured that was to be the fate of them all. They smothered the second child, and the two women had each cut their own throats in attempted suicide. However, they didn't sever any vital structures and their lives were probably saved by Navy Lieutenant (j.g.) B.H. Inloes, a former Baltimore physician.

After Lieutenant Slaughter offered them candy and water and proved his friendliness, the aged trio consented to go to a stockade for protection, providing the Americans buried their babies immediately. The natives held brief ceremonies and the babies were laid to rest by a Marine graves registration group.

Another patrol of riflemen fired on two figures darting from a brush pile toward a cave. When the couple was captured it was discovered they were a man and teen-aged son, wearing caps and khaki jackets identical to the Jap army uniform. The boy was a student and the father wore one of the son's outfits.

The boy was hit by the riflemen and it was explained to the father the reason they were fired upon was the resemblance of their clothes to a uniform. The father thought this was funny, chuckled and tossed the cap aside.

When Jap soldiers are found in these caves, killing them is routine. When the occupants are found to be civilians, convincing them requires a lot of tact and patience, but saving them is just as routine.

Sgt. Harold T. Boian
Okinawa

"I couldn't move as that Jap with the knife came closer and closer"
This good story for the hometown paper of a Marine went undistributed by the Division of Public Relations because he appeared to be incautious at best or just plain foolhardy.

A quest for souvenirs on Okinawa turned out to be the most harrowing experience of his life for Marine Sergeant Martin B. Martin of Ellenboro, N.C.

Sergeant Martin, accompanied by two other Marines, started into a tiny village on Northern Okinawa looking for souvenirs. The village was behind their own lines and Martin didn't bother to take along a weapon, although his two buddies carried carbines.

Rounding a bend in the road, they suddenly saw three Japs lying in a ditch. Two of them were armed with rifles. The Japs were as surprised as the Marines, but the Leathernecks recovered quicker. They shot the Japs with the rifles.

The third Jap, seeing Martin unarmed, charged at him—pulling a wicked-looking hari-kari knife as he ran.

"I've been scared before," Martin said, "but I've never been that scared before in my whole life. I couldn't move a muscle and I stood rooted to the spot as that Jap with the knife came closer and closer."

Luckily, his buddies did act. They shot the Jap six times before he tumbled into the ground dead—12 feet away from Martin.

Sgt. Harold W. Twitty
Nago, Okinawa

"Many things of interest were found"

Besides encouraging reckless behavior, the quest for souvenirs on Okinawa created an image problem. With its large noncombatant population, the island presented opportunities for souvenir hunting that went beyond the belongings of enemy troops. Marines were warned to respect civilian property. Some stories sent to the public relations division were either not used or the looting angle was deleted in editing. The following paragraphs were cut from a day-of-invasion story that noted Marines had time on their hands because of the relative ease of the landing.

After the Marines dug in, many of them started out on souvenir hunting missions. The thatched roof homes of the poorer farmers held little of interest, but in the tile-covered houses of the better-to-do Okinawans, many things of interest were found.

Sergeant Raymond H. Neltner, of Peoria, Ill., found a beautiful one-half carat diamond ring in a dresser drawer sitting in an onion patch.

"I'm gonna send that to my wife," he said.

Sgt. Harold W. Twitty
Nago, Okinawa

A little more than a week later, a group of Marines looking for souvenirs explored a private home. The Navy rejected the story below, perhaps in part because of its enemy propaganda value as an example of Americans violating the privacy of civilians. At some point the reference to souvenir hunting was penciled out; the practice had been listed as a prohibited topic long before Okinawa.

Something about Mr. Kaneshiro's house made it stand out from the rest. Maybe it was just a little neater, a little more attractive.

The village had been shelled and bombed before the Marines moved in. Some houses still were smoking ruins, but Mr. Kaneshiro's house stood proudly on his small knoll untouched.

We didn't know it was Mr. Kaneshiro's house, of course, when we trudged past it in the dust. None of us had ever heard of Mr. Kaneshiro. But going back to it later in a search for souvenirs, it was very easy to learn the house had been lived in by the Kaneshiro family.

The furniture had been moved out into the yard—to save it if the house were hit—and there were papers and letters scattered about the ground.

Sight of a Sears, Roebuck catalogue made us want to know more about the man who had lived here. There were letters and cards among the papers, a discarded wallet, and a cake of Palmolive soap.

His name was on some of the letters, many of which were written—in English—from Hawaii. There were Christmas cards from Colorado Springs, Col., and Glendale, Calif. There was a picture card folder of Chattanooga, Tennessee, showing in postcard colors the scenic beauty of the southern city.

One letter was addressed both in English and Japanese. It was from Mr. Kaneshiro's brother in Hawaii.

"Do you remember your English language yet," the letter asked. "If you think Japanese language is easier, you can write to me that way next time you wish to write to me.

"Since Japan and U.S.A. is getting unfriendly as time goes on, in the future it is possible that we might not be able to write each other. Even right now it is hard to send anything to Japan.

"But anyway, let's pray that war will never come," the letter concluded.

It was postmarked September 15, 1941.

From other papers we learned that Mr. Kaneshiro himself had at one time lived in Hawaii where he once bought a Dodge truck, registered for the draft in the last war and bought a $5 war savings stamp.

Mr. Kaneshiro didn't come home while we were there and we didn't get to know him; but the visit to his neat tile-roof home 350 miles from Japan and finding articles that are familiar in everyday American life made it seem indeed a small world.

Sgt. Harold W. Twitty
Nago, Okinawa

"Marines had been pinned down for hours, the wounded were dying"

Time could be a story's highest hurdle in the race toward distribution. Weeks went by as CINCPAC held up a seven-page dispatch about a Marine advance. The delay may have been due to checking the casualty status of the numerous men named in the story. By the time the DPR received it, more than a month had passed, and the civilian press had already published their own accounts. This CC's version went unused. Fully identified in the story, though not in this excerpt, were First Lieutenants Daniel B. Brewster of Baltimore, Maryland; Marvin C. Plock of Lincoln, Nebraska; Charles W. Flannery of Dallas, Texas; Marvin D. Perskie of Atlantic City, New Jersey; and Platoon Sergeant Elmer P. Imus of Kingman, Arizona.

As yet the Jap caves had not been located by anyone outside Brewster's platoon. Perskie decided to use a smoke screen and withdraw his men. Under cover of smoke grenades a stretcher team dashed across the narrow opening and pulled out Plock's casualties. Plock brought his men snaking back up the ridge out of the ravine. But attempts to move in toward Brewster's position failed. At each try enemy machine gun bullets streamed through the smoke and held the men back.

Next Perskie tried artillery. He called for a barrage on the far slopes of the ravine. But the big guns were unable to pull their fire down on the ravine without endangering the lives of men in the second platoon.

Meanwhile, up the ravine in the rice paddie, Brewster's platoon was being mercilessly cut to pieces by the enemy. Here the men knew where the Japs were. They could hear them and sometimes they could see them. But each attempt to raise to a firing position drew a hail of bullets from nearby caves.

They knocked down a few Japs. One became careless and leaned out over the small knoll where Brewster's Marines lay. A BAR (automatic rifle) spoke and the Jap tumbled into the cave with the Marines. One was hit as he tried to run from one cave to another. Others were killed in the entrances to caves.

But mostly the men could do nothing but hug the mud, get wounded and die. The cave where the platoon was situated became sticky with blood. The ground was covered with it. Scarcely a dozen men of the platoon were still alive and unwounded.

Brewster himself was hit twice. In moving about to keep his men organized and look after the wounded he had drawn fire to himself numerous times. Once a bullet crashed through his helmet barely creasing his head. Another time he was hit in the foot.

Private First Class Anthony Caso of Jersey City, N.J., asked permission to attempt to break out. Too many men had been killed in the attempt. Brewster refused to allow him to go. Caso insisted. Brewster gave his permission. They didn't expect him to make it. But Caso rolled into the small, muddy stream that skirted the rice paddie and snaked his way out. Most of the way he was underwater.

With Caso's arrival, Perskie received his first appraisal of the desperate situation in the ravine. Also men on the outside learned for the first time the location of the caves and sources of enemy fire.

Perskie drew his two platoons up along the rim of the high ridge. To Plock and Imus he pointed out the caves as identified by Caso. The company was going to charge over the ridge to sweep down into the ravine and save what was left of Brewster's platoon.

The entire area was completely controlled by enemy machine guns and rifles. It seemed almost suicide to charge into the face of such fire. But there was nothing else left to do. The battle had been going on all day. Few Japs had been killed. The Marines had been pinned down for seven hours and the wounded were dying from lack of care. Not a man in the company flinched.

Plock's platoon led the charge. Imus' men followed. When Perskie dashed over the ridge top the double line of Marines went forward. What followed was a blazing few minutes of fighting too fast and furious to follow and which left more than 150 Japs dead.

As the two platoons crashed down into the ravine, Flannery pushed his machine guns over the top of the ridge and sent a spray of lead down in front of the charging men.

Plock's men crashed down through the brush to the first cave and poured lead and flame into it with hardly a pause. In a matter of seconds they were down and past Brewster's position. Stretcher bearers moved down on the heels of the attack and began evacuating the wounded men while the fighting blazed around them.

In one small draw of the ravine twenty Japs were swept down with one blast of the flame thrower. Six more were cut down by rifle fire a few yards farther on. Caves were blasted by hand grenades and bazookas and left smoldering by flame throwers.

In a matter of minutes it was over. The attack evidently had been too swift and unexpected for the Japs. Few more Marines were hit. Dead Japs sprawled in crevices and ditches everywhere in the area.

The Marines tramped back out of the ravine carrying the last of their wounded. For three hundred yards, the entire length of the ravine, they tracked blood along the path back.

Sgt. George R. Voigt
Okinawa

Checking all casualties before identifying them in stories was worth the delay, especially given public relations goals. Staff Sergeant Vic Kalman wrote an item on Corporal William T. McGonigle, twenty-four, of Darby, Pennsylvania, and how he had suffered thirty shrapnel fragments while aboard a transport under attack off the coast of Okinawa. "Why do I consider myself lucky?" McGonigle told Kalman. "Not a piece hit a vital organ." A week later McGonigle died of his wounds, and the story went unused.

"They do not make attractive roommates"

An unusual feature of Okinawa's hilly southern landscape were concrete tombs. For weary Marines they were shelter from rain and a place to rest in the relatively quiet opening days of the invasion. Cut from a story about a Marine patrol were macabre details of sheltering in a tomb.

Marines in one area had a difficult choice to make. They were bivouacked in the midst of Japanese burial vaults—concrete vaults whose insides would remain warm and dry.

But a Marine could not sleep in one of these tombs alone. He had to share it with the ancestors of the island's population. Charred bones remaining from cremations, whole skeletons—they do not make attractive roommates. One Leatherneck, driven on by the rain, gingerly started to remove a box from a tomb to make way for his tired and dripping body. In the box were the remains of an old woman, a ghastly looking skeleton still clothed in a tattered dress. The Marine would start to move the box, turn away in disgust, look at the soaking terrain outside, and then start to move the box again. His unhappiness about the whole thing was very obvious.

This story, incidentally, is being written in one of these tombs, but it is one of the better locations. Only a few urns containing bones are present to turn the stomach.

Technical Sgt. Stanford Opotowsky
Okinawa

"The battle ceased only when the last Jap was dead"

A powerful report on fighting in the south's cave-infested Awacha Pocket appeared to be rewritten for space, to remove names of casualties who could not be confirmed, and to delete battlefield gore. The challenge of confirming casualties in time for publication probably meant that some Marines were dropped from stories even though they were indeed wounded. This excerpt from the original dispatch includes Marine Private First Class Thomas M. Hegerty, but he was dropped from the released version when his casualty status could not be confirmed. Hegerty was later awarded the Navy Cross for his actions, the citation noting his injuries.

A "Banzai" attack on the sector of the line held by Fox company revealed the desperation of the Japs as they fought to break the beginning of the battle of Awacha Pocket.

More than 200 enemy soldiers formed the attack force led by a lieutenant colonel. Six Marines and a Navy corpsman broke the full strength of the charge.

These men fired a borrowed machine gun and mowed down 55 Japs. One Marine was killed and four were wounded.

The dead Marine, Clayton E. Nessan, 19, the son of Mrs. Tilda Nessan of 1109 North Duluth Avenue, Sioux Falls, S.D., fired into the Japs after his legs were blown off and died after a grenade blew off his arm.

Corporal Donald C. Munroe, 21, of Kalamazoo, Mich., fired the machine gun until he was hit. His place was taken by Private First Class Thomas M. Hegerty, 19, of Middlesex, N.Y., suffering from a shoulder wound.

Private First Class Robert R. Switzer, 22, of 613 Lynn Street, Findley, Ohio, moved to the assistant gunner position though wounded. The corpsman, Pharmacist's Mate 2/c Billy Cox, 21, of 2864 Reynolds Street, Omaha, Neb., his medical gear destroyed by shrapnel, moved from man to man treating them with makeshift dressings while the Marines continued fighting.

A hand grenade wounded Private First Class Robert F. Gorshing, 28, of Custer City, Okla., but he continued to fight. Private First Class Carl Hollingsworth, 31, of 421 West Willingham Street, Cleburne, Texas, unhurt, joined the charging Japs in an attempt to reach the Marine lines and bring back aid.

He was discovered and killed one of the enemy. For the remainder of the battle he played dead. At daybreak he succeeded.

The main body of Japs came screaming at the Marine line. Terrific fire broke the first wave within 25 feet of the closest Marine.

The Japs retreated, using "knee mortars" to cover their flight. Twice more they attacked the face of the ridge, but the Marines held fast. The battle raged for more than four hours in the pre-dawn and ceased only when the last Jap was dead.

Staff Sgt. Leo T. Batt and Sgt. Walter Wood
Okinawa

"The Japanese diligently mined the house containing sleeping Marines"

The "believe it or not" qualities of events were mainstays of American newspapers. However, a wartime story that would likely upset readers, especially those with relatives and friends in the fight, would understandably go unused by the Marines' public relations operation.

Japanese soldiers infiltrated through the outposts of one Marine unit here, and painstakingly blew up a house in which the only occupants were already dead.

A Marine Graves Registration Unit reported that they had laid several bodies in a house, pending their transfer to the cemetery the next day. That night the Japanese infiltrated, and evidently mistaking the bodies for sleeping members of the unit, diligently mined the house on all sides with dynamite and destroyed it.

Private First Class Stanley R. Leppard
Okinawa

"He described the experience as worse than a nightmare"

Another casualty of time was a report, excerpted here, on the battle for Kunishi Ridge, filed in mid-June but declared "outdated" when received weeks later at division headquarters. Even after five days of day and night fighting, the flat land approaching the ridge was still described as "a bloody no man's land."

At night the ridge was hellish beyond description. At times Marines found Japs advancing on them from all sides, singly and in groups of three or four as they came out of caves for infiltration efforts.

When a group of about 100 Japs pulled a banzai charge, 27 were killed before the others fled.

Private Gene M. Wilson of West Chestnut Street, Oxford, Ohio, who helped break up the charge described the experience as "worse than a nightmare."

He was just going on watch at about 3 a.m., he said, when he saw two men coming toward him. "They were dressed in Marine uniforms, complete to packs and camouflaged helmets."

When Wilson shouted, "Hey Mates, what outfit you with?" he heard a lot of Jap jabbering and the approaching men opened fire. The attack lasted until just before dawn.

"I saw at least 75 Japs moving around," said Wilson. "And they all had bayonets fixed."

The forward slopes of Kunishi Ridge, where Marines are alternately digging in to avoid sniperfire and rushing Jap sniper positions, is a riot of color that gives it a carnival appearance. Red, blue, yellow and white parachutes, used for dropping supplies from planes, are strewn all over an area of 500 yards.

But it's the devil's carnival that's playing on Kunishi Ridge and the heights of Mezado and Kuwanga beyond. In the five days and nights of battle the rifle companies of an entire battalion have been reduced to the strength of a single company. And only three of the original officer complement of the companies are still in action.

Sgt. Joseph P. Donahue
Okinawa

"Select the biggest ship you see and crash dive it"

Two stories, written about a week apart, described Japanese pilots taken prisoner. Both were rejected by CINCPAC, which in keeping with censorship regulations forbade stories about prisoner interrogations.

When a Jap pilot learned his was a suicide mission he decided living with Americans was better than dying for the emperor, so bailed out over Yontan airfield.

The young airman was a commercial pilot, called into military service four months ago. After indoctrination his first combat assignment was over Okinawa. He was told to take off and orders would be sent by radio as he reached the target.

As American ack-ack greeted him, the orders were radioed, "Select the biggest ship you see and crash dive it."

The reaction he explained to a language officer was, "T'hell with this."

Sgt. Harold T. Boian
Okinawa

A novice Japanese airman, captured after his plane was shot down here, expressed great surprise when told he was on Okinawa.

"I was instructed to follow another plane—which I did," he explained to Marines. He said he was "absolutely ignorant of my mission's objective."

The Japanese, a master sergeant, told Marines he was 30 years old and had never flown a combat mission before. He added his flying time totaled only 250 hours.

Staff Sgt. Ed Meagher
Okinawa

Captain John N. Popham, a Marine public relations officer, attached a typed appeal of CINCPAC's general order not to write about enemy interrogations. He contended that the order should be reconsidered for such stories because they suggest that "the Japs are on their last legs in the air, are using obsolescent aircraft and poorly trained or untrained flyers." Nonetheless, CINCPAC killed the story.

"Is that a Jap? What if that's a Marine?"

DPR headquarters may have decided not to use this story of a close encounter with a Japanese soldier because the Marine's "burning ambition" appeared unseemly—or his handling of the situation deemed inadequate. Censorship regulations had warned against indications of "timidity."

On Motobu Peninsula, Corporal Robert A. Siegel, of 59 S. 10th Street, Brooklyn, N.Y., was close enough to part a Jap's hair with one shot, his burning ambition for 17 months.

But when the 35-year-old corporal spoke in the dead of night, the enemy departed the scene and was killed by another Leatherneck.

Since he entered the Corps, in November 1943, Siegel has let it be known generally, "If I could get just one Jap my two daughters would think I was the greatest Marine in the world."

Along toward morning his chance came. He awoke and found a Jap standing 20 feet from his foxhole. Siegel quietly raised his rifle. All he had to do was squeeze the trigger.

Suddenly, he thought, 'What if that's a Marine?' He roused Corporal Pete Ferretti, of Cementon, N.Y., his foxhole buddy. When he asked Ferretti, "Is that a Jap?" the prowler ran.

Another Leatherneck shot him.

Sgt. Harold T. Boian
Okinawa

"The patch of earth surrounding the Jap erupted violently"

An edited version of this Marine's confrontation with a Japanese soldier trimmed details of the soldier's gruesome death. But DPR headquarters withheld the piece when the Marine was reported killed in action three weeks later, his own death making the final paragraph ironic.

The duel was uneven—a bean shooter versus an elephant gun sort of thing—but, after all, the Jap soldier started it.

His opponent was Marine Private Donal B. Liebermann, 21, son of Mr. and Mrs. Ben Liebermann, of 2337 Benton Way, Santa Ana, Calif., a veteran demolitions man of the Sixth Marine Division's Fourth Regiment. He had been hit on the arm by a machine gun bullet the day before, but refused to be evacuated.

The Jap popped from a cave that Liebermann was on his way to seal. The Jap threw a grenade—a strategic error, for the Californian promptly hurled what he was carrying in his hand. He was carrying a stiff charge of TNT.

The patch of earth immediately surrounding the Jap erupted violently before Liebermann's eyes. Dirt—and the Jap—shot upward in a furious cascade. The enemy soldier rose fully 20 feet or more before gravity took hold and returned him—in sections—to the ground.

Liebermann, who fought with a Marine Raider battalion on New Georgia and received a letter of commendation for bomb disposal work on Guam, was hit, but not critically, by fragments of the Jap's grenade.

This time, however, with his second wound in as many days, Navy corpsmen evacuated him. They couldn't keep him out of the action, however. He was back on the line the next day.

Staff Sgt. Ed Meagher
Naha, Okinawa

"The camouflaged enemy runway was perfect"

Information that could benefit the Japanese continued to find its way into dispatches. Telling the enemy what was known about troops and their activities was to be avoided. The first of the following excerpts from stories with content drawing such notations as "killed by CINCPAC" or "do not release" made the stakes clear. "Not released," a censor wrote. "Gives aid and comfort to enemy, showing effectiveness of camouflage." Usually no detailed explanation was provided, only scrawled words "security" or "intelligence."

A ghost-like Japanese fighter strip, which had defied American naval and air bombardment, was found by four Marine Corps officers who were searching for culvert timbers.

So perfect was the camouflage that Yank evacuation planes were using an adjacent concrete highway as a runway.

The fighter strip was disguised as a rice paddy, near the Southern Okinawa town of Itoman, with a drainage ditch, sod banks, bamboo sprouts and several "farmhouses" which could be removed at a moment's notice.

The Japanese diverted a natural stream beneath the coral runway, substituting an imitation one above the culvert.

Staff Sgt. A. D. Hawkins
Okinawa

An Easter present from the Japanese saved the United States many thousands of dollars during the first of the invasion of this important airport island.

The "eggs," delivered into our hands Easter afternoon, were in the form of giant Nippon bombs and, of course, it was the enemy's intention that they be "laid" on our Pacific Armies and Allied ships at sea, but they backfired, Tojo.

Instead, the bombs are being used as demolition charges for the destruction of the Jap military emplacements on this strategic island, which they once termed "the Gibraltar of the China Sea."

When the First and Sixth Marine Divisions stormed the shores of Okinawa on Easter Sunday they succeeded in capturing the Yontan Airfield during the daylight hours.

Near the strip the Leathernecks learned they had not been forgotten by the Easter Bunny. They found an ammo dump with "eggs" of all sizes, bantam up to turkey.

On previous operations, the Marines used dynamite, TNT and other explosives, costing thousands of dollars, to destroy caves, gun emplacements and other strongholds. On Okinawa, the Jap bombs found at Yontan Airfield were used for demolitions work.

Sgt. William Boniface
Okinawa

Out of Okinawa's labyrinth of caves have come death-dealing Japs, frightened civilians and abandoned enemy armament, but Marine Gunnery Sergeant Glen D. Sturges, 32, of Cortaro, Ariz., hit the Jack-pot.

While on a routine patrol of the hillside caverns, the Arizona Marine found 20 cases of Formosan pineapple, and five cases of swordfish, which the Japs left behind in their retreat.

Sturges, whose buddies now are supplementing their "C" and "K" rations with the Jap canned goods, is also a First Marine Division veteran of Cape Gloucester and Peleliu, and an old hand at probing enemy defenses.

Staff Sgt. A.D. Hawkins
Okinawa

In this instance a Navy censor made clear why a section of the story was being cut, writing in red pencil, "No mention permitted of Marines eating Jap food." The rationale was not provided; such information might have encouraged the enemy to leave behind poisoned provisions in future engagements.

Hellcats, the Second Marine Air Wing's night fighter squadron, are getting new bolts of trained "lightning" in their wings for combat air patrol and night strikes.

Previously equipped only with 50 caliber machine guns in the wings, the Hellcats now are sprouting a couple of 20 mm. cannon. Not all of them have "grown" the additional firepower, but until they do it probably is just as well, for the Japs don't know the "haves" from the "have nots" in this respect.

Night fighters are used principally for defensive work in the Pacific, but now that more of them carry the 20's, they are going on strikes against the enemy on other islands. Too, they are equipped with rockets, the silencers of gun emplacements.

Sgt. Claude R. Canup
Okinawa

Japanese army doctors gave lethal shots of morphine to 20 of their badly wounded soldiers, and left them behind to die when the Nipponese forces retreated southward from Shuri, it has been revealed.

The incident took place in a hospital cave near Shuri where there were more than 100 wounded soldiers when the evacuation began.

As Marines of the First Division pushed the Jap lines back, the wounded were brought in and laid on the mud. Water seeped, and sometimes flowed in torrents, through the porous coral walls of the cave.

The only light in the cave was that of the doctor's flashlight.

Even the less seriously wounded were not allowed to go outside the cave entrance and filth accumulated.

Medical supplies were low.

The doctor and hospital corpsmen set out with regular troops, but the walking wounded were left to set out for themselves along roads that were being bombarded by American ships and artillery.

Staff Sgt. George E. McMillan
Okinawa

"He wasn't finished killing Japs"
Too good to be true? This story was killed without a stated reason.

Even when Marine First Lieutenant Allen P. Hensley, of Atwater, Ohio, was being carried from the battlefield on a stretcher, with a bullet in his stomach, he wasn't finished killing Japs.

Hensley was shot in the stomach by a sniper during mopping up operations in the final hours of the Okinawa campaign.

As stretcher bearers carried him to a rear line aid station, Hensley spotted a Jap dart from behind a craggy hill. Lifting his pistol he fired once from the swaying stretcher. The Jap fell dead.

Staff Sgt. George R. Voigt
Okinawa

When Marine combat correspondent Sergeant Joseph Dube polled a handful of Marine veterans of Okinawa after the news of a secret superweapon striking Japan, he found some of them worried. "If this—wachamecallit—secondary irradiation gizmo keeps killing people for years, we'll be stuck here a long time before we can land in Japan," one of them complained. Another told Dube, "I suppose the Air Corps will be getting all the credit for beating the Nips now." Still others had their own parochial view: "Theyda still been looking for someplace to fly their planes from if the Marines hadn't taken Guam, Iwo and Okinawa." Dube reported that a more optimistic strain of thought had it that the war would be over in fewer than thirty days.

Those views were expressed for a story Dube wrote on August 8, 1945, two days after an atomic bomb destroyed the city of Hiroshima and a day before a second atomic bomb was unleashed on Nagasaki. The prediction of Japan's capitulation was accurate, but its decision was not immediate despite the possibility of more atomic strikes. Pushing Emperor Hirohito to accept defeat on American terms—his announcement came August 15—was the added pressure of a Soviet invasion from the north, new doubts that a defensive action could succeed, and questions over whether civil order and the imperial institution itself could survive continued conventional bombing and the prospect of a famine-inducing blockade.

Marine veterans of battles from Guadalcanal to Okinawa rightly took a share of the credit for enabling the bombers carrying their nuclear payloads to hit Japan and return safely. The fight for the Marianas had led to the establishment of an American base at Tinian, the island where the atomic flight crews trained. It was there the bomber named *Enola Gay* was outfitted to carry the uranium bomb "Little Boy" to Hiroshima and then the bomber *Bockscar* with a plutonium cousin, "Fat Man," for its flight to Nagasaki. Support aircraft would rendezvous with each of the B-29 A-bombers over Iwo Jima. When the *Bockscar* ran short of fuel, it landed safely on Okinawa. All the Marines on those and other Pacific islands could look back with pride on their role in bringing the war with Japan to an end.

11

Life in the Marine Corps

Sergeant Bill Ross was among the Marine combat correspondents who witnessed his fellow CCs at their best but also knew them to be complicated human beings. Like his fighter-writer colleagues, the former United Press newsman saw in Marines a deep well of what civilian journalists called "human interest" stories. They could range from the poignant to the comical, from the heartwarming to the tragic, from the serious to the silly. Yet the Marine editors at the Division of Public Relations, at times at the urging of Navy censors, waved off anything that showed Marines in an unflattering light. After all, their purpose was not to entertain readers but to build support for the Marine Corps.

Lost in that PR effort were many stories that depicted day-to-day life in the Marine Corps. A particular victim was the humorous anecdote. A sense of humor, Ross told readers in a dispatch, "is probably one of the Marines' greatest 'secret weapons.'" Laughter, he added, helped keep them from cracking up. "And there really is no telling just how much of a 'weapon' has been the Leathernecks' ability to laugh at infinitely serious situations confronted in the hard-fought Pacific war." That sentiment was struck from Ross's story.

A section of a Navy memo on censored subjects captured the wide swath of potential violations that might arise in everyday stories about Marine life: "Criticism of equipment, appearance, physical condition, or morale of the collective or individual armed forces of the United States or her Allies." The memo added: "Any press dispatch which indicates alleged disunity, timidity, lack of leadership, administrative incompetency, or presumed political interferences within the armed forces of the United States comes within the meaning of this statement." While the memo stated that such material could be used in enemy propaganda, unstated was the likely concern about the response of American readers to such stories.

The following stories are slices of Marine Corps life that drew the attention of Marine writers because of their journalistic training to recognize a story or a colorful character that would engage readers. Many have the qualities of humor that Ross believed were essential for men under the stress of combat. These stories either were not passed by a Navy censor or were put aside by editors at division headquarters. Often such vignettes, many presented here without titles because of their brevity, were withheld from distribution to American media for no stated reason. Context or a rationale has been included here if expressed or if outside the kinds of concerns noted earlier in this collection.

"It's Father O'Neill to you"

No one would deny that the Marine Corps was stocked with vivid or eccentric personalities. A profile of a cantankerous Irish Catholic priest, Father William Richard O'Neill, lost some of its color when it strayed into describing violations of military regulations, including insubordination. The following segments were cut from the original six-page feature story, as were the descriptions of O'Neill's "hair-trigger temper" and the time the Navy chaplain quieted the foul talk in a nearby tent by letting the Marines have it "in their own language."

Thus, it is not the least surprising that Father O'Neill lost his temper one day on the front lines at Guadalcanal, as he was being fired upon by Japanese snipers while holding confession in a fox-hole. Father O'Neill muttered softly yet eloquently at the Japs.

So acrid was the Padre's ire that he grabbed the gun that was lying at his side, aiming it in the general direction of the Japs. In a voice which revealed the Irish of his forebears and the Manhattan of his nativity, "I'll teach those undersized, bowlegged sons of the Devil to interrupt confession," the Padre shouted.

Then the Padre remembered that chaplains are noncombatants. With a reluctant effort of self-denial he lowered the rifle, crowded his considerable bulk even lower in the foxhole and heard the remainder of the confession . . .

The padre narrowly avoided being kicked out of the Navy only a week after he enlisted. The Navy gives all prospective chaplains a six-week course of instruction in military courtesy, Naval customs, and the manual of arms. It was the latter which caused difficulty, not only to the Padre but to all other priests as well. When the order, "right shoulder arms" was shouted by the officer in charge, the result was chaotic. One or two executed the order correctly, but the rest placed their weapon on their left shoulders or dropped it on the deck.

Father O'Neill was the target of scorn. As the Padre tells the story, he was no worse off than the rest, but he was singled out because his six-foot-three build made him so conspicuous.

"Hey, you, O'Neill," the lieutenant shouted. But he got no further. The Padre threw his rifle on the ground, broke ranks, walked up to the officer, shook a gigantic finger under the instructor's nose and said:

"Look here, I studied for fourteen years to become a priest. It's Father O'Neill to you."

Then he executed an about-face, picked up his rifle and took his place in the ranks with an angelic expression on his face while the countenance of the young Lieutenant grew purple with anger and frustration.

"The Commanding Officer," the Padre relates, "called me up on the carpet for that breach of military etiquette and debated whether to kick me out of the service. 'Don't you realize,' he said sternly, 'that we're trying to make a military man out of you?' He let me go, but thereafter I was called Father O'Neill."

Staff Sgt. Samuel Shaffer
A U.S. Marine Base in New Zealand

"This Shangri-la is as real as beer, baseball, and hamburgers"

A Navy censor had no objection to distributing this story of a pleasure island operating in the Pacific theater. Yet at DPR headquarters it was marked "file" and "not used." Public relations officers may have thought the description of American servicemen at play when the war news in mid-1943 was often grim would not sit well with the public. In the author James Hilton's popular novel Lost Horizon, *published in 1933 and filmed in 1937, Shangri-La was a faraway utopian society.*

James Hilton's Shangri-la is still a romantic dream. President Roosevelt's Shangri-la turned out to be the aircraft carrier Hornet.

But this Shangri-la, somewhere in the Pacific, is as real as beer, baseball, and hamburgers.

Thousands of miles from home, this Shangri-la lies in a natural amphitheater facing the sea, in the outer harbor of an advanced Allied naval base.

The Navy discovered the spot, and lost no time in converting it into a playground for sailors, Marines, and merchant ship crews, whose vessels were anchored in the harbor.

The entire Pacific is in the war zone, and at sea there is neither time or space for recreation.

But this quiet bay, where the ships are being refueled, or unloaded, or provisioned, the tense ready-for-battle routine is eased up enough for the crews of ships to go ashore in small parties and relax in the way they used to back in the States.

There are half a dozen baseball diamonds on Shangri-la, basketball courts, horseshoe lanes, tag-football fields, with ample ground for all kinds of sports events. The Pacific's on hand for swimming, and the multicolored foothills forming a semicircle around Shangri-la, are fine for climbing and shaking off the sea-legs.

Recreation parties get either the morning or afternoon at Shangri-la. Every sailor and Marine, no sooner does he get his feet ashore, is given two bottles of beer as an appertif for the day's fun. (Drinking is not permitted on Navy warships.) Soon, too, the barbecue pits are ready with the hot dogs, or hamburgers, or on a particularly lucky day, with the steaks, together with the onions, mustard, and catsup.

Usually, there's a big baseball game, between two ships, and after, the ship's band together with their own entertainers put on a show. Corny? Sure! This ain't Broadway, brother.

The lads are mellow when they pile into the launches at dusk and start chugging out to their ships, and between the songs and chanteys, between the spray and cool evening air, the crews return with high spirits and healthy appetites, and wondering what they'll have for chow.

Staff Sgt. Samuel E. Stavisky
Somewhere in the Pacific

"Things looked pretty dark until the bride-to-be appeared at camp"

Love has found a way under many unusual circumstances but seldom does it find a solution in a wash bucket full of soiled Marine clothing as it did in the case of Private Fred M. Sellers, 20, and Clara Mae McCoy.

Caught unprepared by a surprise inspection of clothing, Private Sellers was confined to his quarters because he had only dirty clothes to display. That wouldn't have been a major catastrophe had it not been for the fact that he was to marry Miss McCoy of P.O. Box 696, Abilene, Texas, the following day.

Things looked pretty dark until the attractive 19-year-old bride-to-be appeared at this desert camp, demanded the clothes and proceeded to turn out as beautiful a washing as has ever been seen in the 2nd Airdrome Battalion.

When Private Sellers proudly displayed his future wife's handiwork to his Gunnery Sergeant, the hard-boiled "Gunny" relented and lifted the restriction.

The couple were married in Yuma, Arizona, on Sunday, May 16 with the blessing of the officer of the day who fell prey to the bride's smile and released the Leatherneck from a tour of guard duty for the occasion.

A native of Abilene, Texas, Private Sellers is the son of Mr. and Mrs. Fred M. Sellers, P.O. Box 56, Eastland, Texas.

Sgt. Bob Stinson
Camp Dunlap, California

"I don't know if it was my fault or the censor's"

This story suggesting a mistake may have been made by a censor checking Marine mail for security issues was killed by another censor.

One Marine corporal out here is in trouble, and it has nothing to do with the Japs.

This corporal, who must go unnamed for "security" reasons, wrote two letters recently. One was to his wife back in the States. The other was to a girl acquaintance he made in New Zealand, where he was stationed before coming to this tropical island.

The letters got mixed up.

"I don't know whether it was my fault, or the censor's," says the corporal, "but the letter to my wife got in the envelope to the New Zealand girl, and this girl's letter ended up in the envelope to my wife.

"I found out about it just today. The New Zealand girl returned my wife's letter, with a note saying, 'Guess you're in the soup now.'

"All I did in the New Zealand letter was thank this girl for sending me some cookies. I hope my wife understands when she gets the letter."

Staff Sgt. Milburn McCarty Jr.
Guadalcanal

"A Marine staff sergeant has been doing a lot of explaining"

Somewhere on the seven seas there is probably a mighty embarrassed sailor.

For at this remote outpost is a Marine Staff Sergeant who has been doing a lot of explaining, via the mails, to his wife because of that sailor and a clothing store's error.

Staff Sergeant Aldon J. Sexton is a 28-year-old communications man who is about to become a father.

Some time ago he made arrangements with a women's clothing establishment back in civilization to send a maternity dress to his wife at Maysville, Oklahoma.

At the same time a sailor (name and address unknown) sent his girlfriend a box of sports clothes and "unmentionables."

A mixup caused the sailor's gift to be sent to the Sexton home. And the supposition is that the maternity dress went to the seaman's girl friend.

Sgt. Bob Stinson
Nukufetau

"Transported from the grim business at hand by movie magic"

Seeing a movie in the South Pacific is a far cry from seeing it in the lush comfort of Radio City Music Hall in New York or, for that matter, in any movie palace back home, but make no mistake about it, movies rank right behind mail as the overseas morale boosters.

The men may have to sit on coconut logs, upturned oil drums, or on the ground or they may have to stand on the jam-packed deck of a transport to see the movie. But those inconveniences are of little moment to troops who are transported from the grim business at hand by the familiar make believe of the motion pictures.

The Marines out in the South Pacific are quite an audience, too. They put up with great discomforts to see the show, spend hours of patient waiting for the movie to begin, and will sit for hours through drenching rain to see the end of the movie.

It is surprising what audiences will flock to the impromptu theaters. One outfit alone drew nightly audiences running into the thousands. The men wandered over to the show right after their evening chow about 5 o'clock although the movie didn't begin until darkness permitted the use of the outdoor screen.

They like their melodrama straight, their love scenes torrid and their chorus girls any old way. The sight of a shapely girl is always sure of a big hand.

Their reactions are like the audiences of the old ten-twenty-thirty "mellers." Ida Lupino would have thrilled as she heard the hisses which greeted her vixen role in "The Hard Way."

At the end when she meets the death which is her just punishment, one Marine shouted:

"Die like a dog, you ——."

On the other hand, it was Yehudi Menuhin's violin playing which got the biggest reception of any of the conglomeration of stars in "Stage Door Canteen" and although most found "The Magnificent Ambersons" much too talkative, many commented that they liked the thoughtful production.

The movies are often interrupted by air raids, particularly when the moon was so bright it dulled the image on the screen but lighted the target for the enemy.

As they crouched in the foxhole, the Marines would shout:

"Let's secure this damn air raid and get on with the movie."

They weren't so afraid of bombs, they were just annoyed at the interruption.

One of the stories they tell about Marine movie audiences can't be vouched for. Here it is though:

Gene Autry's life was in peril during one of the hotter moments of one of his wooly westerns. The villain was creeping up on Autry, bent on dire things for Gene.

Suddenly, a Marine in the audience whipped out a .45, put two neat holes through the image of the villain and called victoriously:

"Never mind, Gene, I got him."

Sgt. James E. Hague
Guadalcanal

"Native elders turned out to inspect this creature from the Bronx"

Taste likely was the main reason this humorous report drew the markings "suggest no!" even though passed by a censor. Another reason may have been the depiction of native islanders as easy targets of mockery.

Should a resident of the Bronx ever find himself on this remote island and have a native shy away from him when he admits the place of his origin is the Bronx, he can thank, or cuss, the Marines were making the Bronx and "bad medicine" synonymous.

Started as a gag, allegedly by a Brooklynite, the legend that anyone hailing from the New York borough is a dangerous warrior, or "bad medicine," has spread throughout a nearby native village.

Uninitiated Leathernecks are amazed when native youngsters suddenly break into a screaming run whenever a Marine is identified as a "Bronx man."

Before the embarrassed Marine can make a hasty withdrawal, he usually must pass through a gauntlet of intermingled looks of awe and speculation. They are looks directed at him by the assembled elders who turn out to inspect this creature from the Bronx.

So hilarious has the joke become that practically every Leatherneck visitor to the village is stamped with the Bronx label, whether he comes from Titusville or Weehawken.

But the crowning surprise is sprung when a loin clothed kid lets go with what he is convinced is the accepted war cry of all Bronx "bad medicine" men—that king of the razzberries, the Bronx Cheer.

Sgt. Bob Stinson
Somewhere in the South Pacific

"As natives go, she could be considered pretty close to beautiful"

Marine combat correspondent Sergeant Bob Stinson wrote another story focused on native islanders the same day he related the joke aimed at Marines from the Bronx. It, too, was not used after it reached DPR headquarters. In this case, it may have been held back for the embarrassment it would have caused the young Marine. Patronizing attitudes toward island natives, including women's physical features, often surfaced in CC dispatches.

Private First Class Ross Scott had his back washed last night by a comely South Sea Island maiden.

He hasn't quite gotten over the surprise. And he "probably never will."

The 22-year-old Marine from Hot Springs, Ark., got involved in the blush-provoking episode when he accepted an invitation to a native dance.

"The girl wasn't exactly the Hollywood version of a Pacific island queen," says the Leatherneck. "But as natives go, she could be considered pretty close to beautiful."

The anti-aircraft gun crew member of a Marine airdrome battalion stationed on this remote island is not only a Marine, but an accomplished painter. His art training has accustomed him to nudity in all forms. Therefore, he's not easily embarrassed by it.

However, to receive an unexpected bath at the hands of a scantly clad girl under the approving eye of her fond father is not in the agendum of either an artist or a Marine.

The bath was administered after a supper of wild bananas and other delicacies identifiable only by a native. The family, of which the Leatherneck was a guest, repaired to the back of their shack where the "Skytilleryman" was invited to bathe.

He didn't exactly feel in need of a bath, but not wishing to offend his host, he made dilatory motions. He assumed, naturally, that the female members of the family would make themselves scarce before he disrobed.

The older daughter, "about 18," tired of the delay and proceeded to assist the amazed Marine with his undressing.

When all his clothing had been removed she began an industrious scrubbing of his back. Mama and papa and the kids performed their ablutions with an occasional approving glance at their guest.

Discreet questioning on the part of Private First Class Scott convinced him he was not the victim of B.O.

It's just a native custom to bathe before dancing, he found out.

"And I guess it's just a human American custom to get kinda upset when a shapely dame washes your back," the former Louisiana Tech student says.

P.S. Private First Class Scott had a "swell" time at the dance, despite the fact the loin cloth his host insisted he wear instead of trousers kept slipping off, he says.

Sgt. Bob Stinson
Somewhere in the South Pacific

"A gun to use when he runs into his first Jap"
A Navy censor suggested not using this story out of concern that shipping a handgun through the mail violated postal regulations.

Marine Private Charles B. Hansford, 26, of 2824 St. Paul Street, Chicago, a Marine intelligence scout, has received a .45-caliber Colt pistol from his brother, John, deputy sheriff of Williamson County, Ill.

The pistol, Deputy Sheriff Hansford wrote, was taken from a small-fry Chicago gangster who became entangled with the county law enforcers. The serial number had been filed off by the gangster, so that its ownership was untraceable. But, added brother sheriff, serial number or not, it probably could be used by brother Marine when he runs into his first Jap.

Private Hansford is the son of Mr. and Mrs. C.O. Hansford, of Johnston City, Ill., where he formerly served as a special policeman. His wife, Flora, lives at 2824 St. Paul Street, Chicago.

Technical Sgt. Samuel E. Stavisky
Somewhere in the Southwest Pacific

"Single words now explain the most adverse conditions"

Ever since Hannibal forgot to shoe his elephants' hooves before crossing the Alps, Armies, Navies, and Marine Corps' have considered themselves all fouled-up.

And they are.

But not until this war did every man in the service have such ready descriptions of the abnormal situations.

With cursing on the wane—at least that which is eloquent enough to be worth listening to—single words now explain the most adverse conditions.

Let's suppose that early in the morning a Marine Sergeant is told to take a truck and ten men on a ten mile ride to a neighboring unit to pick up a half-dozen tents.

Being a good sergeant, he will genially approach his platoon and ignore the fact that no one will volunteer for the job.

Having chosen his ten volunteers with the casual wave of the hand, he walks to the truck.

But the truck isn't to be found.

"Snafu," he spits out, points out a volunteer from his ten-man working party and orders him to find the truck.

Snafu means "situation normal, all fouled up."

The volunteer returns with the truck, but without a driver.

"Snisfu," says the sergeant, and since everyone wants to drive he volunteers for the job himself.

Snisfu means "situation normal, it's still fouled up."

Arriving at the neighboring but unneighborly camp, the sergeant discovers that while the tents are there, they still are pitched.

"Tarfu," the sergeant murmurs.

Tarfu means "things are really fouled up."

Just as the tents have been struck and loaded, a second lieutenant appears to insist that the tents belong to the Army, and that neither the Navy nor the Marine Corps can have them.

"Janfu," shrugs the sergeant.

Janfu means "joint army-navy foul up."

The ten volunteers cheerfully pitch the tents again, slyly poke holes in the canvas as they do.

There is another word covering the opposite of the situation described, but it never has been used.

It is "Sanfu."

Sanfu means "situation abnormal, not fouled up."

> Technical Sgt. Howard E. Biggerstaff
> Munda Field, New Georgia

"Sorry, sir, but I have orders"

Passed by a censor but later marked "kill," the story, abridged here, of a conscientious Marine guard might have been thought to show up a three-star general.

With the assault troops landing under extremely heavy Jap machine-gun and mortar fire here on November 20 were a company of Marine Military Police.

And right up front was the shortest member of the group, whose duty it is to keep the other Marines in check. Private Julius W. Cotten, of North Liberty Street, Canton, Mississippi. He is only five feet five and one-quarter inches tall, but he doesn't have too much trouble with obstreperous Gyrenes. "I can usually take care of them," he says confidently.

Private Cotten was with Colonel Carlson's Raiders in the raid on Makin some months ago, so the Gilberts were familiar territory for him.

At our last base before hitting Tarawa, Private Cotten was detailed to stand guard at the door of the secret planning room, where the strategy for this campaign was being decided on, and to permit no one to enter without the proper pass.

One day Lieutenant General Vandegrift paid a brief visit to Headquarters and accompanied Major General Julian C. Smith, Commanding General of the Second Marine Division, and Brigadier General Leo D. Hermle, Assistant Division Commander, to the Planning Room.

Generals Smith and Hermle showed their passes. General Vandegrift attempted to cross the threshold but was stopped by Private Cotten, who prodded his carbine into the General's ribs.

"Sorry, sir," he said, "but I have orders not to admit anyone without a pass."

Lieutenant General Vandegrift identified himself, but Private Cotten was adamant.

Finally a Colonel had to go down to the office on the deck below and have a pass made out and signed by the proper officers. Only then was he admitted by the short MP.

When he came out, General Vandegrift complimented Private Cotten on his conscientious performance of his duty.

"It's the only time in my life," recalls Private Cotten, "that I only stuck a carbine into the ribs of a three-star general."

Staff Sgt. Fred Feldkamp
Tarawa

Marines will have their joke—regardless of place, time or conditions.

Near a bivouac area on Cape Gloucester is a straddle trench with a neat pile of dirt beside it. On a shovel stuck into the dirt is a sign, printed in block letters. It reads:

"Please Flush."

Staff Sgt. Joseph L. Alli
New Britain

"I hope Mom doesn't find out I'm down here"

Seldom did a Navy censor or the editors at the public relations newsroom comment on the impact a story might have on the subject or his family. This story presented no security issues, but a censor pointed to the young Marine being quoted and suggested that those evaluating the story for publication "consider his own desires as expressed." Subsequently, the Navy killed the piece.

"Gee, I hope Mom don't know where I am—she'd be scared stiff!"

No, it wasn't his imminent meeting with the Japs that had Private First Class George W. Rambow, 20-year-old Marine of Solen, N.D., frightened—it was the fact that his mother might find out where he was and "get worried all over the place."

Private First Class Rambow was punching cows on his uncle's ranch a year ago—and now he'd "like to punch a Jap—or slit his throat."

"Yeah," he said in a slow drawl, "I liked punchin' cows—you see Dad died, Mom is teaching school and there are the kids—and what I did brought in a little more." The "kids," as Private First Class Rambow fondly refers to his two younger brothers and three sisters, are James, 18, a Seaman, second class, U.S. Navy, who is stationed at Navy Pier in Chicago; Charles, 11, Peggy, 16, Mary Ellen, 14 and Helen, 9.

"I saw some of those Japs at Makin Island (Gilbert Group) and they're not so hot! I'm not a bit afraid of 'em," Private First Class Rambow drawled. "But I didn't write Mom that I'd been there," he added with caution. "I hope she doesn't find out I'm down here."

"Mom" is Mrs. Henry L. Rambow, who teaches in the Cannonball, N.D., country school "where the farmers' kids go to class."

Private First Class Rambow enlisted in the Marine Corps last April at Mandan, N.D., with "Mom's" consent.

Technical Sgt. Walter C. Cochrane
Aboard Flagship, off Kwajalein, Marshall Islands

"Sweet violets, covered all over from head to toe"

Along about dusk the boys come trodding along the path back from the beer garden, carrying a couple of quarts of brew under their belts. Most of the time they get to putting their croonin' voices together. By straining an ear it can faintly be made out that the tune is "Sweet Violets." The song has a couple of home-made lines which need cleaning up a mite. But it's all in the spirit of fun, and dedicated to Private First Class Salvatore "Sal" Ciuffreda of Washington, D.C.

The story around it began when "Sal" stepped into a ditch on the Namur battlefield, and his feet began to sink down lower every time he wiggled, and tried to get out.

"Sal" was yelling bloody murder and hollering for a rope. When the boys found him, he was all the way up to his ears in what looked like mud.

Well, "Sal" figured he was sinking in quicksand, and that he was a goner for sure. Finally he stopped squirming and his feet hit bottom. The boys stretched out a helping hand and yanked him out.

When "Sal" shook off the "quicksand" he noticed the boys kept away from him just like he was a dengue fever mosquito or even worse. He perked up his nose and got a whiff of what had an odor like a bunch of Japs that had been corpses for a week.

When "Sal" thought about it, he reasoned out that there wasn't any quicksand in the Marshall Islands. It dawned on him just what he had fallen in up to his ears. The boys were between the wind and "Sal," but he could make out what they were croonin'—"Sweet violets, covered all over from head to toe, covered all over with . . ."

"Sal" isn't one to get all worked up over a ribbing, but in a way he's a bit down in the dumps. It doesn't look to "Sal" as though he'll get any rest until there's a pad-lock on the beer house and the place is closed up. For it's only when the boys get dry tonsils that they don't go in for croonin'.

Sgt. Edward F. Ruder
Namur Island, Kwajalein Atoll, Marshall Islands

When the talk in this Fourth Marine Division outfit turns to what medals and ribbons they will rate after six beerless, bathless, breathless weeks fighting in the Marianas, Chief Marine Gunner William Laverty Jr., of 21 Dales Avenue, Jersey City, N.J., has the untoppable answer.

"The only ribbon I'm interested in," drawls the gunner, "is Pabst Blue Ribbon. They can keep the rest for that fighting rear echelon."

Sgt. Bob Cooke
Saipan

Before a Marine fighter pilot landed on this island his mother asked him quite frequently if he couldn't be a little more newsier in his letters home.

During the early weeks of the campaign here, the 21-year-old Marine was able to be a little more explicit. Within the censorship regulations he explained that he was bombing and strafing the enemy among other things.

Today in each of the four letters he received from his mother she asked him if he wouldn't explain what strafing meant.

Technical Sgt. Bill Goodrich
Peleliu

A group of Fourth Marine Division artillery men here are writing Army Air Forces General Arnold, asking him to send a supply of the latest phonograph records along with next bomb load he sends to Tokyo.

A favorite radio program out here is the Jap propaganda broadcaster, "Tokyo Rose," but the boys are beginning to tire of her album of vintage disks and the only way they can think of to get new records to her is via a B-29.

Sgt. John B. T. Campbell Jr.
Tinian

A Marine chaplain sounded the call for worship on this first Sunday since the completion of the Saipan-Tinian campaign. The response was not as enthusiastic as it had been recently and this the chaplain noted as he stepped before the shrunken group.

"I perceive," he said, lugubriously surveying the handful of the faithful, "that the shooting has stopped."

The laughter that followed this remark was so general that even the chaplain had to join in.

Sgt. John B. T. Campbell Jr.
Tinian

Before the battle for Guam, Marine Corporal Charles A. Coleman, 19, of 1305 Park Street, Pierre, S.D., christened his heavy, untried machine gun "The Impatient Virgin."

The second day of the assault found the corporal and his gun, now tested by the heat of battle, in a front line emplacement. Corporal Coleman, paint brush in hand, was busy renaming his weapon "Hot Mama."

Technical Sgt. Donald A. Hallman Sr.
Guam

Navy mail censors are nearly always good for a story and here is the latest to date.

A Marine M.T. Sergeant of this command wrote a thirteen-page sugar report to the little woman back Stateside. To the envelope he attached the following note addressed to the censor:

"During the last eight months I have written but half a dozen short notes in all for censorship, therefore, I hope the censor will bear with me and have patience with this lengthy exposition. Thanks."

Not to be outdone, the censor returned the letter to the Sergeant with the following remarks attached:

"Please limit your letters to two pages. No patience. Air mail overloaded. You're welcome."

Sgt. Herman Chapel
Guam

Lieutenant William F. McClain, 610 West Walnut Street, Lancaster, Pa., a Navy chaplain with the Marine Corps, tells a story on himself.

During the battle of Guam a shell fragment shattered the helmet of a Marine lying next to him. The Marine, fearing the worst had happened, asked the chaplain to pray for him.

The chaplain did.

"Am I going to die?" the Marine then asked.

"I hardly think so," answered the chaplain, "you only have a slight nick on the back of your head."

The Marine looked up questioningly:

"Well, why did you pray for me then?"

Sgt. Edward F. Ruder
Somewhere in the Pacific

Every motion picture shown at the various theater areas of the First Marine Division is assigned a service rating.

Films such as "Mrs. Parkington," and "Once Upon a Time," drew 4.0 top billings from Marine critics. "The Fighting Seabees" was listed as 3.5.

But every time a training film is scheduled, the bulletin board reads:

"Training Film—0.0."

Sgt. Joseph P. Donahue
Somewhere in the South Pacific

An ever-present sense of humor, an invaluable asset to lighten the strain of combat, is increasingly reflected by the number of signs painted by Marines in this war-ravaged island. One sign, situated near the base of Mount Surabachi, reads:

Suribachi Heights Real Estate Company
Ocean view—Cool Breeze
Plenty of Fireworks Free.
———
See Us for Choice Foxhole Sites—Don't Delay!
You May be Sorry!

Over the entrance to one Leatherneck's foxhole "home," you see the words: "Bombs and Slant Eyes, Keep Out!"

And another foxhole "door" bears the legend: "Through these portals pass the most homesick people on earth."

Sgt. Bill Ross
Iwo Jima

A month after the victory at Iwo Jima, Sergeant Bill Ross submitted an eight-page collection of Marine humor during battles over the course of the war. "Wherever the Marines have fought, they have also taken a supply of humor, the American variety," Ross wrote. DPR headquarters later noted that several magazines had rejected the piece. It concluded, "Just not good enough execution of a good idea." Excerpted here are some of the punch lines.

From an amphibious landing: A youthful Leatherneck was lying in a foxhole with an older Marine. Jap mortars were falling hot and heavy and enemy artillery was much in evidence. The whine of ricocheting bullets cut through the air. "This sure as hell is a young man's war," the young Marine said, "but as soon as you get in it, you're an old man—and getting older by the second!"

From Bougainville: Suddenly the jungle seemed to come alive with Jap soldiers. They opened up from everywhere with everything from small arms to mortars to spasmodic artillery shelling. Then all was quiet. A voice was heard through the eerie silence of the hot, steaming jungle: "Does anyone have an old, cold beer they don't want?" asked the unknown Leatherneck.

From Guam: Marines circulated a mimeographed handbill along the front line reading: "Tonight! Banzai Charge! Thrills!!! Chills!!! Suspense!!! See Sake-Crazed Japs Charge at High Port! See Everybody Shoot Everybody. See the Cream of the Marine Corps Play With Live Ammunition. Sponsored by The Athletic & Morale Office. Come Along and Bring a Friend. Don't Miss the Thrilling Spectacle of the Banzai Charge. Starting at 10 p.m. and lasting all night!! Admission Free!!!"

From Peleliu: One Marine unit had to climb a steep hill to seize a crest dominating a wide range of fire. Casualties were heavy. An unidentified Marine had hastily printed a small sign and placed it at the foot of the slope: "Escalator out of order. Please use stairs and proceed at your own risk."

From Iwo Jima: "I missed winning the Purple Heart," the Marine said. "But if they'd seen me getting out of the way of some of those shells, I'd get the Distinguished Flying Cross—and that's damned hard to win in the infantry!"

Also from Iwo Jima: Hidden from view of his comrades by a steep ridge, he was approximately 100 yards from our lines. Asked by his command post what the situation was "up there," the Marine answered over the field telephone: "I'm not married, but I reckon this is like being the bridegroom of the devil's daughter—and living with her folks."

Sgt. Bill Ross
Iwo Jima

A Marine (Private Thomas J. Weiner, Newark, N.J.) tells the story of the doughty warrior who perched a machine gun, automatic rifle and two carbines over the sand bags around his foxhole on the Iwo Jima beach.

"What are all the weapons for?" asked the Marine. "The nearest Jap is a mile from here."

"Well, in case one does come," came the reply, "I want to be sure I get him."

Sgt. Edward F. Ruder
Iwo Jima

Doctors haven't heard of it and neither has Hollywood but battle-weary Marines after days of fighting on this rocky island coined a new name for a minor wound forcing the men to be evacuated from the battlefront.

"It's the 'Hollywood hit' and off you go," says Marine Corporal Donald V. Murphy, 24, whose wife, LaVerne, and mother, Mrs. Mary E. Murphy, live at 15427 Rockford Avenue, San Fernando, Calif.

"When a Marine was hit in the flabby part of the arm or leg by a bullet or shrapnel and the wound necessitated hospital attention, we called it a 'Hollywood Hit.' Off he went in a stretcher or an ambulance jeep to a rear area," Murphy said. "Yes, it got to be a standing joke and the fellows kidded anyone getting a minor wound."

Sgt. Chester H. Smith
Iwo Jima

This story was rejected because editors deemed that it featured "an illegal practice."

Day after day a metallic symphony in one key was played over and again by Marines of the veteran Fourth Division as they fashioned rings from 50-cent pieces on ships returning from Iwo Jima.

This pastime, an energetic outlet from the boredom of life aboard a navy transport, was so popular that the din sounded like a thousand metal-billed woodpeckers pecking at the door of a bank vault.

Marines squatted on hatch covers and any available deck space to pound holes out of Uncle Sam's bullion. Spoons, knife hilts and other strange tools served as hammers.

The hobby was pursued violently from sunrise to sunset each day until interest flagged and finally petered out about the middle of the voyage.

One Marine explained that this unusual practice should be adopted by all members of the armed forces to prevent inflation after the war.

Sgt. Robert A. Hunter
Somewhere in the Pacific

A profit-minded Marine was ready to corner the early souvenir market even before American forces landed at this Japanese inner defensive bastion.

He spent most of his time aboard the transport en route manufacturing "genuine Japanese" souvenirs which he planned to sell at fancy prices on the island.

His stock included carved wooden idols, wood blocks with "Japanese" inscriptions, polished shells, chopsticks and fans. In reserve he had several hundred Japanese postcards captured at Guam and Peleliu.

Staff Sgt. Ray Fitzpatrick
Okinawa

Ten bucks is the limit for American servicemen now headed for the onslaught against the Jap bastion of Okinawa.

That, according to orders, is the maximum amount you can take ashore with you. The purpose is to prevent inflation at Okinawa. American military authorities were concerned with the runaway prices which resulted in the Philippines when U.S. troops spent their money recklessly, and they hope to prevent the same thing from occurring again.

It should be pointed out that everything a Marine, or soldier needs at Okinawa will be provided, and that he will have little real need for spending money. And if he does have to make an emergency touch, the paymasters will be ashore not many days after the assault troops.

2nd Lt. Milburn McCarty Jr.
En route to Okinawa

The first letter a Marine received here contained a ten dollar bill and a note explaining he could use it to make purchases.

On Okinawa the only stores which may be open are in Naha, still in enemy hands and under a terrific Marine and Navy artillery barrage.

Sgt. Leo T. Batt
Okinawa

She married another guy.

Her explanation and a bill for a toilet set which he never ordered, reached Marine Private First Class John P. Terrence, 23, of 1416 Beverly Road, Brooklyn, N.Y., in his last mail before he hit the beach here.

Terrence read the last line of the letter, "I love my husband, and God Bless you."

Then he ripped open the other letter. It was a bill from the same store where he had purchased the girl's Christmas present. A new item was listed: One toilet set, $2.75.

Across the bottom of the slip Terrence wrote, "What toilet set? Besides, she married another guy."

Then he returned the slip and the letter from the girl to the company.

Sgt. Harold T. Boian
Okinawa

"Beans and bombs: How to make foxhole coffee"

A prime example of a slice of Marine life is Technical Sergeant Murray Lewis's story on how Marines could make coffee in a foxhole. Why was it not distributed? Submitted as the battle for Okinawa began its third month and the war in the Pacific halfway through its fourth year, the story may have seemed too light.

A few of the Marines in this unit are coffee lovers. From watching them, this correspondent has been able to find out just what that means.

Three days after landing here, one of them "scrounged" a 20 pound tin of coffee grounds. It has been with us ever since, through heavy rains and permeating mud.

First, we had to have a coffee pot. Nothing else being available, the grounds were poured into a cardboard box and the tin became our "Joe pot."

How it has ever remained in condition suitable for use, no one will ever know. All of us were indoctrinated, by good old American advertising, to believe that the only coffee worth buying was either "vacuum-sealed," homogenized, dated, or concocted by a long tradition of experts.

We also remember that we were constantly cautioned to brew the potent liquid in specific types of containers, or to maintain certain hygienic precautions if we were after "that delicious aroma."

Well, the copy writers could come out here for some facts. We have learned that coffee is coffee, wet or dry, muddy or not, and the blacker the better. It is the only accepted way to face the day after a night in a foxhole, or to mentally blot out the rain or the cold.

They might be appalled if they looked into our coffee box and saw the crust of slime that we have learned protects it from the elements. Instead of the recommended mathematical method of measuring out the grounds, we use the "fist rule"—so many fists to a pot of water.

Making the coffee is simple. When the water reaches the boiling point, the grounds are dropped in and stirred into the liquid. About half a canteen of cold water is poured into the pot immediately. This settles the grounds to the bottom.

Here is the only controversial point. One school of foxhole coffee-making insists that the grounds should be in the pot while the water is still cold, thus allowing a more perfect blend. Either way, the result is always hot, and good.

We will have to concede the point about cleanliness, however, even if we can't detect any loss of aroma. The water scarcity being what it is, we have dispensed with frequent washing of the coffee pot. Fresh water is poured over the old grounds and a new batch is on the way. When the amount of grounds is greater than the quantity of water (by volume, that is, according to precipitation and doodad), we know it is time to wash the pot.

Some day, of course, all of us expect to get home. When that happens, we don't know how we're going to take to the scientifically correct, perfectly proportioned potion that we used to smack our lips over. Perhaps the manufacturers may be forced to market a special service men's brand.

If so, instead of the hothouse variety ordinarily dispensed, the bean would be thoroughly saturated with murky water, dragged through mud and pulverized into the proper grind by a steam roller on a sandy road.

Technical Sgt. Murray Lewis
Okinawa

Epilogue

When the US Marine Corps transitioned from a wartime footing to peacetime pursuits, its Division of Public Relations underwent significant changes. The estimated average overseas tour of a combat correspondent had been two years; in early 1945, many DPR personnel were already returning to the States to join division operations in Washington or offices around the country. Some were receiving medical discharges or being released after having reached the age of thirty-eight. As the nation's war machine wound down following Japan's surrender, the DPR began reducing its personnel at a faster pace. Division demands were changing as well, the most notable being the decision to stop requiring the "Joe Blow" stories so favored by hometown media. Public interest was shifting to postwar issues; what the local boys were doing after the shooting stopped was probably of little interest to readers. By September 1946, the DPR's ranks had been reduced by nearly half. Two other important changes had taken place during that first postwar year: It was renamed the Division of Public Information, and its commander, General Robert L. Denig, retired. His idea for seeding the Corps with journalists trained as Marines lived on, though continually modified during peacetime years interrupted by Korea and wars to follow.

Many of Denig's "fighter writers" returned to the news business when they resumed their civilian lives. Some pursued work in other forms of media, including television and motion pictures, and some in public relations. Several went on to write memoirs, novels, or battlefield history that encompassed their experiences in the Pacific war. For example, James W. Hurlbut, who had shipped out to Guadalcanal and became the first Marine combat correspondent to report from a war zone, took a job with NBC's staff in Chicago and appeared on news programs. In 1965, twenty years after he was released from active duty, Hurlbut returned to the Marines at the request of the commandant to produce film reports on the Vietnam War as the chief of the service's pictorial branch. He died unexpectedly in 1967 at age fifty-seven, by then a Marine colonel, and was buried at Arlington National Cemetery.

Herbert Merillat, the first Marine public relations officer on Guadalcanal, left the military and wrote for *Time* magazine, later worked for US government foreign aid organizations, and pursued a career in international law. He eventually turned to writing articles for various publications as a full-time freelancer. In 1982 he published a more personal look at his experiences in the country's first offensive of the war, *Guadalcanal Remembered*, a companion of sorts to his first book on the battle, *The Island*, published in 1944. He died in 2010 at age ninety-four in Washington, DC.

Pete Zurlinden had worked for Ohio newspapers and in the Annapolis, Maryland, bureau of the Associated Press before joining the Marines. When he returned from the service, he worked in the news business in Chicago and Ohio before becoming press secretary to the governor of Ohio in 1948. He later worked in public relations in Ohio and California before joining the *Los Angeles Times* in 1955. Zurlinden was in that newsroom when he suffered a fatal heart attack in 1957. He was forty-two and had just written the banner-line story for the morning's final edition.

Hy Hurwitz rejoined the *Boston Globe* shortly before the Japanese surrender, which he covered. He was back on the *Globe* sports staff in time for the 1946 Red Sox season. At fifty-six Hurwitz died of a heart attack in 1966, his fortieth year with the newspaper.

Dick Hannah left newspapers and joined a public relations firm. He became the spokesman for the business interests of the reclusive billionaire Howard Hughes for two decades until his death at sixty in January 1976, three months before Hughes himself died.

Fred Feldkamp became an editor for *Life* magazine and a writer for the newsreel "The March of Time." In the 1950s he wrote two documentary television series about the war, *Crusade in Europe* and *Crusade in the Pacific*, and then went into motion picture production. He died at sixty-seven in 1981.

Gene Ward returned to the *New York Daily News* and became one its best-known sportswriters and columnists. He covered hockey, boxing, football, and thoroughbred racing, including twenty-nine consecutive Kentucky Derbies. He died in 1992 at age seventy-eight.

Alfred E. Lewis was one of the young men who left the *Washington Post* to join the Marines. He returned to the *Post* newsroom after the war and remained on the police beat until he retired in 1985. His close but professional ties with the police allowed him to join investigators of a break-in at Democratic National Committee headquarters at the Watergate building in 1972, which scored the *Post* an early beat on the political scandal of the century. Lewis was eighty-one when he died of cancer in 1994.

Bill D. Ross wrote a history of the battle for Iwo Jima four decades after fighting in it, then a book about Peleliu. He had returned to journalism after the war and later worked in public relations and as a freelance writer. He died in 1994 at seventy-three.

Samuel Shaffer joined the staff of *Newsweek* after the war and was the magazine's chief congressional correspondent for thirty years. He covered fourteen presidential nominating conventions and four presidential campaigns. He was eighty-five when he died in 1995.

John N. Popham had left the *New York Times* to serve as a Marine public relations officer. He returned to the *Times* and reported from the American South during the racial turbulence of the 1950s, the first northern newspaper correspondent to cover the region regularly. He began a twenty-year run, in 1958, as the managing editor of the *Chattanooga Times*. In retirement Popham earned a law degree at seventy-two. He died in 1999 at age eighty-nine.

Earl J. Wilson, a public relations officer, joined the US Information Agency after the war. In thirty years with the USIA he served in Shanghai, Manila, Mexico City, Hong Kong, Madrid, and Malaysia. He was eighty-one when he died in 1999.

Alvin M. Josephy Jr., who wrote battlefield dispatches but was best known for his radio recordings under fire on Iwo Jima and Guam, became a prominent historian, particularly of Native Americans. He served as chairman of the board of trustees of the Smithsonian Institution's National Museum of the American Indian. In his 2000 memoir, *A Walk Toward Oregon*, he recounted his efforts to get the news about Marines under fire. He was ninety when he died in 2005.

When Samuel E. Stavisky returned to the *Washington Post*, he eventually shifted to editorial and column writing. In 1954 he started his own public relations firm, which operated for thirty-five years. In retirement Stavisky wrote *Combat Correspondent*, a memoir about his stint as a CC. He died in 2008 at age ninety-three.

Millard Kaufman, a public relations officer, did not return to the newsroom. Instead, he became a Hollywood screenwriter and producer and was nominated for Academy Awards for his screenplays for *Take the High Ground!* (1953) and *Bad Day at Black Rock* (1955). He also helped create the cartoon character Mr. Magoo. In 2007 he published his first novel, *Bowl of Cherries*, two years before he died at age ninety-two.

Cyril J. O'Brien returned to the *Camden Courier-Post* (New Jersey) and worked for several other newspapers on the East Coast before moving to Washington, DC, to cover Congress for a Texas news service. In 1949 he began writing for the Johns Hopkins Applied Physics Laboratory, a stint that turned into a thirty-four-year career in science and technology writing for the APL. He spent much of his retirement years writing about the war and providing accounts to historians and documentarians. When O'Brien died in January 2011, he was considered the oldest known living Marine combat correspondent.

That distinction apparently passed, if briefly, to Irving Schlossenberg, who had been a photographer for the *Washington Post* when he left the newsroom to write and take pictures for the Marine Corps. After the war, he sold the *Encyclopedia Britannica* door to door and ascended to national sales director and executive assistant to the company president. When Schlossenberg died, at age ninety-two in 2011, a Marine writer reported in his obituary that he had been the oldest of the CCs still alive.

Among the Marine combat correspondents who continued in the craft of journalism, two in particular rose to prominence while covering America's next two major conflicts. One was William K. Beech, who had adopted the byline Keyes Beech as a CC and kept it while reporting for the *Chicago Daily News*, beginning in 1947. He was one of six reporters who won the Pulitzer Prize for international reporting in 1951 for their coverage of the Korean War. He also covered the entire Vietnam War for the *Daily News* and later reported on Asia for the *Los Angeles Times* until his retirement in 1983. Beech died in 1990 at seventy-six. "He prided himself on being a battlefield correspondent," a colleague said. "He believed the real story was out where the troops were and not in the briefing room."

That also could be said of the combat correspondent–turned–public relations officer Jim G. Lucas. He too found himself under fire in Korea, reporting on the war for Scripps-Howard newspapers. In the tradition of their legendary combat writer Ernie Pyle, Lucas wrote about the average man in uniform, twice winning an award dedicated to Pyle's memory. Lucas's stories from Korea won the Pulitzer for international reporting in 1954, the citation noting his "front-line human interest reporting." He returned to combat reporting in Vietnam even before the buildup of American troops and continued to cover the war throughout the 1960s. Going from battlefield to battlefield apparently took a toll on the man who had left Tulsa, Oklahoma, as a young reporter to become a Marine combat correspondent. Friends remembered Lucas's struggle with binge drinking and night terrors, which they linked to the horrors he had experienced over three decades as a witness to war. Among them was the death of the renowned photographer Robert Capa. Lucas was there when Capa stepped on a land mine south of Hanoi in 1954.

Lucas was dying of colon cancer in 1971 when he made his final trip to a veterans hospital in Washington, DC. "You know," he told the friend who drove him there, "all the mud and blood and battle I've seen and I've got to die like this." Lucas was fifty-six.

Were the deaths, the wounds, and the terrible memories suffered by the Marine combat correspondents and other writers worth their efforts on behalf of the Division of Public Relations? At first glance it would be difficult to reconcile such sacrifices with the ephemeral goal of advancing a favorable image for an organization. But then the Marine Corps was not selling cornflakes; it was an essential bulwark against an enemy threatening the nation. Yet like a business that relied on the goodwill of the public for operating capital and highly qualified personnel, the Marine Corps had a keen interest in promoting its strengths and downplaying its flaws. Hence, the men who oversaw the Division of Public Relations and the journalists-turned-Marines who wrote for it were willing to tamp down the journalistic impulse to report the whole story. Calling their dispatches "press releases" was a subtle nod by the division to the difference between journalism and public relations, though when the stories appeared in newspapers and other media they had the attributes of a news report—and not by accident.

When Denig and Major George Van der Hoef conceived the idea of a fighting and writing Marine recruited from the newsroom to promote the Corps, they may not have appreciated the professional tension inherent in such a hybrid. The DPR bulletin, which was full of advice for what to cover and how to write, did not address the ethical dilemma that faced the journalist who had become a public relations practitioner. Most likely Denig and Van der Hoef assumed, and with good reason, that any American would understand that achieving the aim of the war effort—victory—was the final consideration whenever the practice of public relations compromised the practice of journalism. The bulletin never advised combat correspondents and others to be dishonest or to publish a falsehood, and no memoir or oral history suggested dishonesty was part of their training. However, the demand that they not damage the reputation of the Marine Corps turned the CCs away from journalism and toward public relations even if their work was truthful and accurate. On hand to keep them from straying were Navy censors and like-minded division editors.

Truth and accuracy had been central to the discussions of ethical conduct for journalism and public relations that had emerged during the two decades before World War II. As part of newspapers' transition from a party-aligned press in the eighteenth century to objective reporting, the American Society of Newspaper Editors (ASNE) in 1923 adopted an influential "canons of journalism" that included truthfulness, accuracy, independence, impartiality, and decency. While not as specific, the pioneering public relations practitioner Ivy Lee's groundbreaking "Declaration of Principles" in 1905 had included accuracy but focused on the practice of providing guidance to reporters seeking information about a client on subjects of value and interest to the public. In later years Lee would add advocacy to the practitioner's craft. Missing from Lee's declaration, understandably, were the ASNE standards of independence and impartiality, two points that separated journalism and public relations even if truth and accuracy did not.

Denig and others who developed the Marine combat correspondent initiative showed their lack of expertise in both journalism and public relations by setting an unrealistic standard. "Absolute accuracy and absolute truth must never fail to govern the preparation of all photographic and news material issued by this Division," stated the internal bulletin of April 7, 1943. By then, a full year after Denig began recruiting, the division should have recognized that absolute truth and accuracy were impossible under the best of circumstances, let alone a world war. The brutal realities that combat Marines in the Pacific had already experienced would only worsen on Tarawa and not end until victory on Okinawa. At headquarters and elsewhere, officers weighing the potential impact of Marine combat correspondents' stories on discipline, morale, and recruiting curtailed the pursuit of absolute accuracy and absolute truth, not to mention establishing a historical record. This is not to criticize the Marine writers themselves, only to acknowledge that they were being guided by unrealistic expectations from the same superior officers who, by necessity, had their reports censored.

The professional divide between journalism and public relations in regard to accuracy and truth was evident in the division's guidance for Marine writers and in the editing of their stories. For example, public relations demanded that they not report that Marines fired upon each other by accident or that Marines suffered from what could later be called post-traumatic stress. There were stories that acknowledged or described such occurrences, and they were not distributed for publication. The failure to tell such truths to the American public during wartime was arguably a lie of omission justified by the need for a strong defense. The journalists who joined the DPR could hardly be faulted for accepting the "shared sacrifice," as the journalism historian Michael S. Sweeney called it, that the civilian press willingly undertook while the United States fought for its survival. Civilian editors who published the CCs' stories apparently did not disapprove of the blending of journalism and public relations, especially given readers' appreciation of the hometown focus of such stories.

Hovering over all the Marine writers (and civilian reporters) was Navy censorship, which in retrospect stands as the largest impediment to the Division of Public Relations' lofty goal of complete truth and accuracy. How could that goal possibly be achieved when Marine writers were under orders not to describe a multitude of events and instructed to adhere to broadly written regulations on matters such as taste, timidity, and criticism of the service? The censor's role in maintaining control over what information from the theater of war reached the American public but also enemy forces was understandable and essential in time of war. That the lies of omission and outright false or misleading statements could be debated after victory was a powerful argument in favor of censorship. Yet so much of the Marine writers' work remaining classified for so many years indicated that events casting a shadow on the Marine Corps were more likely to remain hidden than to be shared openly. In this way the division lived up to its public relations mission while deploying its journalism-based personnel.

Another blow to accuracy becomes apparent, at least with hindsight, when reviewing the original dispatches stored at the National Archives. Marine editors and Navy censors had little problem changing quotations. One might excuse altering quotations that contain a few words that identify troop strength or deployment, the use of certain weapons, and the names of fellow Marines whose wounds or deaths had yet to be confirmed or reported to next of kin. However, quotations that were changed included those that could draw criticism of the Marine Corps and its men. "Nips" was usually changed to "Japs" (why one racial slur was accepted over another was not explained), but racial references to "yellow" skin were usually deleted. Minor cursing such as "damn" and "hell" was usually eliminated; the writer himself most likely scrubbed fouler language from quotations before submitting a story.

A minor issue? Not to journalists who are trained to record and report what people say. If quotations could be changed routinely, then readers could question what else had been manipulated to fit a narrative that strayed from the facts at hand. However, one wrinkle is worth considering. The public relations profession allows its practitioners to develop statements released under the names of clients who then claim the words to be their own. One might argue that Marines in the field were clients and that the Division of Public Relations decided how best to present them to the public. Such a relationship was unique in public relations: As a client under orders to obey higher-ranking personnel, Marines had little say in the matter. Again, the combat correspondent initiative was closer to public relations than journalism.

While the Division of Public Relations achieved its goal of promoting the Marine Corps as a fighting force, the division fell short of its goal to collect military information and facts of significant historical value to the Corps. By discouraging its writers to record nearly everything significant they witnessed or were told, the division sanctioned an incomplete Marine chronicle. Just as any authorized institutional history might overlook less exemplary events, the CC stories from the battlefield and elsewhere avoided recording flaws and failings or even the colorful if sometimes cringe-worthy facts of Marine life. Furthermore, in adhering to the segregationist practices of some segments of the news media, the division diminished the collection and dissemination of the contributions of African American Marines to the war effort and to Marine Corps history. When only approved versions of their stories reached the news media and were made easily accessible for historians, the Marine combat correspondents helped place a distinctly incomplete version of reality into its historical archives and into the public record.

The goal of contributing to the historical record of the Marine Corps suffered even more under the system for collecting and saving battlefield copy. A strong argument existed during the war for holding back information for security reasons, although in retrospect some DPR personnel thought those concerns were overblown. In his 1967 history of the CCs, Benis M. Frank noted that a top DPR official believed security consciousness was "exaggerated" and was "usually concerned with trivialities." Many CC reports withheld for security reasons were not declassified until 1958; whether that was true for their reports as a whole is unclear. Moreover, declassified as well as unused reports apparently were filed in archives and untapped by historians, who may have decided that "press releases" held little interest and were not worth the time it would take to slog through thousands of pages—assuming the stories' existence was even known to them. What historians missed were the kinds of human-interest details that make the story of Marines in the Pacific come alive and justify the work the CCs and other Marine writers and photographers carried out under perilous conditions.

The public relations division's success in placing news about Marines in local and national media during World War II may have helped inspire greater efforts by the US military to create its own journalism in the form of public information and public relations. Within a few years, the military services were sending personnel to their own separate schools for training in journalism or public information or both. Consolidating the services' developmental goals for communications duties led to the creation, in 1964, of the Defense Information School, which operates today at Fort Meade, Maryland, with the motto "Strength Through Truth." If there was indeed tension in turning an experienced journalist into a Marine writer, one way to relieve it would be to turn Marines into writers. Uniform regulations for public relations in the armed services ended the era of Denig's Demons more than the retirement of Denig himself. "Never again would the prerogatives, initiative, and free-wheeling individualism of World War II Marine combat correspondents be experienced," according to Frank.

To their credit, journalists trained at Parris Island did not accept their orders without complaint. "Most of the combat correspondents were most unhappy at having to confine themselves to the writing of Joe Blow stories," Frank wrote in his CC history. "Not that all of them dreamed of someday writing *the* great war story or of producing *the* scoop of the war, most believed that there was more to the job than just grinding out the Joe Blows, that there were other stories to be told. And many of them did write them." Stories of courage and sacrifice, such as Jim Lucas's first-person report from the bloody beaches of Tarawa, informed the public and generated support for the Marine Corps and the war against the Japanese. Only time would reveal the harshest realities of the Pacific war and the flaws within the heroes who fought it.

Acknowledgments

Many people provided assistance and encouragement as I researched and wrote this book.

It began with my interest in the life and work of the journalist Jim G. Lucas, which introduced me to the history of the Marine Corps combat correspondents. Seeking out friends and colleagues of Lucas led me to contact the World War II–era Marine writers Millard Kaufman and Cyril J. O'Brien and the Marine combat cameraman Norman Hatch. When we spoke, they were among the few men still living who had worked with the Division of Public Relations during the war. They were generous with their time and memories.

Most of my research occurred at facilities of the National Archives and Records Administration in College Park, Maryland, where the CC dispatches are held, and in St. Louis, where military personnel records are stored. I found the archivists overseeing collections in all the various media to be extremely helpful. I am most grateful for their ongoing work to retain the nation's historical records and make them available to researchers.

Similarly, I was warmly welcomed at the Marine Corps History Division in Quantico, Virginia. The staff of its archives branch provided essential materials as well as expertise. The division's publications, particularly its series of booklets on the Marine Corps in World War II, are fine examples of concise military history.

I would be remiss if I did not include my appreciation for the invaluable resources available, in person and online, through the Library of Congress in Washington, DC. My local library, the C. Burr Artz Public Library of the Frederick County, Maryland, Public Libraries system, has been another valuable source of assistance in gaining access to information.

Speaking of archives, I also thank Phillip Daniel for his many hours of research assistance and for discussing the subject and how to approach it. Special thanks, also, to Hamilton Bean of the University of Colorado–Denver for sharing his book *Nimitz's Newsman: Waldo Drake and the Navy's Censored War in the Pacific* ahead of its publication.

Another helping hand came from my friend Alan Wild, a longtime newspaper copy editor who applied his professional skills to the manuscript. He has done so for nearly all my books and, in my view, is batting a thousand.

This book grew out of my contribution to a collection of essays, *Reporting World War II*, edited by G. Kurt Piehler and Ingo Trauschweizer and published by Fordham University Press. I benefited from their support as I sought to delve deeper into the subject.

Away from archives and libraries, I am grateful for encouragement from my family, essential ingredients for success in a long-term writing project. I thank my mother, Dorothy Daniel, and my siblings, Holly Daniel and Phillip Daniel. I also owe a debt of gratitude to many friends, among them Marilyn Greenwald, Nick Hirshon, Joe Kennedy, Larry Lamb, Mark Lemke, Jason Schaff, Terri Utley, and Pat Washburn.

I dedicate this book to the members of my family—a grandfather, my father, my uncles and an aunt, and a cousin—who served in the armed forces. Their service helped make it possible for our family to enjoy peace and freedom.

Notes

Introduction

"They were your boys": June 20, 1944, Lucas files, among news release submission files within Records of the Division of Information and its predecessor, the Division of Public Relations; Record Group 127, Records of the United States Marine Corps, National Archives and Record Administration, College Park, Maryland. News releases hereafter noted as within NARA. Lucas had been a reporter for the *Tulsa Tribune* (Oklahoma).

Merillat memoir: Herbert Christian Merillat, *Guadalcanal Remembered* (University of Alabama Press, 2003; originally Dodd & Mead, 1982), 3. As he explained in his memoir, at the time of the war Merillat went by the middle name Laing, his mother's preference, while his birth certificate gave it as Christian, his father's preference and, after the war, the writer's own.

Institutional histories: See Benis M. Frank, *Denig's Demons and How They Grew: The Story of Marine Combat Correspondents, Photographers, and Artists* (Moore & Moore, 1967); and Garry M. Cameron, *Last to Know, First to Go: The United States Marine Corps' Combat Correspondents* (Charger Books, 1988). The latter was updated as *First to Go: The History of the USMC Combat Correspondents Association* (St. Johann Press, 2018).

1. A Dangerous Publicity Campaign

For background on Wake Island and the attack, see Donald L. Miller, *D-Days in the Pacific* (Simon & Schuster, 2005), 30–31; Arthur Zich, *The Rising Sun* (Time-Life, 1978), 89–91; and Robert J. Cressman, *A Magnificent Fight: Marines in the Battle for Wake Island* (Marine Corps Historical Center, 1992).

Newspaper reports: "Wake and Guam Reported Taken," *New York Times*, December 9, 1941; "Marines Still Hold Wake and Midway," *Los Angeles Times*, December 13, 1941; and "John Fisher, "Japs Again Raid Wake Island," *Chicago Tribune*, December 15, 1941; "U.S. Marines Beat Off 2 More Jap Attacks on Wake," *Chicago Tribune*, December 20, 1941.

"A laconic statement": Hal Foust, "Japs on Wake Island," *Chicago Tribune*, December 24, 1941.

Division headquarters: The Marine Corps moved into the Navy Annex in November 1941 and remained there for more than fifty years. See Steve Vogel,

"Navy Annex Being Razed After 70 Years of Service," *Washington Post*, December 30, 2012. As Washington is the seat of the federal government, even though its bureaucracy spread into the Virginia and Maryland suburbs in search of land, notably the Arlington-based Pentagon, casual references to the location of Marine Corps headquarters and the operations of the Division of Public Relations will be to Washington in this text.

Early Marine Corps publicity: Robert G. Lindsay, *This High Name: Public Relations and the U.S. Marine Corps* (University of Wisconsin Press, 1956), 9.

National Recruiting Publicity Bureau: Lindsay, *This High Name*, 10–11.

Public relations gains credence: See Scott M. Cutlip, *The Unseen Power: Public Relations: A History* (Lawrence Erlbaum Associates, 1994).

Dedicated public relations section: Lindsay, *This High Name*, 4.

"I went in there": Robert L. Denig, oral history conducted May 24, 1967, US Marine Corps Oral History Program, Marine Corps Archives, Marine Corps History Division, 3–4. Hereafter referred to as MCA, MCHD.

Denig's promotion: Benis M. Frank, *Denig's Demons and How They Grew: The Story of Marine Combat Correspondents, Photographers, and Artists* (Moore & Moore, 1967), 3.

Division's priorities: John W. Thomason III, "Public Relations Division Makes Rapid Progress," *Marine Recruiter*, December 1941, 1.

"He put me wise": Denig oral history, 13.

Idea to place journalists with divisions: Denig oral history, 13.

Initiative's goals and authorization: See memo, "News Coverage Throughout the Marine Corps," March 22, 1942, Combat Correspondents File 1, MCA, MCHD; and Frank, *Denig's Demons*, 6.

Recruiting in newsrooms: Frank, *Denig's Demons*, 6–7.

"I liked the idea": Herbert Christian Merillat, *Guadalcanal Remembered* (University of Alabama Press, 2003; originally Dodd & Mead, 1982), 9. At the time of the war, Merillat went by the middle name Laing and later by Christian.

Hurlbut background: "Names of Many D.C. Men Go on Promotion Lists," *Washington Post*, November 23, 1942.

Hurlbut teaches Merillat: Merillat, *Guadalcanal Remembered*, 7–11.

Holcomb announces initiative: Jim Lucas, *Combat Correspondent* (Reynal & Hitchcock, 1944), 1. While the announcement cited six weeks of training, Lucas would recall spending eight weeks at Parris Island.

Ages of first recruits: "4 of Post Staff to Be Combat Writers," *Washington Post*, August 15, 1942.

Denig allows medical waivers: See Samuel E. Stavisky, *Marine Combat Correspondent: World War II in the Pacific* (Ivy Books, 1999), 7–8; and Merillat, *Guadalcanal Remembered*, 9.

"You're in": Stavisky, *Marine Combat Correspondent*, 6.

Murphy's eyesight: Jessica Contrera, "Seventy-Four Years After His Death in WWII, a Marine Is Returned Home," *Washington Post*, December 1, 2018.

Josephy's waiver: Alvin M. Josephy Jr., *A Walk Toward Oregon: A Memoir* (Knopf, 2000), 180.

"If you were in there as a major": O'Brien interview with author, August 26, 2005.

Bulletin, August 8, 1942, Combat Correspondent file 1, MCA, MCHD. Hereafter, CC file 1–3, MCA.

First recruits return to Washington: See Bulletin, August 8, 1942, Combat Correspondent file 1, MCA, MCHD. Hereafter, CC file 1–3, MCA.

Typewriters in combat: Jim Lucas noted that CCs were first issued Remington typewriters, which he described as bulky and difficult to carry under fire; later they turned to the smaller Royal typewriter and then the Hermes portable, which Lucas said was issued to newer CCs. Lucas, *Combat Correspondent*, 34.

"Woefully ignorant": Bulletin, second July edition, 1942, CC file 1, MCA.

Wary of government competition: Bulletin, December 8, 1942, CC file 1, MCA.

Use of CC material by civilian press: Bulletin, February 17, 1944, CC file 2, MCA.

"Even unhappier": Frank, *Denig's Demons*, 37.

Nopper background: "AP Editors Join Military Forces," *Hagerstown Daily Mail* (Maryland), July 1, 1942.

Operation of division story distribution: See bulletins of January 6 and May 4, 1943; special bulletin of May 18, 1943, CC file 1, MCA.

"He believed he needed to control": See Hamilton Bean, *Nimitz's Newsman: Waldo Drake and the Navy's Censored War in the Pacific* (Naval Institute Press, 2024), 2.

Use of clipsheet: Bulletin, August 3, 1944, CC file 3, MCA.

Establishment of office for magazine distribution: Bulletin, April 17, 1944, CC file 2, MCA.

Magazine use of exclusive material: Bulletin, June 2, 1943, CC file 1, MCA.

Pay for stories not allowed: Bulletin, September 1, 1944, CC file 3, MCA.

Initial stories from Guadalcanal: Bulletin, December 8, 1942, CC file 1, MCA.

Distribution of stories from Saipan: Bulletin, July 17 and August 3, 1944, CC file 3, MCA.

"While the daily activities": Official Style Book for Marine Corps Public Relations Officers and Combat Correspondents, Box 3, A1 1006 1007 1008, USMC, NARA. The guide is not dated; a bulletin noted it had been distributed in mid-June 1943.

"We don't want": Bulletin, April 7, 1943, CC file 1, MCA.

Discouraged storylines: See bulletins of January 6, 1943, CC file 1; August 12 and August 25, 1943, CC Bulletin file, Vol. 2, NARA; and March 20, 1945, CC Bulletin file, Vol. 4, NARA.

References to girlfriends: 45 Bulletin, August 12, 1943, CC Bulletin file, Vol. 2, NARA.

"At that rate": Bulletin, May 4, 1943, CC file 1, MCA.

"The only training": O'Brien interview.

"We don't appreciate": Bulletin, December 8, 1942, CC file 1, MCA.

"Write as you please": Bulletin, October 9, 1944, CC file3, MCA.

Press releases, not news stories: Bulletin, February 24, 1943, CC file 1, MCA.

"Remember, you are always writing": Bulletin, August 12, 1943, CC Bulletin file, Vol. 2, NARA.

Wartime censorship: See Jean Folkerts and Dwight L. Teeter Jr., *Voices of a Nation: A History of Mass Media in the United States,* 3rd ed. (Allyn and Bacon, 1998), 422–23.

"One of the shared sacrifices": See Michael S. Sweeney, *Secrets of Victory: The Office of Censorship and the American Press and Radio in World War II* (University of North Carolina Press, 2001), 3.

"Certain matters of policy": See security guide file, Box 3, A1 1008 370/23/20/03, NARA.

"The censorship was mostly for taste": O'Brien interview.

"Stories in obvious bad taste": Bulletin, August 12, 1943, CC Bulletin file, Vol. 2, NARA.

Prohibition of dogs' graves: Bulletin, December 1, 1944, CC Bulletin file, Vol. 3, NARA.

"Little yeller fellers": The rhyme may have originated with the comedian Bob Hope, whose radio show was sponsored by the toothpaste Pepsodent. Hope assured his audience the product would prevent "little yeller fellers under your smeller."

"Slick in spic": Bulletin, June 1942, CC file 1, MCA.

Listing prohibited subjects due to security: Bulletin, June 2, 1943, CC file 1, MCA.

Stories cited for prohibited subjects: See bulletins of July 26, 1943, CC file 2, MCA; and October 9, 1944, CC file 3, MCA.

Story subjects to be treated with care: See bulletins of January 20, February 17, and March 20, 1944, CC file 2, MCA.

"Does not injure the morale": See Pacific Fleet Letter 14L-42, April 12, 1942, Enclosure (B), page 5, in Public Relations General Policy (folder 1 of 2), Records Relating to Public Relations, c. October 1943–April 1946, Commander-in-Chief, Pacific Fleet (CINCPAC), Records of Naval Operating Forces ("Flag Flies"), Record Group 313, NARA. Henceforth noted as Records Relating to Public Relations, CINCPAC, NARA.

Not permitted to send "bad news": Stavisky, *Combat Correspondent,* 33.

"I didn't give the censors": Stavisky, *Combat Correspondent,* 37.

"Our dispatches avoided": Dan Levin, *From the Battlefield: Dispatches of a World War II Marine* (Naval Institute Press, 1995), 97.

"Let the guy write" and "All this stuff": Millard Kaufman, interview with author, 2005.

Casualties among DPR personnel: See memo, Robert L. Denig to commandant of the Marine Corps, April 15, 1944, in combat correspondent file 2 of 6, MCHD; and list of casualties, May 1, 1944, in combat correspondent file 6 of 6, MCHD.

Deaths among DPR personnel: See report, "World War II Marines in Public Relations and Affiliated Assignments," September 6, 1991, in combat correspondent file 4 of 6, MCHD; and *First to Go*, dedication page. The 1991 report by the Marine Corps Combat Correspondents Association sought to compile a comprehensive list of all personnel assigned at one time or another to the Division of Public Relations, including women reservists and stateside personnel; the number of names went beyond 800, about one-fourth of them CCs and public relations officers. The report concluded that at least six additional Marines had been killed during their service but had not been included in a previous estimate of thirteen as listed in *First to Go*.

2. In the Jungles of Guadalcanal

"We were all green troops": James W. Hurlbut interview, March 10, 1943, Office of Naval Records and Library, 1–2. Accessed through the online military records site Fold 3.

"To the Japs on Guadalcanal": Herbert L. Merillat, "D.C. Officer Tells Heroic Story of Marines Who Captured Jap Bases in Solomons," *Washington Sunday Star*, August 30, 1942.

"May be of considerable significance": George Fielding Eliot, "Pacific Attacks Seen as Opening of Offensive," *Los Angeles Times*, August 9, 1942.

On the front pages: See their editions of August 30, 1942.

"He was willing": Hurlbut interview, ONRL, 10.

"Eight months after": Hurlbut, "Epic of Marines at Solomons Described by Arlington Man," *Washington Evening Star*, August 31, 1942.

Banned by Navy decree: Herbert Christian Merillat, *Guadalcanal Remembered* (University of Alabama Press, 2003; originally Dodd & Mead, 1982), 121. At the time of the war, Merillat went by the middle name Laing.

"Guadalcanal was a pretty big beat": Hurlbut interview, ONRL, 11.

"Enemy forces were well dug in": James W. Hurlbut, "Systematic Marine Patrols Wipe Out Jap Stronghold," *Tucson Citizen* (Arizona), September 14, 1942.

Undeveloped focus on rank-and-file Marines: Merillat, *Guadalcanal Remembered*, 187–88.

"We made a mad dash": Merillat interview, March 9, 1943, Office of Naval Records and Library, 15. Accessed through the online military records site Fold 3.

Description of Hurlbut's archived files: See stories dated October 25 and November 15, 1942, among news release submission files within Records of the Division of Information and its predecessor, the Division of Public Relations; Record Group 127, Records of the United States Marine Corps, National Archives and Record Administration, College Park, Maryland. News releases hereafter noted as within NARA.

"Ten men, pooling their activities": Report dated October 18, 1942, but dated as filed November 15, 1942, Hurlbut files, NARA.

Title, "They were pleased with the power of their new weapon": January 18, 1943, Burman files, among news release submission files within Records of the Division of Information and its predecessor, the Division of Public Relations; Record Group 127, Records of the United States Marine Corps, National Archives and Record Administration, College Park, Maryland. News releases hereafter noted as within NARA.

"The taking of any part": See memo, press censorship policy for forthcoming operations, dated March 15, 1945, in file marked Chief Press Censor (Miscellaneous Memoranda), Records Relating to Public Relations, CINCPAC, NARA.

Title, "The great mistake of coming in contact with a Marine": October 27 [1943], Barr files, NARA.

Title, "We seldom see 'em in Brooklyn": January 23, 1943, Hannah files, NARA.

Title, "He looks like the freckle-faced kid next door": December 1 [1942], Miller files, NARA.

Title, "He was picked up and dropped before being buried alive": September 15 [1943], Blechman files, NARA.

Title, "The elements were in control": May 11, 1943, Childress files, NARA.

Navy officials categorized interrogation as secret: See memo on interrogation of prisoners, dated August 27, 1943, from adjutant general's office, War Department, to Commander-in-Chief, Southwest Pacific Area, et al., file marked Censorship Rules/Censorship Policy (Folder 2 of 2), Records Relating to Public Relations, CINCPAC, NARA.

Title, "To have died would have been better": April 14, 1943, Stavisky files, NARA.

Alternative translations: Provided in 2024 by Dr. Yuko Miki, associate professor of history at Fordham University.

Title, "Better to kill fish with dynamite or hand grenades?": August 5 [1943], Blechman files, NARA.

Title, "It's a heck of a note": April 24, 1943, Childress files, NARA.

Title, "He had found his niche at last": September 15 [1943], Blechman files, NARA.

Title, "A future blurred by a shattering Jap bullet": December 1942, Johnson files, NARA.

Title, "A medal for guys who don't do a damn thing": April 1943, Lucas files, NARA.

For Guadalcanal casualty statistics, see Henry I. Shaw Jr., *First Offensive: The Marine Campaign for Guadalcanal* (US Marine Corps, 1992), 51–52.

Stavisky recalls early months: Samuel E. Stavisky, *Marine Combat Correspondent: World War II in the Pacific* (Ivy Books, 1999), 75.

"That's a 'normal' happening": Stavisky, *Marine Combat Correspondent*, 78.

"There's something pretty terrifying": See profile of Burman by Staff Sgt. Fred Feldkamp, undated (probably September–October 1943); Feldkamp files, NARA.

"As a Combat Correspondent": story dated December 26, 1942; Burman files, NARA.

3. Somewhere in the South Pacific

McDevitt's and Marder's actions: See report, Technical Sergeant Jim G. Lucas, Enogai, New Georgia, August 11, 1943, Lucas files, among news release submission files within Records of the Division of Information and its predecessor, the Division of Public Relations; Record Group 127, Records of the United States Marine Corps, National Archives and Record Administration, College Park, Maryland. News releases hereafter noted as within NARA.

McDevitt and Marder commendations: See report by Sgt. Ray Fitzpatrick, Somewhere in the South Pacific, March 16 [1944], Fitzpatrick files, NARA.

"When we were enlisted": See report, Technical Sergeant Jim G. Lucas, Enogai, New Georgia, August 11, 1943, Lucas files, NARA.

Collings incident: See "Marine Combat Photographer Earns Purple Heart but Loses His Film," Navy release, Somewhere in the South Pacific, August 30, 1943, Biggerstaff files, NARA.

Azine and Wexler incident: See report by Technical Sgt. Milburn McCarty Jr., Bougainville, November 29, 1943, McCarty files, NARA.

"No one needs to tell you": See report, Sgt. Charles P. Evans, Bougainville, November 8, 1943, Evans files, NARA.

Stinson aboard observation plane: See report, Sgt. Bob Stinson, Somewhere in the Pacific, July 19 [1943], Stinson files, NARA.

Title, "First they bomb our wounded and now they strafe them!": July 12, 1943, Marder files, NARA.

Marine Raiders as a relatively new force: See Jon T. Hoffman, *From Makin to Bougainville: Marine Raiders in the Pacific War* (Marine Corps History and Museums Division, 1995), 1–6.

Title, "A Marine who thinks he's a Seabee": July 22, 1943, Marder files, NARA.

Title, "A report from aboard 'The Slave Ship'": October 23, 1943, McCarty files, NARA.

Title, "A sailor recognized the pilot as a Jap": November 19 [1943], Blechman files, NARA.

Title, "Don't shoot, I'm a Jap . . .": November 14, 1943, Barr files, NARA.

Title, "If it wasn't for him, we wouldn't be here now": January 4, 1944, Marder files.

Title, "He jest throwed up his hands and began gibbering": November 13, 1943, Pavone files, NARA.

Title, "We were all a little crazy for a while": December 17, 1943, Pavone files, NARA.

258 | Notes to pages 60–70

Title, "Complete with stockade, padlock, and turnkey": November 29, 1943, McCarty files, NARA.

Title, "This method of fighting off sleep is not suggested": December 6 [1943], Blechman files, NARA.

Title, "He just got around the corner": November 5, 1943, Hague files, NARA.

Title, "A flourishing racket aimed at the gullible": June 26, 1943, Stavisky files, NARA.

"Two new medals": November 7, 1943, McCarty files, NARA.

"Marine Sergeant John A. Ross": December 20, 1943, Black files, NARA.

"Wounded on the Bougainville front": December 14, 1943, McCarty files, NARA.

"Pay day being a week off": October 31, 1943, Stavisky files, NARA.

Title, "There's a bit of strategy involved in this action": August 7, 1943. McDevitt files, NARA.

"Marine Raiders have made headlines": November 12, 1943, Pavone files, NARA.

"The harassed Japs on Bougainville": November 16, 1943, McCarty files, NARA.

"Apparently having an extreme shortage": November 29, 1943, Johnson files, NARA.

Title, "Most have already gone through the hell of battle": December 3, 1943, McCarty files, NARA.

"This isn't a Marine Combat Correspondent's paradise": Staff Sgt. Solomon Blechman, November 15 [1943], Blechman files, NARA.

Stinson's disappearance and details: See "Marine Combat Correspondent Missing in Action," Navy Department release, November 26, 1943; "Marine Combat Correspondent Dies in Accident," Navy Department release, December 10, 1943; Stinson files, NARA. See also obituary report dated February 1958, Combat Correspondent files, Marine Corps Archives, Quantico, Virginia.

Letter to Stinson's parents: Lt. Col. Thomas G. McFarland to Zoe M. Stinson, January 28, 1944; Stinson files, National Personnel Records Center, Military Personnel Records, St. Louis.

Baggett death: See carbon copy of certificate of death for Lee E. C. Baggett, marked received December 21, 1942, by Bureau of Medicine and Surgery, Navy Department, Washington; Baggett file, National Personnel Records Center, Military Personnel Records, St. Louis. The death certificate and supporting statements indicated Baggett and others had been on a picnic and swimming party on a Sunday afternoon, November 29, 1942, and were aboard a truck returning to the Guantanamo base when a low-hanging tree branch along a road knocked Baggett over the side. One of the truck's rear tires struck and killed him. His death was erroneously recorded in CC tributes to have occurred during the Guadalcanal campaign.

Marine writers and photographers wounded: See report, Sergeant Francis H. Barr, Somewhere in the South Pacific, April 3, 1944, Barr files, NARA.

Additional losses early in war: Division headquarters had felt a loss at the very beginning of the Pacific war. Second Lieutenant Eugene M. Key, who left the *Dallas Times-Herald* to enlist, had served as a public relations officer in Washington for three months before leaving the public relations operation in March 1942 to join the First Marine Raider Battalion. A month later, the battalion embarked for the Pacific. Key, then a first lieutenant, died on Tulagi on August 7 when enemy snipers attacked his platoon, but not before he destroyed the nest with grenades. He was awarded the Navy Cross posthumously. See the Marine statement on his death in Combat Correspondents File 2, Marine Corps History Division, Quantico, Virginia.

Casualties in New Georgia and Bougainville campaigns: See casualties table, Henry I. Shaw Jr. and Maj. Douglas T. Kane, *Isolation of Rabaul: History of U.S. Marine Corps Operations in World War II* (U.S. Marine Corps Historical Branch, 1963), 2:587.

4. Four Bloody Days on Tarawa

"As the sky brightened": Sgt. Pete Zurlinden, "Marine Writer Describes Tarawa Invasion," official release, December 5, 1943, among news release submission files within Records of the Division of Information and its predecessor, the Division of Public Relations; Record Group 127, Records of the United States Marine Corps, National Archives and Record Administration, College Park, Maryland. News releases hereafter noted as within NARA.

The massive clash: For details of the preparations for defending and assaulting Tarawa and the difficulties both sides encountered, see Joseph H. Alexander, *Across the Reef: The Marine Assault on Tarawa* (U.S. Marine Corps, 1993; Donald L. Miller, *D-Days in the Pacific* (Simon & Schuster, 2005); Joseph H. Alexander, *Utmost Savagery: The Three Days of Tarawa* (Ivy, 1995); and Rafael Steinberg, *Island Fighting* (Time-Life Books, 1978).

Front-page headlines: The Lucas story appeared in some late editions of the three newspapers on December 3 and was more widely carried on December 4. Others publishing the story on their front pages of December 4 included the *Cincinnati Enquirer* and the *Baltimore Sun*, both spreading it across six of their eight columns.

"Five minutes ago": See "How U.S. Won Tarawa! Story by a Marine," *Chicago Tribune*, December 4, 1943.

Imperial Japanese dead: The figure of 6,000 was changed in editing to 4,000.

Title, "I never expected to live to write this story": November 23, 1943, Lucas files, NARA.

Title, "It was necessary to shoot all of them to remove that nuisance": November 26, 1943, Shaffer files, NARA.

Title, "All I could do was yell. Then I hit him with my fist": November 28, 1943, Murphy files, NARA.

Title, "He made up his mind to sneak into the first shorebound boat": November 24, 1943, Zurlinden files, NARA.

Title, "We're goners but we gotta stay here and keep cool": Undated, Shaffer files, NARA.

Title, "I saw he was a Jap and let him have it": January 19, 1944, Murphy files, NARA.

Title, "Caught in the cross fire of one of their own": November 24, 1943, Lucas files, NARA.

Title, "Hey, captain, what'll I do with these prisoners?": January 31, 1944, Beech files, NARA.

Removing personal items subject to censorship: See memo, dated October 3, 1944, from chief fleet censor, in file marked A7-2 Censorship and Security (Folder 2 or 3), Records Relating to Public Relations, CINCPAC, NARA.

Title, "The best souvenir on this island": December 2, 1943, Feldkamp files, NARA.

Title, "The island by now is practically stripped clean": November 25, 1943, Murphy files, NARA.

Earlier story identifying tipsy man as a Marine: See Capt. Earl J. Wilson story dated November 24, 1943, Wilson files, NARA.

Title, "I was there too and I didn't see you": November 24, 1943, Feldkamp files, NARA.

Title, "To these men . . . this seems the height of luxury": December 16, 1943, Murphy files, NARA.

Title, "Ski and Jim": Undated, Wilson files, NARA.

Title, "The kind of men who are making the biggest sacrifices": Undated, Balaban files, NARA.

American casualties: Alexander, *Across the Reef*, 50.

Japanese casualties: Alexander, *Across the Reef*, 7.

Identifying and relocating dead: See "Tarawa: Fact Sheet," Defense POW/MIA Accounting Agency, U.S. Department of Defense, https://www.dpaa.mil/Resources/Fact-Sheets/Article-View/Article/569615/tarawa/.

Newsreel footage from Tarawa: See Charles Jones, *War Shots: Norm Hatch and the U.S. Marine Corps Combat Cameramen of World War II* (Stackpole, 2011).

Kroenung's death: Missing Marines website, https://missingmarines.com/wesley-l-kroenung-jr/.

"The worst night of my life" and "I used to think": Report, Staff Sgt. Richard J. Murphy, Tarawa, November 25, 1943, Murphy files, NARA.

5. From New Britain to the Marshalls

For general information on New Britain, see Bernard C. Nalty, *Cape Gloucester: The Green Inferno* (Marine Corps Historical Center, 1994).

For general information on the Marshall Islands, see John C. Chapin, *Breaking the Outer Ring: Marine Landings in the Marshall Islands* (Marine Corps Historical Center, 1994).

"Smoke from the explosion": Sgt. Murray Lewis, undated story, Lewis files, among news release submission files within Records of the Division of Information and its predecessor, the Division of Public Relations; Record Group 127, Records of the United States Marine Corps, National Archives and Record Administration, College Park, Maryland. News releases hereafter noted as within NARA.

Title, "A survey of the foul odors of war": January 18, 1944, Black files, NARA.

Title, "I figure the Lord was with me": January 4, 1944, Stavisky files, NARA.

Title, "He got some measure of revenge": January 5, 1944, Stavisky files, NARA.

Title, "Leaflets show Australians drowning in a sea of battle": December 30, 1943, Stavisky files, NARA.

Title, "One was driving, one bailing, a third firing at dive bombers": March 2, 1944, Stavisky files, NARA.

Title, "I knew then what outfit I was meant to be in": Undated [1944], Mielke files, NARA.

Censorship policies on enemy action: See enclosure B, subjects not to be released for publication, Pacific Fleet Letter 2L-43, February 10, 1943, Records Relating to Public Relations, CINCPAC, NARA.

Title, "The incident proves the enemy is still breathing": May 28, 1944, Olszyk files, NARA.

Title, "He could see that the firing was coming from his own outfit": February 10, 1944, Ruder files, NARA.

Title, "Like moving through a nightmare in technicolor": March 8, 1944, Cooke files, NARA.

Title, "Flame-throwers used on Roi did have many faults": March 8, 1944, Cooke files, NARA.

Title, "He felt himself lifted off the ground in a confusion of flying metal": February 25, 1944, Lewis files, NARA.

Title, "We had to admire them, but we shot them, too": February 26, 1944, Lewis files, NARA.

Title, "She saved my life, even if she didn't know it": Undated [1944], Lewis files, NARA.

Title, "Carrier pigeons, Japanese rifles, and Mrs. Roosevelt": February 1944, Cooke files, NARA.

"The Marines had been on Roi Island": February 1944, Cooke files, NARA.

Title, "The Minnesota Marine stood up and charged the nest alone": February 1, 1944, Cooke files, NARA.

Title, "They were just asking to be killed": February 5, 1944, Lewis files, NARA.

Title, "A modern fairy tale without a dragon or an ogre": February 8, 1944, Rasor files, NARA.

Title, "Temptation just seemed to reach out and grab him": February 11, 1944, Ruder files, NARA.

Title, "The Jap never was told the name of the song": January 18, 1944, Stavisky files, NARA.

"The wounded Japanese soldier": February 22, 1944, Lewis files, NARA.

"Not that the Marines ever had to be told": April 14, 1944, Lewis files, NARA.

"An air of mystery": February 12, 1944, Vandergrift files, NARA.

General prohibition on releasing information on captured documents: See War Department letter of August 27, 1943, under heading Captured Material, Information from Prisoners, in Instructions for Field Press Officers, Pacific Oceans Area, in file marked same (Folder 1 of 2), Records Relating to Public Relations, CINCPAC, NARA.

Title, "My dear American soldiers, this is my last message": November 28, 1944, Kaufman files, NARA.

Marine casualties: Nalty, *Cape Gloucester*, 31.

Japanese casualties: Chapin, *Breaking the Outer Ring*, 16.

"Being on the lines" and "How is it?": Goldberg's story, written from Cape Gloucester, did not carry a date, but it closely followed an article written in March 1944, Goldberg files, NARA.

"We are living luxuriously": See the story marked for distribution to the *Boston Post* and news media publications, March 22, 1944, Goldberg files, NARA.

6. Sweeping the Marianas: Saipan, Guam, and Tinian

"Saipan will be still another 'first,'": report, Staff Sgt. Richard J. Murphy, June 11, 1944, Murphy files, among news release submission files within Records of the Division of Information and its predecessor, the Division of Public Relations; Record Group 127, Records of the United States Marine Corps, National Archives and Record Administration, College Park, Maryland. News releases hereafter noted as within NARA.

Booklet on Saipan: report, Staff Sgt. Richard J. Murphy, June 11, 1944, Murphy files, NARA.

For general information on the Marianas battles, see John C. Chapin, *Breaching the Marianas: The Battle for Saipan* (Marine Corps Historical Center, 1994); Richard Harwood, *A Close Encounter: The Marine Landing on Tinian* (Marine Corps Historical Center, 1994); and Cyril J. O'Brien, *Liberation: Marines in the Recapture of Guam* (Marine Corps Historical Center, 1994).

Title, "I was ready to take a gulp of water and have it over with": May 22, 1944, Shultz files, NARA.

Title, "Cries of the dying, moans of the wounded": June 17, 1944, Ruder files, NARA.

Title, "Japanese prisoners of war dug graves for our men": June 17, 1944, Lucas files, NARA.

Atrocity stories policy: See heading for atrocity stories, memo from Joint Security Council, February 8, 1944; in Instructions for Field Press Officers, Pacific Oceans Area, in file marked same (Folder 1 of 2), Records Relating to Public Relations, CINCPAC, NARA.

Title, "About midnight, the baby started to cry": June 18, 1944, Schlossenberg files, NARA.

Title, "They were your boys. You never saw them like this": June 20, 1944, Lucas files, NARA.

Title, "I thought I would like to have this": June 27, 1944, Gordon files, NARA.

Title, "They didn't laugh long": June 20, 1944, Vandergrift files, NARA.

Title, "A gentlemanly duel at 10 paces on a front line roadway": June 27, 1944, Vandergrift files, NARA.

Title, "The strain of self-control has become terrific": July 1, 1944, Tenelly files, NARA.

Title, "Nature was a military genius when she carved this island for defense": July 1, 1944, Tenelly files, NARA.

Title, "The Jap captive was very happy to oblige": July 12, 1944, Kalman files, NARA.

Title, "Were they mad? Heck, no. They thanked us!": July 18, 1944, Kalman files, NARA.

Title, "Some of our boys would like to use them": July 10, 1944, Vincent files, NARA.

Title, "Still think I'm a Japanese spy, captain?": July 8, 1944, Cooke files, NARA.

Title, "The first time I ever really hated war": July 15, 1944, Acosta files, NARA.

Title, "Japs had told him Americans always torture natives": July 28, 1944, McCarty files, NARA.

Title, "Constantly hearing death scream overhead in bullets and shells": July 25, 1944, Cooke files, NARA.

Title, "I realize we have to kill them, but I just can't get myself to do it": July 31, 1944, Kalman files, NARA.

Policy on first-person stories: See division bulletins of June 1 and July 17, 1944.

Title, "We were subjected to intense mortar fire all the way": July 21, 1944, Kaufman files, NARA.

Title, "The most horrible sight he had seen": August 8, 1944, Barr files, NARA.

Title, "He was much too busy to sit around counting the money": October 28, 1944, Weaver files, NARA.

Title, "We'll give you some work to do": August 14, 1944, Marston files, NARA.

Title, "Come along for a visit to the Stump Ward": July 29, 1944, McCarty files, NARA.

Saipan casualties: Chapin, *Breaching the Marianas*, 36.

Tinian casualties: Harwood, *Close Encounter*, 29–30.

Guam casualties and holdouts: O'Brien, *Liberation*, 43–44.

Final straggler surrenders: "Japanese, Long in Cave, Now Hopes to Meditate," *New York Times*, January 26, 1972.

Blechman death: See obituary, Combat Correspondents File 1, Marine Corps History Division.

Murphy death and identification: See "Sgt. Dick Murphy, Jr., Former Star Reporter, Listed Missing," *Washington Evening Star*, September 4, 1944; and Jessica Contrera, "Seventy-Four Years After His Death in WWII, a Marine Is Returned Home," *Washington Post*, December 1, 2018.

7. Payback at Peleliu

For an overview of the battle, see Gordon D. Gayle, *Bloody Beaches: The Marines at Peleliu* (U.S. Marine Corps History and Museums Division, 1996); and Rafael Steinberg, *Island Fighting* (Time-Life Books, 1978).

"Is it really impossible": Report, Sgt. William Boniface, Peleliu, September 16, 1944, Boniface files, among news release submission files within Records of the Division of Information and its predecessor, the Division of Public Relations; Record Group 127, Records of the United States Marine Corps, National Archives and Record Administration, College Park, Maryland. News releases hereafter noted as within NARA. The first two quotations were crossed out in the initial version of the story. The conclusion, that the most difficult part of the invasion was over, was retained.

"Three days and two nights: Tech. Sgt. Benjamin Goldberg, Peleliu, September 18, 1944, Goldberg files, NARA.

"Japanese soldiers would dig in": Gayle, *Bloody Beaches*, 5.

Title, "A tongue of flame shot out like a hundred flame throwers": October 30, 1944, Wilson files, NARA.

Title, "A contest to see who would get the most Japs": Undated [1944], Conway files, NARA.

Title, "You're going to be surprised when you try to land at Palau": September 18, 1944, Goldberg files, NARA.

Title, "They thought he was equipped with an outboard motor": November 5, 1944, Goodrich files, NARA.

Title, "If we got sick, we were shot": October 9, 1944, Kalman files, NARA.

Title, "They were running with a case of bottles between them": October 17, 1944, Walker files, NARA.

Title, "He was badly wounded, then the ants came . . .": November 21, 1944, Moser files, NARA.

Title, "Japanese caves were outfitted almost luxuriously": September 29, 1944, Kelly files, NARA.

Title, "All of the heroes of a fighter squadron are not in the air": October 30, 1944, Goodrich files, NARA.

Peleliu casualties: See Gayle, *Bloody Beaches*, 48; and Steinberg, *Island Fighting*, 183.

Peleliu as a "forgotten battle": See Bill D. Ross, *Peleliu: Tragic Triumph: The Untold Story of the Pacific War's Forgotten Battle* (Random House, 1991). Ross, a Marine combat correspondent on Iwo Jima, was among those who saw Peleliu that way.

"Night of hell": Edited versions of Hallman's report, marked for release October 1, 1944, can be found in his files at NARA.

Hallman's service and background and his son's death: See Sgt. James E. Hague's undated story about the CCs in his NARA files; Hallman's unused story dated October 4, 1943, in Hallman's files, NARA; and "Marine at National Rites for Son," *Amarillo Daily News*, c. April 1948.

8. Invisible Heroes: Black Marines and Sailors in the Pacific

Dive bomber attack: Moran's report was dated December 26, 1943, while the handwritten note suggesting it not be released was dated January 21, 1944. The rejection may have been because of the age of the item. In the Moran files, among news release submission files within Records of the Division of Information and its predecessor, the Division of Public Relations; Record Group 127, Records of the United States Marine Corps, National Archives and Record Administration, College Park, Maryland. News releases hereafter noted as within NARA.

"Whenever a man": Bulletin, October 30, 1943, CC file 2, Marine Corps Archives, Marine Corps History Division.

"If it were a question": Bernard C. Nalty, *The Right to Fight: African-American Marines in World War II* (Marine Corps Historical Center, 1995), 1.

"Trying to break into a club": Nalty, *The Right to Fight*, 2.

Black Marine defense battalions: For information on defense battalions and depot and ammunition companies, see Nalty, *The Right to Fight*; and Charles D. Melson, *Condition Red: Marine Defense Battalions in World War II* (Marine Corps Historical Center, 1996).

African American casualties: Nalty, *The Right to Fight*, 19.

Roosevelt administration and Black troops: See Steven Casey, *The War Beat, Pacific: The American Media at War Against Japan* (Oxford University Press, 2021), 150–51.

Kalman stories: See stories in 1944 issues of the *St. Louis Argus*, October 27; *Michigan Chronicle* (Detroit), October 28; *New York Age*, November 4; and *Weekly Review* (Birmingham, AL), November 4.

Hallman stories: See stories in 1944 issues of the *California Eagle* (Los Angeles), November 16; and *Michigan Chronicle, Omaha Guide, Weekly Review,* and *Pittsburgh Courier,* all November 18.

Foreman's story: See the *Jackson Advocate* (Mississippi), June 9, 1945.

Kalman's profile of Cullers: See *Weekly Review,* December 23, 1944.

Cullers obituary: See Barbara Sherlock, "Started First Ad Agency in U.S. Owned by Blacks," *Chicago Tribune,* October 10, 2003.

Title, "Negro Marines aid in manning key base in Southwest Pacific": March 1, 1944, Hurley files, NARA.

Title, "They worked around the clock and did a swell job": July 16, 1944, Vandergrift files, NARA.

Title, "There was a time we wouldn't ride in the same street car": Undated [1944], Kalman files, NARA.

Title, "Not a single man has shirked even the toughest and most dangerous job": September 23, 1944, Hallman files, NARA.

Title, "Whenever we get tired of eating rations, we have broiled fish": Undated [1944], Kalman files, NARA.

Title, "Where you all fin' some souvenirs around heah?": Undated [1944], Black files, NARA.

"Two colored Marines": Undated [1945], Vincent files, NARA.

"Then there was the story": Undated [1945], Vincent files, NARA.

"It was the first night" Undated [1944], Goldberg files, NARA.

Title, "Among the more conscientious sniper hunters are Negro Marines": June 29, 1944, Opotowsky files, NARA.

Title, "Marine, is my husband there?": Undated, Goldberg files, NARA.

Title, "Just plain tired of being the men behind the guns": April 1945, Chester H. Smith files, NARA.

Title, "They have been pinned down while carrying wounded Marines": May 6, 1945, Foreman files, NARA.

Title, "I have to be with the boys in action": November 3, 1944, Kalman files, NARA.

Title, "We tried to dodge them mortar shells, but they just kep' on coming": October 30, 1944, Moser files, NARA.

Title, "His unit loaded much of the cargo for the Tarawa raid": Undated, Nicholson files, NARA.

Title, "He helped to wipe out a cave of Imperial Engineers": December 3, 1944, Nicholson files, NARA.

Title, "Someone heard a faint cry for help": January 4, 1945, Nicholson files, NARA.

Nicholson background: See Michael Hurd, *Collie J., Grambling's Man with the Golden Pen* (St. Johann Press, 2007), chap. 2, "Of Sawmills, Kingfish, and 'Funi-Funi.'"

Obituary: Frank Litsky, "Colie J. Nicholson, 85, Who Promoted Grambling's Teams, Is Dead," *New York Times*, September 16, 2006.

Nicholson in American-controlled areas: See Hurd, *Collie J.*

Not deployed to any island assault: See Hurd, *Collie J.*

"Being in the Marine Corps": See Hurd, *Collie J.*

9. Thirty-Six Days on Iwo Jima

Genaust and the famous flag raising: The event took place a few hours after Marines raised a smaller flag on Suribachi. For details of the controversies over whether either flag raising was staged (they were not) and the misidentifying of the flag raisers, see Breanne Robertson, "Iwo Jima and the Struggle for Historical Truth," in *Investigating Iwo: The Flag Raisings in Myth, Memory, and Esprit de Corps*, ed. Breanne Robertson (Marine Corps History Division, 2019). The moment the photographers took their pictures is described in Charles P. Neimeyer, "Black Sand and Blood: The 36-Day Battle for Iwo Jima, 19 February–26 March 1945," in Robertson, ed., *Investigating Iwo*, 15–16.

"Rallied the American public": Citation from Navy Secretary James Forrestal, October 27, 1945. See Image 201, Official Military Personnel File for William H. Genaust, Series: Official Military Personnel Files, 1905–1998, National Archives Catalog, National Archives and Records Administration, https://catalog.archives.gov/id/57287326.

"I feel he has done his part": Jessie Genaust to Franklin Roosevelt, October 14, 1944. Image 168, Genaust personnel file, National Archives Catalog.

Plea politely denied: Walter R. Hooper to Jessie Genaust, October 27, 1944. Image 170, Genaust personnel file, National Archives Catalog.

Genaust on Saipan: He received the Bronze Star posthumously for his actions against the snipers on Saipan on July 9, 1944. For details, see the citation dated November 14, 1947. Image 206, Genaust personnel file, National Archives Catalog.

Forces strength: See Robertson, "Iwo Jima and the Struggle for Historical Truth," xvii; and Neimeyer, "Black Sand and Blood," 8.

American casualties: Robertson, "Iwo Jima and the Struggle for Historical Truth," xviii.

"It ate up men": Report, Sgt. Bob Cooke, March 4, 1945, Cooke files, among news release submission files within Records of the Division of Information and its predecessor, the Division of Public Relations; Record Group 127, Records of the United States Marine Corps, National Archives and Record Administration, College Park, Maryland. News releases hereafter noted as within NARA.

Title, "Unexpectedly tough Jap opposition resulted in considerable confusion": March 2, 1945, Campbell files, NARA.

Title, "Their dead and wounded demonstrated their bravery under fire": Undated, Vincent files, NARA.

Title, "The boy lost his mind": Undated, Lucas files, NARA.

Title, "Honey I know you will write as soon as you can": Undated, Levin files, NARA.

Title, "At least one Jap agrees with the Marines": March 5, 1945, Weaver files, NARA.

"Ration biscuits have always been the source": Sgt. Henry A. Weaver, April 2, 1945, Weaver files, NARA.

Title, "Don't ask me why I left the galley": Undated, O'Donnell files, NARA.

Title, "I'll not even take off my helmet to scratch my head": March 11, 1945, Barr files, NARA.

"It was less than a week": Report, undated, Dashiell files, NARA.

Title, "The cost of one artillery unit firing one day to win Iwo Jima": March 4, 1945, Ross files, NARA.

Title, "A strategy being used extensively in this operation for the first time": March 1, 1945, Campbell files, NARA.

"The Japanese mined one Iwo Jima beach": Report, March 7, 1945, Ruder files, NARA.

"When the Japanese trapped": Report, undated, Lucas files, NARA.

"Call it curiosity": Report, July 1, 1945, Kirby files, NARA.

Title, "Almost no use killing those damn gooks just for postcards!": March 4, 1945, Cooke files, NARA.

Title, "That one didn't have our number on it": March 23, 1945, Ruder files, NARA.

Title, "Orders are orders": Undated, Chester Smith files, NARA.

Title, "I want to be accepted as an American, because that's what I am": Undated, Dashiell files, NARA.

Title, "Marines kill the Japs, Marines should bury them": March 13, 1945, Weaver files, NARA.

Title, "White sheets fell limp over what was once his legs": March 21, 1945, Ruder files, NARA.

Title, "One of the more touching things were baby shoes": Undated, Dashiell files, NARA.

Iwo Jima casualties and aftermath: See Joseph H. Alexander, *Closing In: Marines in the Seizure of Iwo Jima* (Marine Corps Historical Center, 1994), 47–48, 50–51.

"Out of countless tales": Sgt. Keyes Beech, "Pittsburgher and 60 Men Start Across Iwo, 3 Make It," *Pittsburgh Press*, March 1, 1945.

Processing stories about Iwo Jima: Bulletin, March 20, 1945, CC Bulletin file, Vol. 4, NARA.

CCs killed during the Iwo Jima campaign: See official Marine Corps press releases for Barberio in Combat Correspondent file 1 and for McElroy and Vessey in Combat Correspondent file 2, MCHDA. Middlebrooks' death is referenced in his NARA file.

Deaths of cameramen: The Marine officer who oversaw photo coverage on Iwo Jima, Norman Hatch, recalled that four cameramen were killed on the island: William H. Genaust, Donald Fox, Leo Harry McGrath, and Donovan R. Raddatz. (Navy records show that Harry Leo McGrath was a Navy photographer.) See Charles Jones, *War Shots: Norm Hatch and the U.S. Marine Corps Combat Cameramen of World War II* (Stackpole, 2011), 175.

Details of Genaust's death: See statement by Robert R. Campbell, May 3, 1945, Image 61, Genaust personnel file, National Archives Catalog.

10. Okinawa and Imperial Japan's Last Stand

"We are a bewildered lot of Marines": Report, Sgt. Harold E. Foreman, April 5, 1945, Henna, Okinawa, Foreman files, among news release submission files within Records of the Division of Information and its predecessor, the Division of Public Relations; Record Group 127, Records of the United States Marine Corps, National Archives and Record Administration, College Park, Maryland. News releases hereafter noted as within NARA.

"We fought the elements": Report, John P. Schediwy, Okinawa, July 20, 1945, Schediwy files, NARA.

American casualties: Donald L. Miller, *D-Days in the Pacific* (Simon & Schuster, 2005), 311.

Japanese losses: Joseph H. Alexander, *The Final Campaign: Marines in the Victory on Okinawa* (Marine Corps Historical Center, 1996), 22.

Noncombatant deaths: See Alexander, *The Final Campaign*, 51; and Miller, *D-Days in the Pacific*, 308.

After Okinawa: For a discussion of the post-Okinawa plans of both the United States and Japan, see Richard B. Frank, "Ending the Pacific War," in *The Pacific War: From Pearl Harbor to Hiroshima*, ed. Daniel Marston (Osprey, 2006), 227–45.

Title, "Convincing civilians to surrender is bringing headaches": April 8, 1945, Boian files, NARA.

Title, "I couldn't move as that Jap with the knife came closer and closer": Undated, Twitty files, NARA.

Title, "Many things of interest were found": April 1, 1945, Twitty files, NARA.

Souvenir hunting as a prohibited topic: See Navy Department Public Relations Bulletin, June 1, 1944, in file marked Public Relations Bulletin (May–August 1944), Records Relating to Public Relations, CINCPAC, NARA.

"Something about Mr. Kaneshiro's house": Report, April 9, 1945, Twitty files, NARA.

Title, "Marines had been pinned down for hours, the wounded were dying": April 20, 1945, Voigt files, NARA.

"Why do I consider myself lucky?": Report, May 5, 1945, Kalman files, NARA.

Title, "They do not make attractive roommates": June 4, 1945, Opotowsky files, NARA.

270 | Notes to pages 210–21

Title, "The battle ceased only when the last Jap was dead": Undated, Batt files, NARA.

Title, "The Japanese diligently mined the house containing sleeping Marines": April 27, 1945, Leppard files, NARA.

Title, "He described the experience as worse than a nightmare": June 16, 1945, Donahue files, NARA.

Title, "Select the biggest ship you see and crash dive it": May 10, 1945, Boian files, NARA.

"A novice Japanese airman": Report, May 19, 1945, Meagher files, NARA.

Popham note: See John H. Popham, undated note, in Meagher files, NARA.

Timidity as censorship subject: See memo on censorship regulations, dated January 5, 1945, in file marked A7-2 Censorship and Security (Folder 1 of 3), Records Relating to Public Relations, CINCPAC, NARA.

Title, "Is that a Jap? What if that's a Marine?": April 19, 1945, Boian files, NARA.

Title, "The patch of earth surrounding the Jap erupted violently": May 27, 1945, Meagher files, NARA.

Title, "The camouflaged enemy runway was perfect": June 16, 1945, Hawkins files, NARA.

"An Easter present from the Japanese": Report, April 29, 1945, Boniface files, NARA.

"Out of Okinawa's labyrinth": Report, May 24, 1945, Hawkins files, NARA.

"Hellcats, the Second Marine Air Wing's": Report, May 17, 1945, Canup files, NARA.

"Japanese army doctors": June 5, 1945, McMillan files, NARA.

Title, "He wasn't finished killing Japs": July 3, 1945, Voigt files, NARA.

"If this—wachamecallit": Report, August 8, 1945, Dube files, NARA.

Frank, "Ending the Pacific War," 243–45.

11. Life in the Marine Corps

Laughter "is probably one of the Marines' greatest 'secret weapons.'": See Ross, "Laughing Leathernecks," April 19, 1945, Ross files, among news release submission files within Records of the Division of Information and its predecessor, the Division of Public Relations; Record Group 127, Records of the United States Marine Corps, National Archives and Record Administration, College Park, Maryland. News releases hereafter noted as within NARA.

"Criticism of equipment": See Memo on censorship regulations, dated January 5, 1945, in file marked A7-2 Censorship and Security (Folder 1 of 3), Records Relating to Public Relations, CINCPAC, NARA.

Title, "It's Father O'Neill to you": May 8, 1943, Shaffer files, NARA.

Title, "This Shangri-la is as real as beer, baseball, and hamburgers": May 10, 1943, Stavisky files, NARA.

Title, "Things looked pretty dark until the bride-to-be appeared at camp": May 18, 1943, Stinson files, NARA.

Title, "I don't know if it was my fault or the censor's": September 16, 1943, McCarty files, NARA.

Title, "A Marine staff sergeant has been doing a lot of explaining": October 7, 1943, Stinson files, NARA.

Title, "Transported from the grim business at hand by movie magic": October 23, 1943, Hague files, NARA.

Title, "Native elders turned out to inspect this creature from the Bronx": November 7, 1943, Stinson files, NARA.

Title, "As natives go, she could be considered pretty close to beautiful": November 7, 1943, Stinson files, NARA.

Title, "A gun to use when he runs into his first Jap": November 24, 1943, Stavisky files, NARA.

Title, "Single words now explain the most adverse conditions": November 25, 1943, Biggerstaff files, NARA.

Title, "Sorry, sir, but I have orders": December 2, 1943, Feldkamp files, NARA.

"Marines will have their joke": Report, January 16 [1944], Alli files, NARA.

Title, "I hope Mom doesn't find out I'm down here": January 30, 1944, Cochrane files, NARA.

Title, "Sweet violets, covered all over from head to toe": February 8, 1944, Ruder files, NARA.

"When the talk": Report, July 18, 1944, Cooke files, NARA.

"Before a Marine fighter pilot landed": Report, November 1, 1944, Goodrich files, NARA.

"A group of Fourth Marine Division": Report, August 3, 1944, Campbell files, NARA.

"A Marine chaplain sounded the call": Report, August 6, 1944, Campbell files, NARA.

"Before the battle for Guam": Report, undated, Hallman files, NARA.

"Navy mail censors" Report, undated, Chapel files, NARA.

"Lieutenant William F. McClain": Report, February 29, 1945, Ruder files, NARA.

"Every motion picture shown": December 12, 1944, Donahue files, NARA.

"An ever-present sense of humor": March 11, 1945, Ross files, NARA.

"Wherever the Marines have fought" and punch lines: Report, April 19, 1945, Ross files, NARA.

"A Marine . . . tells the story": Report, February 28, 1945, Ruder files, NARA.

"Doctors haven't heard of it": Report, undated, Chester H. Smith files, NARA.

"Day after day a metallic symphony": Report, undated, Hunter files, NARA.

"A profit-minded Marine": Report, undated, Fitzpatrick files, NARA.

"Ten bucks is the limit": Report, March 18, 1945, McCarty files, NARA.

"The first letter a Marine received": Report, April 8, 1945, Batt files, NARA.

"She married another guy": Report, April 17, 1945, Boian files, NARA.

Title, "Beans and bombs: How to make foxhole coffee": Undated, Lewis files, NARA.

Epilogue

DPR personnel return to United States or receive discharge: Benis M. Frank, *Denig's Demons and How They Grew: The Story of Marine Combat Correspondents, Photographers, and Artists* (Moore & Moore, 1967), 49.

DPR ranks halved: Frank, *Denig's Demons*, 52.

Hurlbut postscript: "Jim Hurlbut, Ex-Newsman Here, Is Dead," *Chicago Tribune*, March 27, 1967.

Merillat postscript: Adam Bernstein, "Marine Had Career as an Author," *Washington Post*, April 29, 2010.

Zurlinden postscript: "Pete Zurlinden Jr., 42, Times Reporter, Dies," *Los Angeles Times*, May 9, 1957.

Hurwitz postscript: Harold Kaese, "Hy Hurwitz Dies," *Boston Globe*, May 2, 1966.

Hannah postscript: "Billionaire Recluse's Spokesman," *Washington Post*, January 17, 1976.

Feldkamp postscript: "Fred Feldkamp, 67, Writer, Dies," *New York Times*, December 8, 1981.

Ward postscript: "Gene Ward, 78, Dies," *New York Times*, March 31, 1992.

Lewis postscript: Martin Weil, "Legendary Police Reporter Alfred E. Lewis Dies," *Washington Post*, May 4, 1994.

Ross postscript: "Bill D. Ross, 73," *New York Times*, September 16, 1994.

Shaffer postscript: "Samuel Shaffer Dies at 85," *Washington Post*, October 21, 1995.

Popham postscript: Douglas Martin, "John Popham, 89, Dies," *New York Times*, December 14, 1999.

Wilson postscript: "USIA Official Earl J. Wilson Dies," *Washington Post*, March 28, 1999.

Josephy postscript: Margalit Fox, "Alvin M. Josephy Jr., Historian on Indian Life, Dies," *New York Times*, October 18, 2005.

Stavisky postscript: Patricia Sullivan, "Samuel Stavisky," *Washington Post*, September 24, 2008.

Kaufman postscript: William Grimes, "Millard Kaufman, 92, a Creator of Mr. Magoo, Dies," *New York Times*, March 19, 2009.

O'Brien postscript: "Cyril J. Obrien, Oldest Marine War Correspondent, Dies at 92," press release, Johns Hopkins Applied Physics Laboratory, December 2, 2011.

Schlossenberg postscript: See obituary, *Kansas City Jewish Chronicle*, February 18, 2011; and Jeffrey Cordero, "Irving Schlossenberg, 92," an article published online by the 9th Marine Corps District, February 19, 2011. The Marine article carried the claim that he had been the oldest living CC.

Beech postscript and "He prided himself": John T. McQuiston, "Keyes Beech, 76, Correspondent in Asia for Five Decades, Is Dead," *New York Times*, February 16, 1990.

Lucas's drinking and night terrors: Barry Zorthian to the author, c. 2005. Zorthian knew Lucas while serving as press officer for the US embassy in Saigon during the Vietnam War and hosted Lucas as an overnight guest at his home.

"You know, all the mud and blood and battle": Dan Thomasson to the author, January 14, 2005.

ASNE canons of journalism: See "A Newspaper Code," *New York Times*, April 29, 1923.

Lee's principles: The text of the declaration and Lee's other views are included in Karen Miller Russell and Carl O. Bishop, "Understanding Ivy Lee's Declaration of Principles: U.S. Newspaper and Magazine Coverage of Publicity and Press Agentry, 1865–1904," *Public Relations Review* 35 (2009): 91–92.

"Shared sacrifice": Michael S. Sweeney, *Secrets of Victory: The Office of Censorship and the American Press and Radio in World War II* (University of North Carolina Press, 2001), 3.

DPR official on security concerns: Frank, *Denig's Demons*, 36.

Development of Defense Information School: See school's history page on its website, https://www.dinfos.dma.mil/.

"Never again would the prerogatives": Frank, *Denig's Demons*, 53.

"Most of the combat correspondents": Frank, *Denig's Demons*, 28.

Select Bibliography

Alexander, Joseph H. *Across the Reef: The Marine Assault on Tarawa.* U.S. Marine Corps, 1993.
———. *Closing In: Marines in the Seizure of Iwo Jima.* Marine Corps Historical Center, 1994.
———. *The Final Campaign: Marines in the Victory on Okinawa.* Marine Corps Historical Center, 1996.
———. *Utmost Savagery: The Three Days of Tarawa.* Ivy Books, 1995.
Bean, Hamilton. *Nimitz's Newsman: Waldo Drake and the Navy's Censored War in the Pacific.* Naval Institute Press, 2024.
Cameron, Garry M. *Last to Know, First to Go: The United States Marine Corps' Combat Correspondents.* Charger Books, 1988. Updated as *First to Go: The History of the USMC Combat Correspondents Association.* St. Johann Press, 2018.
Casey, Steven. *The War Beat, Pacific: The American Media at War Against Japan.* Oxford University Press, 2021.
Chapin, John C. *Breaching the Marianas: The Battle for Saipan.* Marine Corps Historical Center, 1994.
———. *Breaking the Outer Ring: Marine Landings in the Marshall Islands.* Marine Corps Historical Center, 1994.
Colbourn, Colin. "Esprit de Marine Corps: The Making of the Modern Marine Corps Through Public Relations, 1898–1945." PhD diss., University of Southern Mississippi, 2018.
Cressman, Robert J. *A Magnificent Fight: Marines in the Battle for Wake Island.* Marine Corps Historical Center, 1992.
Cutlip, Scott M. *The Unseen Power: Public Relations: A History.* Lawrence Erlbaum, 1994.
Dower, John W. *War Without Mercy: Race and Power in the Pacific War.* 1986; Pantheon, 1993.
Folkerts, Jean, and Dwight L. Teeter Jr. *Voices of a Nation: A History of Mass Media in the United States.* 3rd ed. Allyn and Bacon, 1998.
Frank, Benis M. *Denig's Demons and How They Grew: The Story of Marine Combat Correspondents, Photographers, and Artists.* Moore & Moore, 1967.

276 | Select Bibliography

Gayle, Gordon D. *Bloody Beaches: The Marines at Peleliu.* U.S. Marine Corps History and Museums Division, 1996.

Harwood, Richard. *A Close Encounter: The Marine Landing on Tinian.* Marine Corps Historical Center, 1994.

Heinrichs, Waldo, and Marc Gallicchio. *Implacable Foes: War in the Pacific, 1944–1945.* Oxford, 2017.

Henri, Raymond, and Jim G. Lucas, W. Keyes Beech, David K. Dempsey, and Alvin M. Josephy Jr. *The U.S. Marines on Iwo Jima.* 1945. Kindle edition, 2019.

Hoffman, Jon T. *From Makin to Bougainville: Marine Raiders in the Pacific War.* U.S. Marine Corps History and Museums Division, 1995.

Hurd, Michael. *Collie J., Grambling's Man with the Golden Pen.* St. Johann Press, 2007.

Jones, Charles. *War Shots: Norm Hatch and the U.S. Marine Corps Combat Cameramen of World War II.* Stackpole, 2011.

Josephy, Alvin M., Jr. *The Long and the Short and the Tall: Marines in Combat on Guam and Iwo Jima.* Knopf, 1946. Repr. Burford Books, 2000.

———. *A Walk Toward Oregon: A Memoir.* Knopf, 2000.

Keaton-Lima, Linda M. Canup, ed. *War Is Not Just for Heroes: World War II Dispatches and Letters of U.S. Marine Corps Combat Correspondent Claude R. 'Red' Canup.* University of South Carolina Press, 2012.

Leckie, Robert. *Helmet for My Pillow.* 1957; repr. Arcadia Press, 2019.

Levin, Dan. *From the Battlefield: Dispatches of a World War II Marine.* Naval Institute Press, 1995.

Lindsay, Robert G. *This High Name: Public Relations and the U.S. Marine Corps.* University of Wisconsin Press, 1956.

Lucas, Jim. *Combat Correspondent.* Reynal & Hitchcock, 1944.

Marston, Daniel, ed, *The Pacific War: From Pearl Harbor to Hiroshima.* Osprey, 2006.

Melson, Charles D. *Condition Red: Marine Defense Battalions in World War II.* Marine Corps Historical Center, 1996.

Merillat, Herbert Christian. *Guadalcanal Remembered.* 1982. Repr. University of Alabama Press, 2003.

Merillat, Herbert Laing. *The Island: A History of the First Marine Division on Guadalcanal.* 1944. Repr. Westholme, 2010.

Miller, Donald L. *D-Days in the Pacific.* Simon & Schuster, 2005.

Nalty, Bernard C. *Cape Gloucester: The Green Inferno.* Marine Corps Historical Center, 1994.

———. *The Right to Fight: African-American Marines in World War II.* Marine Corps Historical Center, 1995.

O'Brien, Cyril J. *Liberation: Marines in the Recapture of Guam.* Marine Corps Historical Center, 1994.

O'Connell, Aaron B. *Underdogs: The Making of the Modern Marine Corps.* Harvard University Press, 2012.

O'Sheel, Patrick, ed. *Semper Fidelis: The U.S. Marines in the Pacific, 1942–1945.* William Sloane, 1947.

Robertson, Breanne, ed. *Investigating Iwo: The Flag Raisings in Myth, Memory, and Esprit de Corps.* Marine Corps History Division, 2019.

Ross, Bill D. *Iwo Jima: Legacy of Valor.* 1985. Repr. Vintage, 1986.

———. *Peleliu: Tragic Triumph: The Untold Story of the Pacific War's Forgotten Battle.* Random House, 1991.

Shaw, Henry I., Jr. *First Offensive: The Marine Campaign for Guadalcanal.* U.S. Marine Corps, 1992.

Shaw, Henry I., Jr., and Maj. Douglas T. Kane. *Isolation of Rabaul: History of U.S. Marine Corps Operations in World War II.* Vol. 2. U.S. Marine Corps Historical Branch, 1963.

Sledge, E. B. *With the Old Breed: At Peleliu and Okinawa.* 1981; repr., Presidio, 2007.

Smith, Larry. *Iwo Jima: World War II Veterans Remember the Greatest Battle of the Pacific.* Norton, 2008.

Soule, Thayer. *Shooting the Pacific War: Marine Corps Combat Photography in WWII.* University Press of Kentucky, 2000.

Stavisky, Samuel E. *Marine Combat Correspondent: World War II in the Pacific.* Ivy Books, 1999.

Steinberg, Rafael. *Island Fighting.* Time-Life Books, 1978.

Sweeney, Michael S. *Secrets of Victory: The Office of Censorship and the American Press and Radio in World War II.* University of North Carolina Press, 2001.

Tatum, Charles W. *Red Blood, Black Sand: Fighting Alongside John Basilone from Boot Camp to Iwo Jima.* Dutton Caliber, 2012.

Wilson, Earl J., and Jim G. Lucas, Samuel Shaffer, and C. Peter Zurlinden. *Betio Beachhead: U.S. Marines' Own Story of the Battle for Tarawa.* 1945; repr., Pickle Partners, 2016.

Zich, Arthur. *The Rising Sun.* Time-Life, 1977.

Index

Acosta, Frank Jr. (CC): byline of, 136–38 (Saipan)
Alli, Joseph L. (CC): byline of, 229 (New Britain)
American Red Cross, 37, 90, 198
American Society of Newspaper Editors, 243–44
Associated Negro Press, 181
Associated Press, 11, 14, 73, 74, 164, 182, 240
Atlanta Journal, 164
atomic weapons, 159, 190, 217–18
Australia, 25, 70, 88, 100–1, 113
Azine, Harold (CC), 46

Baggett, Lee E. C. (CC), 70, 258n
Balaban, Burt (CP): byline of, 92–94 (Pearl Harbor)
Baltimore Sun, 14, 259n
Barberio, John M. (CC), 201
Barr, Francis H. (CC): byline of, 30 (Guadalcanal), 55 (Bougainville), 143–44 (Guam), 188–89 (Iwo Jima)
Batt, Leo T. (CC): byline of, 210–11, 236–37 (Okinawa)
Beech, Keyes (CC): byline of, 86 (Marine Base/Pacific), 200 (Iwo Jima); postscript, 242
Betio, 71–72, 80, 92, 94–95. *See also* Tarawa
Biggerstaff, Howard E. (CC): byline of, 227–28 (New Georgia)
Black, John W. (CC): byline of, 63 (Somewhere/SW Pacific), 98–99, 172 (New Britain)
Blechman, Solomon I. (CC): 69; byline of, 32–33, 36–38, 39 (Guadalcanal), 54–55, 61 (Bougainville); death of, 147–48
Boian, Harold T. (CC): byline of, 203–4, 212, 213, 236–37 (Okinawa)
Boniface, William (CC), 149; byline of, 215 (Okinawa)
Boston Globe, 24, 74, 240
Bougainville, 43, 45, 46, 47, 69, 147, 160; casualties on, 70; dateline of, 52–54, 54–55, 55, 56, 57, 57–60, 60–61, 61, 61–62, 63, 63–64, 65, 65–66, 66, 66–69, 234. *See also* Solomon Islands
Brunson, Mason (CC), 74
Burman, Edward J. (CC), 27, 43–44; byline of, 27–30 (Guadalcanal)

Camden Courier-Post (New Jersey), 17, 241
Campbell, John T. (CC), 128; byline of, 183–84, 190–91 (Iwo Jima), 232 (Tinian)
Canup, Claude R. (CC): byline of, 216 (Okinawa)
Capa, Robert, 242
Cape Gloucester, 97, 101–2, 121, 153, 160, 169; dateline of, 98–99, 99–100, 100, 100–1, 102–4, 118, 172, 216, 229. *See also* New Britain
Casey, Steven, 164
censored or rejected stories, subjects of: absence without leave, 38–39, 39, 49–52, 80–82, 102–4, 188; accidents, 110, 123–24, 158–59; alcohol use, 87–88, 117–18, 155–56, 231; anti-war sentiment, 1–3, 5–6, 127–29, 136–38; atrocities by enemy, 126–27, 136–38, 138–39, 143–44, 154–55;

280 | Index

censored or rejected stories *(continued)* battlefield horror, 125; bland anecdotes, 231, 232, 233, 233–34, 234–35, 237–38; blunders and questionable judgment, 55, 63, 90–92, 193–94; brutality against enemy, 27–30, 30, 54–55, 57, 83–84, 110–11, 153–53; criticism of armed forces, 52–54, 227–28, 232–33; criticism of civilian press, 88–89; disorganization, 82–83, 101–2, 183–84; dubious material, 32, 32–33, 151–52, 186, 217; embarrassing incidents, 63, 130–31, 226–27, 228–29; enemy civilians, interactions with, 203–4, 205–7; female relationships, 222–23, 223, 223–24; flamethrowers, 27–30, 108–9, 130; friendly fire, 79–80, 85–86, 105–6; focusing on Marine writers, 73–77, 141–43; frivolous material, 113, 189–90, 229–30; gallows humor, 193; identifying casualties, 73, 76, 207–9, 210–11, 214; illegal or dishonest acts, 30, 62, 129, 134–35, 144–45, 205–7, 227, 235–36; information that could aid enemy, 31–32, 33–35, 64–66, 113–14, 115–17, 123–25, 132–33, 150–51, 152–53, 157–58, 190–92, 194–95, 214–17; insubordination, 60–61, 80–82, 86, 220–21; intense combat, 56, 57–60, 79–80, 110–11, 131–32, 141–43, 210–11, 211–12; interservice rivalry, 36–37, 38–39, 77–79, 145; Japanese American divided loyalty, 135–36, 194–95; Japanese propaganda, 100–1, 152–53; Japanese resolve, 45, 85, 110–11, 114–15, 119, 119–20, 125, 131, 136–38, 149–50, 159, 183, 203, 217; morbid details, 189, 196, 197–99, 209–10, 211; napalm, use of, 150–51; native people, interactions with, 36–38, 38–39, 138–39, 143–44, 166, 203–4; 225, 226–27; personalizing enemy, 35–36, 111–12, 119–20, 187; prisoners of war, 35–36, 38–39, 54–55, 77–79, 86, 118–19, 125–26, 133–34, 138–39, 187, 194–95, 212–13; reckless behavior, 36–37, 61, 61–62, 63, 117–18, 130–31, 134, 155–56, 188–89, 204–5; recreational activities, 89–90, 221–22, 224–25; religious practices and views, 99–100, 220–21, 232; results of enemy action, 47–49, 105, 106–8, 110, 124, 132–33, 139–40, 184–85; retaliation, fear of, 100; sentimentality, 41–42, 186, 197–99; souvenir hunting, 38–39, 86–87, 87–88, 129, 134, 192, 205–7; treatment of enemy dead, 30, 86–87; vulgarity, 64, 98–99, 227–28, 229, 230–31, 232; weakness in Marines, 40–41, 140–41, 213; wounds, descriptions of, 40–41, 63–64, 66–69, 92–94, 127–29, 131–32, 145–47, 156–57, 185, 196–97. *See also* US Marine Corps combat correspondent initiative; US Navy censors

Chapel, Herman (CC): byline of, 232–33 (Guam)
Chicago Daily News, 242
Chicago Defender, 181
Chicago News, 10
Chicago Tribune, 8, 10, 24, 72, 129, 165
Childress, Henry F. (PRO): byline of, 33–35, 38–39 (Guadalcanal)
Cleveland Plain Dealer, 74
Cochrane, Walter C. (CC): byline of, 229–30 (Marshall Islands)
Colliers, 15
Collings, Cyrus P. (CP), 46
Conway, Walter F. (CC): byline of, 151–52 (Peleliu)
Cooke, Bob (CC), 184; byline of, 107–8, 108–9 (Advance Pacific Base), 113, 113–14 (Marshall Islands), 135–36, 231 (Saipan), 139–40 (Tinian), 192 (Iwo Jima)
Cullers, Vincent T., 165, 176–77

Daily Oklahoman, 74
Dashiell, Dick (CC): byline of, 189, 194–95, 197–99 (Iwo Jima)
Dayton Daily News (Ohio), 164
Denig, Robert L. (PRO), assumes public relations post, 9–10; background of, 9; conceives initiative, 9–10, 24, 243, 244; issues physical waivers, 11;

promotes initiative, 12–13; recruits reporters, 11–12; retires, 239, 247
Diet, Ernest J. (CP), 74–75
Donahue, Joseph P. (CC): byline of, 211–12 (Okinawa), 233 (Somewhere/S. Pacific)
Dube, Joseph (CC), 217

Ellice Islands (Tuvalu), 69–70, 180
Eniwetok, 97, 98, 118–19, 119–20. *See also* Marshall Islands
Enogai, 45, 47–49, 49. *See also* New Georgia
Evans, Charles P. (CC), 46

Feldkamp, Fred (CC): byline of, 86–87; 88–89; 228–29 (Tarawa); postscript, 240
Filan, Frank, 88
Fitzpatrick, Ray (CC): byline of, 236 (Okinawa)
Foreman, Harold E. (CC), 165, 202; byline of, 175–76 (Okinawa)
Forrestal, James, 182
Frank, Benis M., 13, 246, 247

Gavutu, 24. *See also* Solomon Islands
Gayle, Gordon D., 150
Genaust, William H., 182, 201, 267n
Gilbert Islands (Kiribati), 71, 72, 75, 92, 178, 180, 229, 230. *See also* Tarawa
Goldberg, Benjamin (CC), 120–21, 149–50; byline of, 152–53, 173, 174 (Peleliu)
Goodrich, Bill or W. F. (CC): byline of, 153–54, 158–59, 231 (Peleliu)
Gordon, Gerald D. (CC): byline of, 129 (Saipan)
Guadalcanal, 4, 39–40, 41–42, 44, 46, 49–50, 60–61, 62, 63, 68, 76, 77, 78, 85, 91, 95, 99, 100, 101, 122, 131, 137, 138, 153, 157, 159, 166, 169, 218, 220; casualties on, 42–43; censorship of Marine reports from, 26, 26–27, 43; copy flow from, 15, 26–27; dateline of, 27–30, 30, 31, 32, 32–33, 33–35, 35–40, 36–38, 38–39, 39, 223, 224–25, 239, 240; initial Marine writers' reports from, 23–24, 25–26; problems covering news from, 16, 43–44; strategy and tactics on, 25, 43. *See also* Solomon Islands
Guam, 21, 22, 123, 146, 160, 195, 200, 214, 236, 241; Black Marines on, 179, 181; casualties on, 147; dateline of, 141–43, 143–44, 144–45, 145, 232, 232–33, 233, 234; Marine writer killed on, 147–48; strategy and tactics on, 122–23, 217. *See also* Mariana Islands

Hague, James E. (CC): byline of, 61–62 (Bougainville), 224–25 (Guadalcanal)
Hallman, Donald A. Sr. (CC), 159–50, 165; byline of, 170–71 (Peleliu), 232 (Guam)
Hannah, Dick (CC): byline of, 31 (Guadalcanal); postscript, 240
Hatch, Norman (CP), 95
Hawkins, A.D. (CC): byline of, 214–15, 215–16 (Okinawa)
Henderson Field, 26, 35, 43
Henry, John, 88
Hipple, Bill, 88
Hirohito, Emperor of Japan, 59, 217
Holcomb, Thomas, 9, 10, 11, 162–63
Hurlbut, James W. (CC), 10, 22, 23, 24–27; postscript, 239
Hunter, Robert A. (CC): byline of, 235–36 (Somewhere/Pacific)
Hunter Liggett, 23
Hurley, John R. (CC), 164; byline of, 165–66 (Somewhere/S. Pacific)
Hurwitz, Hy, 5 (CC); postscript, 240

International News Service, 10
Iwo Jima, 21, 22, 95, 159, 160, 241; casualties on, 183, 199; copy flow from, 200; dateline of, 172–73, 173, 175, 183–84, 184–85, 185, 186, 187, 188, 188–89, 189, 189–90, 190–91, 191, 191–92, 192, 193, 193–94, 194–95, 196, 196–97, 197–99, 200, 233–34, 234, 234–35, 235; flag raising on, 182–83, 199, 201; Marine writers killed on, 183, 200–1; strategy and tactics on, 150, 159, 218

Japanese Americans, 135–36, 194–95
Japanese armed forces: atrocities ascribed to, 126–27, 136–38, 138–39, 143–44, 154–55; casualties sustained by, 7, 42–43, 70, 94, 120, 147, 159, 183, 199, 203; defensive strategies of, 24–25, 43, 45, 47, 71–72, 98, 122–23, 132–33, 149–50, 157–58, 183, 190–92, 202–3; killing their own wounded, 216–17; Korean laborers used by, 94, 154–55; opening offensives by, 7–8; as prisoners of war, 35–36, 38–39, 54–55, 77–79, 86, 118–19, 125–26, 133–34, 138–39, 187, 194–95, 212–13; propaganda and, 100–1, 152–53; resolve of, 45, 85, 110–11, 114–15, 119, 119–20, 125, 131, 136–38, 149–50, 159, 183, 203, 217; racial slurs against, 19, 29, 192, 202, 245; views expressed by members of, 35–36, 119–20, 187. *See also* censored or rejected stories, subjects of; *individual battles by location*
Joe Blow stories, 9, 13, 26, 27, 186, 239, 247
Johnson, Earle W. (CC): byline of, 40–41 (San Diego), 66 (Bougainville)
Johnston, Dick, 88
Josephy, Alvin M. Jr. (CC), 11; postscript, 241

Kalman, Vic (CC), 164–65, 209; byline of, 133–34, 134 (Saipan), 140–41 (Tinian), 154–55, 169–70, 171–72, 176–77 (Peleliu)
Kaufman, Millard (PRO), 4, 21; byline of, 119–20 (Somewhere/S. Pacific), 141–43 (Guam); postscript, 241
Kelly, James A. (PRO): byline of, 157–58 (Peleliu)
Kirby, John T. (CC): byline of, 192 (Iwo Jima)
Knox, Frank, 163
Korean laborers, 94, 154–55
Kroenung, Wesley L. (CP), 95
Kwajalein, 97–98, 120; dateline of, 105–6, 113, 113–14, 114–15, 117–18, 229–30, 230–31

Leppard, Stanley R. (MW): byline of, 211 (Okinawa)
Levin, Dan (CC), 21; byline of, 186 (Iwo Jima)
Lewis, Murray (CC): byline of, 110, 110–11, 111–12, 118, 118–19 (Somewhere/Pacific), 114–15 (Marshall Islands), 237–38 (Okinawa)
Link, Theodore C. (CC), 70
Los Angeles Times, 14, 24, 240, 242
Lucas, Jim G. (CC, PIO), 1–3, 5, 46, 72–73, 90, 94–95, 247; byline of, 41–42 (S. Pacific Marine Base), 73–77, 85–86 (Tarawa), 125–26, 127–29 (Saipan), 185, 191–92 (Iwo Jima); postscript, 242–43

MacArthur, Douglas, 97, 159
Majuro, 97, 98; dateline of, 105, 115–17. *See also* Marshall Islands
Mamaroneck Daily Times (New York), 147
Marder, Murrey (CC), 46; byline of, 47–49, 49–52 (New Georgia), 56 (Bougainville)
Mariana Islands, 122–23, 146, 147, 148, 179, 185, 218, 231. *See also* Guam; Saipan; Tinian
Marshall Islands, 97–98, 110, 110–11, 119, 119–20, 120, 138, 180, 185; casualties on, 120. *See also* Eniwetok; Kwajalein; Majuro; Namur; Roi
Marston, Gordon D. (CC): byline of, 145 (Guam)
Matjasic, Raymond (CP), 74, 75–76
Matthews, Ernest A. Jr. (PRO), 73, 74, 76, 95
Maurer, Richard H., 49–52
McCarty, Milburn Jr. (CC, PIO): byline of, 52–54 (en route to Bougainville), 60–61, 63, 63–64, 65–66, 66–69 (Bougainville), 138–39, 145–47 (Base Hospital/Pacific), 223 (Guadalcanal), 236 (en route to Okinawa)
McDevitt, Frank J. (CC), 45–46; byline of, 64–65 (New Georgia)
McElroy, James J. (CC), 200–1
McMillan, George E. (CC): byline of, 216–17 (Okinawa)

Index | 283

Meagher, Ed (CC): byline of, 212–13, 214 (Okinawa)
Merillat, Herbert C. or Herbert L. (PRO), 4, 10, 22, 23–24, 26–27; postscript, 240
Middlebrooks, William J. (MW), 201
Mielke, Arthur E. (CC): byline of, 104 (New Britain)
Miller, Norman A. (CC): byline of, 32 (Guadalcanal)
Moran, Maurice E. (CC), 161–62
Moser, James F. Jr. (CC): byline of, 156–57, 177–78 (Somewhere/S. Pacific)
Mount Vernon Daily Argus (New York), 21
Munda Point, 45, 47. *See also* New Georgia
Murphy, Richard J. Jr. (CC), 11, 73, 96, 122; byline of, 79–80 (transport/C. Pacific), 83–85 (Marine Pacific Base), 87–88 (Tarawa), 89–90 (Somewhere/C. Pacific); death of, 148

Namur, 97, 105–6, 108, 110, 111, 113, 184; dateline of, 108–9, 114–15, 117–18, 230–31. *See also* Marshall Islands
National Archives and Records Administration, 3–4, 6, 26, 162, 181, 245
Navajo Indians, 31–32
New Britain, 43, 97–98, 120, 120–21, 157, 229; casualties on, 120. *See also* Cape Gloucester; Rabaul
New Georgia, 46, 47, 68, 214; casualties on, 70; datelines of, 47–49, 49–52, 64–65, 227–28; strategy and tactics on, 43, 45. *See also* Solomon Islands
New York Daily News, 21, 72, 159, 240
New York Times, 24, 180, 241
New Yorker, 88
Newsweek, 70, 241
Nicholson, Collie J. (MW), 180–81; byline of, 178, 179 (Somewhere/Pacific)

O'Brien, Cyril J. (CC): 4, 11, 17, 18, 19–20; postscript, 241–42
O'Donnell, Red (CC): byline of, 188 (Iwo Jima)

Okinawa, 21, 22, 163, 165, 217–18, 244; casualties on, 203; dateline of, 175–76, 203–4, 204–5, 205, 206–7, 207–9, 209–10, 210–11, 211, 211–12, 212, 213, 214, 214–15, 215, 215–16, 216, 216–17, 217, 236, 237, 237–38; strategy and tactics on, 159, 202–3
Olszyk, Louis (PRO): byline of, 105 (Marshall Islands)
Olund, Roy E. (CP), 75
Opotowsky, Stanford (CC): byline of, 173–74 (Saipan), 209–10 (Okinawa)
O'Sheel, Patrick (PRO), 70

Palau Islands, 149, 152–53, 155, 177. *See also* Peleliu
Palmer, Keith, 70
Pavone, Peter Jr. (CC): byline of, 57, 57–60, 65 (Bougainville)
Pearl Harbor: attack on, 7, 10, 11, 17, 18, 19, 75, 162; dateline of, 93–94; postattack operations on, 14, 22, 26
Peleliu, 22, 156–57, 183, 216, 236, 241; Black Marines and Seabees on, 164–65, 169–70, 170–71, 171–72, 173, 176, 176–77, 177–78, 181; casualties on, 159; dateline of, 150–51, 151–52, 152–53, 153–54, 154–55, 155–56, 157–58, 158–59; 169–70, 170–71, 171–72, 173, 176–77, 231, 234; as forgotten battle, 159; strategy and tactics on, 149; unexpected resistance on, 149–50. *See also* Palau Islands
Pensacola News-Journal (Florida), 201
Pepper, Jack (CC), 74
Philadelphia Evening Public Ledger, 49
Philadelphia Inquirer, 70
Pittsburgh Courier, 181

Rabaul, 97, 120. *See also* New Britain
Rasor, Mac Roy (PRO): byline of, 115–17 (Marshall Islands)
Red Bank Daily Standard (New Jersey), 201
Reher, Charles F. (CP), 98
Rendova, 45. *See also* Solomon Islands
Roi, 97, 106–8, 108–9, 111, 184; dateline of, 113, 113–14. *See also* Marshall Islands

Roosevelt, Eleanor, 113
Roosevelt, Franklin D., 7, 95, 100–1, 163, 164, 182, 199, 201, 221
Rosenthal, Joe, 182, 199
Ross, Bill (CC), 219–20; byline of, 189–90, 233–34, 234–35 (Iwo Jima); postscript, 241
Ruder, Edward F. (CC): byline of, 105–6, 117–18, 230–31 (Marshall Islands), 125 (Saipan), 191, 193, 196–97, 235 (Iwo Jima), 233 (Somewhere/Pacific)

Saipan, 1–2, 5, 138, 139–40, 141, 144, 146, 154, 159, 184, 185, 201, 232; Black Marines on, 163, 164, 166–68; 173–74, 181; casualties on, 147; dateline of, 125, 126–27, 127–29, 129, 130, 130–31, 131–32, 132–33, 133–34, 134, 134–35, 135–46, 136–38, 166–68, 173–74, 231; Marine writer killed on, 22, 148; processing stories from, 15; strategy and tactics on, 122–23. *See also* Mariana Islands
Saturday Evening Post, 15, 70
Schlossenberg, Irving (CC): byline of, 126–27 (Saipan); postscript, 242
Scripps-Howard, 242
Shaffer, Samuel (CC), 74, 95–96; byline of, 77–79, 82–83 (Tarawa), 220–21 (Marine Base/New Zealand); postscript, 241
Sherrod, Robert, 88, 95, 129
Shreveport Sun (Louisiana), 180, 181
Shultz, Herb (CC): byline of, 123–25 (Somewhere/Pacific)
Smith, Chester A. (CC): byline of, 193–94 (Iwo Jima)
Smith, Chester H. (CC): byline of, 175 (en route to Iwo Jima), 25 (Iwo Jima)
Smith, Harold P., 129
Solomon Islands, 23, 24, 35, 41–42, 43, 45, 47, 51, 89, 97. *See also* Bougainville; Gavutu; Guadalcanal; New Georgia; Tanambogo; Tulagi
Stackpole, Pete, 129
Stavisky, Samuel E. (CC), 11, 20, 43; byline of, 35–36 (prison camp S.Pacific), 62 (transport/S. Pacific), 64 (Goodenough Island), 99–100, 100, 100–1, 118 (New Britain), 101–2 (Somewhere/S. Pacific), 221–22 (Somewhere/Pacific), 227 (Somewhere/SW Pacific); postscript, 241
Stinson, Bob (CC), 46–47; byline of, 222–23 (Camp Dunlap), 223–24 (Nukufetau), 225, 226–27 (Somewhere/S. Pacific); death of, 69–70
Sweeney, Michael S., 18, 244

Tanambogo, 24. *See also* Solomon Islands
Tarawa, 70, 83–85, 89–90, 90–92, 92–94, 95–96; casualties on, 94; dateline of, 77–79, 79–80, 80–82, 82–83, 85–86, 86, 86–87, 87–88, 88–89; film footage from, 95; impact on home front of, 94–95; Lucas report from, 72–77, 94–95; Marine writer killed on, 22, 73, 75, 77; strategy and tactics on, 71. *See also* Gilbert Islands
Tenelly, Dick (CC): byline of, 131–32, 132–33 (Saipan)
Thomas, Archie, 88
Time magazine, 129, 240
Tinian, 22, 122, 123, 147, 150, 184, 185, 218; dateline of, 139–40, 140–41, 232. *See also* Mariana Islands
To the Shores of Iwo Jima (film), 182
Tojo, Hideki, 19, 28, 59, 78–79, 113, 152, 215
Tokyo (Tokio), 24, 71, 105, 113, 183, 185, 187, 232
Tokyo Rose, 152–53, 232
Truman, Harry, 163
Tulagi, 23, 24, 25, 42. *See also* Solomon Islands
Tulsa Tribune (Oklahoma), 1
Twitty, Harold W. (CC): byline of, 204–5, 205, 206–7 (Okinawa)

United Press, 88, 164, 219
US Army, 7, 55, 103, 108, 123; air forces of, 108, 150, 232; censorship and, 18; competition with Marines, 1, 9, 10, 11; criticized in Marine stories, 20, 31, 36–37, 38–39, 55, 194–95, 228; Guadalcanal and, 28, 34; Iwo Jima

and, 183; Mariana Islands and, 132, 147; New Britain and, 97, 101; Okinawa and, 203; Pearl Harbor and, 8; Peleliu and, 159; prisoner interrogation by, 194–95

US Marine Corps combat correspondent initiative: accuracy and truth as goals of, 243–46; casualties among personnel in, 22, 69–70, 73, 147–48, 160–61, 183, 200–1; censorship guidance for, 2–3, 4–5, 18–22, 43, 219–20; coverage of African Americans by, 19, 161–81; derogatory racial terms and, 19, 29, 192, 202, 245; development of, 1, 9–12, 13–14, 25–26, 27, 43, 47; editorial system of, 2, 3, 13–15, 23–24, 200; historical record as goal of, 1, 246; military training for, 1, 11, 12, 46; promotion and publicity as goal of, 1, 2, 9–10, 13, 15, 16, 17, 243–44, 246; recruiting journalists for, 10–12; relationship with civilian press, 2, 12–13; self-censorship and, 20–21, 247; writing guidance for, 15–17. *See also* censored or rejected stories, subjects of

US Marine Corps combat correspondents (CC), combat photographers and cameramen (CP), public relations officers (PRO), and writers (MW): *see individual names*

US Marine Corps Divisions, 9, 12: First, 10, 22, 23, 24, 25, 97, 152, 153, 158, 172, 176, 177, 215, 216, 233; Second, 70, 72, 87, 90, 122, 123, 132, 147, 229; Third, 123, 188, 189, 190, 194, 198; Fourth, 97, 123, 132, 135, 139, 147, 183, 186, 190, 192, 231, 232; Fifth, 187, 193, 196; Sixth, 204, 214, 215

US Marine Corps Division of Public Relations, 2; background of, 8–9; postwar changes in, 239, 246–47; records of, 4–5. *See also* US Marine Corps combat correspondent initiative

US Navy: Black personnel expanded, 163; competing for recruits, 9, 10, 11; Ellice Islands and, 69–70; Guadalcanal and, 23; Iwo Jima and, 182, 183, 199; Mariana Islands and, 123; Marshall Islands and, 97, 106–8, 115–17; New Britain and, 97; Okinawa and, 203; Pacific area unspecified and, 46; Peleliu and, 159; publicity and, 1, 8, 14, 24; Tarawa and, 72, 84, 90, 94; Wake Island and, 7–8

US Navy censors: censorship regulations and, 2, 3, 4–5, 18–20, 24, 43; civilian press and, 14, 18, 21–22, 24; role in evaluating Marine dispatches, 2, 2–3, 3, 14, 26, 26–27, 219, 243, 245. *See also* censored or rejected stories, subjects of

US Navy chaplains, 77, 126, 128, 220–21, 232, 233

US Navy corpsmen, 124, 147; on Bougainville, 56, 64, 68–69; on Guadalcanal, 41; on Guam, 142–43; on Iwo Jima, 182; on New Georgia, 49–50; on Okinawa, 210–11; on Tarawa, 76

US Navy Seabees, 33, 34, 39, 49–52, 68, 90, 107–8, 163–64, 170–71, 173, 177–78

Van der Hoef, George (PRO), 9–10, 12–13, 24, 243

Vandergrift, Charles R. (CC), 164; byline of, 119 (aboard US Transport), 130, 130–31, 166–68 (Saipan)

Vessey, William T. (CC), 201

Vincent, Jack (CC): byline of, 134–35 (Saipan), 172–73, 173, 184–85 (Iwo Jima)

Voigt, George R. (CC): byline of, 207–9, 217 (Okinawa)

Wake Island, 7–8, 9–10, 24

Walker, Ward (CC): byline of, 155–56 (Peleliu)

Ward, Gene (CC), 74; postscript, 240

Washington Evening Star, 11, 24, 122

Washington News, 10

Washington Post, 11, 14, 24, 72, 90, 240, 241, 242

Washington Times-Herald, 10, 74
Weaver, Henry A. III (CC): byline of, 144–43 (Somewhere/Pacific), 187, 196 (Iwo Jima)
Wheeler, Keith, 88
Wilson, Earl J. (PRO), 88; byline of, 90–92 (Tarawa), 150–51 (Peleliu); postscript, 241

With the Marines at Tarawa (film), 95
WJSV, 10
Wood, Walter (CC): byline of, 210–11 (Okinawa)

Zurlinden, Pete (CC), 71, 73–74, 75; byline of, 80–82 (Tarawa); postscript, 240

Douglass K. Daniel has practiced journalism and studied and written about media and history. He was a reporter and editor for the Associated Press for nearly three decades. Daniel also taught journalism as an assistant professor at Kansas State University and Ohio University. He is the author of several books, including biographies of the *60 Minutes* correspondent Harry Reasoner, Oscar-winning writer and director Richard Brooks, and celebrated actress Anne Bancroft.

World War II: The Global, Human, and Ethical Dimension
G. Kurt Piehler, *series editor*

Lawrence Cane, David E. Cane, Judy Barrett Litoff, and David C. Smith, eds., *Fighting Fascism in Europe: The World War II Letters of an American Veteran of the Spanish Civil War*
Angelo M. Spinelli and Lewis H. Carlson, *Life behind Barbed Wire: The Secret World War II Photographs of Prisoner of War Angelo M. Spinelli*
Don Whitehead and John B. Romeiser, *"Beachhead Don": Reporting the War from the European Theater, 1942–1945*
Scott H. Bennett, ed., *Army GI, Pacifist CO: The World War II Letters of Frank and Albert Dietrich*
Alexander Jefferson with Lewis H. Carlson, *Red Tail Captured, Red Tail Free: Memoirs of a Tuskegee Airman and POW*
Jonathan G. Utley, *Going to War with Japan, 1937–1941*
Grant K. Goodman, *America's Japan: The First Year, 1945–1946*
Patricia Kollander with John O'Sullivan, *"I Must Be a Part of This War": One Man's Fight against Hitler and Nazism*
Judy Barrett Litoff, *An American Heroine in the French Resistance: The Diary and Memoir of Virginia d'Albert-Lake*
Thomas R. Christofferson and Michael S. Christofferson, *France during World War II: From Defeat to Liberation*
Don Whitehead, *Combat Reporter: Don Whitehead's World War II Diary and Memoirs*, edited by John B. Romeiser
James M. Gavin, *The General and His Daughter: The Wartime Letters of General James M. Gavin to His Daughter Barbara*, edited by Barbara Gavin Fauntleroy et al.
Carol Adele Kelly, ed., *Voices of My Comrades: America's Reserve Officers Remember World War II*, foreword by Senators Ted Stevens and Daniel K. Inouye
John J. Toffey IV, *Jack Toffey's War: A Son's Memoir*
Lt. General James V. Edmundson, *Letters to Lee: From Pearl Harbor to the War's Final Mission*, edited by Dr. Celia Edmundson
John K. Stutterheim, *The Diary of Prisoner 17326: A Boy's Life in a Japanese Labor Camp*, foreword by Mark Parillo
G. Kurt Piehler and Sidney Pash, eds., *The United States and the Second World War: New Perspectives on Diplomacy, War, and the Home Front*
Susan E. Wiant, *Between the Bylines: A Father's Legacy*, Foreword by Walter Cronkite
Deborah S. Cornelius, *Hungary in World War II: Caught in the Cauldron*
Gilya Gerda Schmidt, *Süssen Is Now Free of Jews: World War II, The Holocaust, and Rural Judaism*

Emanuel Rota, *A Pact with Vichy: Angelo Tasca from Italian Socialism to French Collaboration*

Panteleymon Anastasakis, *The Church of Greece under Axis Occupation*

Louise DeSalvo, *Chasing Ghosts: A Memoir of a Father, Gone to War*

Alexander Jefferson with Lewis H. Carlson, *Red Tail Captured, Red Tail Free: Memoirs of a Tuskegee Airman and POW, Revised Edition*

Kent Puckett, *War Pictures: Cinema, Violence, and Style in Britain, 1939–1945*

Marisa Escolar, *Allied Encounters: The Gendered Redemption of World War II Italy*

Courtney A. Short, *The Most Vital Question: Race and Identity in the U.S. Occupation of Okinawa, 1945–1946*

James Cassidy, *NBC Goes to War: The Diary of Radio Correspondent James Cassidy from London to the Bulge*, edited by Michael S. Sweeney

Rebecca Schwartz Greene, *Breaking Point: The Ironic Evolution of Psychiatry in World War II*

Franco Baldasso, *Against Redemption: Democracy, Memory, and Literature in Post-Fascist Italy*

G. Kurt Piehler and Ingo Trauschweizer, eds., *Reporting World War II*

Kevin T Hall, *Forgotten Casualties: Downed American Airmen and Axis Violence in World War II*

Chad R. Diehl, ed., *Shadows of Nagasaki: Trauma, Religion, and Memory after the Atomic Bombing*

Raffaella Perin, *The Popes on Air: The History of Vatican Radio from Its Origins to World War II*

Daniel McKay, *Beyond Hostile Islands: The Pacific War in American and New Zealand Fiction Writing*, foreword by Patrick Porter

Robert Sommer, *The Concentration Camp Brothel: Forced Sexual Labor under Nazi Rule*, translated by Dominic Bonfiglio, foreword by Annette F. Timm

Lawrence R. Samuel, *The World War II Bond Campaign*

Douglass K. Daniel, *Kill–Do Not Release: Censored Marine Corps Stories from World War II*